CIVIL WAR QUOTATIONS

CIVIL WAR QUOTATIONS

Darryl Lyman

COMBINED BOOKS
Pennsylvania

PUBLISHER'S NOTE

Combined Books, Inc., is dedicated to publishing books of distinction in history and military history. We are proud of the quality of writing and the quantity of information found in our books. Our books are manufactured with style and durability and are prited on acid-free paper. We like to think of our books as soldiers: not infantry grunts, but well dressed and well equipped avant garde. Our logo reflects our commitment to the modern and yet historic art of bookmaking.

We call ourselves Combined Books because we view the publishing enterprise as a "combined" effort of authors, publishers and readers. And we promise to bridge the gap between us—a gab which is all too seldom closed in contemporary publishing.

We would like to hear from our readers and invite you to write to us at our offices in Pennsylvania with your reactions, queries, comments, even complaints. All of our correspondence will be answered directly by a member of the Editorial Board or by the author.

We encourage all of our readers to purchase our books from their local booksellers, and we hope that you let us know of booksellers in your area that might be interested in carrying our books. If you are unable to find a book in your area, please write us.

For information, address:
Combined Books, Inc.
151 East 10th Avenue
Conshohocken, PA 19428

Library of Congress Cataloging-in-Publication Data
Civil War quotations / [compiled by] Darryl Lyman.
                    p.   cm.
            Includes index.
            ISBN 0-938289-45-4
            1. United States—History—Civil War, 1861-1865—Quotations, maxims,
etc.   I. Lyman, Darryl, 1944-
E468.9.C48   1995
973.7—dc20   95-15520

Combined Books Edition   1   2   3   4   5
First published in the USA in 1995 by Combined Books and distributed in North America by Stackpole Books, Inc., 5067 Ritter Road, Mechanicsburg, PA 17055.

Printed in the United States of America

To my brother
DALLAS

INTRODUCTION

The fire of the American Civil War forged not only a new national identity but also a new national language and literature. Erudite orators, literary lions, unyielding politicians, gritty generals, boys in the trenches, women on the homefront (and in the field)—all, singed by the fire, spoke and wrote in urgent tones about the flaming grandeur engulfing them. This was not an ordinary war. It was a brothers' war. Love and hate were fused and confused. And out of the heights and depths of those mixed emotions came an incredibly rich range of cries and quips, poems and songs, prayers and speeches, reports and dispatches, letters and diaries. Thus was created a language and literature of the people, not of the scholars; heated and hammered out by the raw experience of life and death, not by study.

This book is a compendium of Civil War quotations. A "Civil War quotation" is here defined as a verbal unit that pertains in some way to the Civil War and was first recorded, by hand or in print, during the war or was first spoken during the war, even if it was not recorded till after the war. Most of the quotations fall between Abraham Lincoln's first inauguration, 4 March 1861, and his death, 15 April 1865; however, some examples are drawn from as early as January 1861 and as late as July 1865.

Under each quotee's name, quotations are arranged, to the extent possible, in chronological order. Undated quotations are listed in alphabetic order after the dated ones.

Because oral quotations are often recorded by different witnesses in different forms, and printed quotations frequently vary in different editions, some of the quotations in this book may have slightly altered versions elsewhere. But there has been very little editing here. The quotations are presented as found in familiar sources.

An "attributed" quotation is one that may or may not be authentic. Some familiar quotations are omitted because they are definitely fictitious. An example is Lincoln's supposed reply when someone said that Grant drank too much: "Tell me the brand of whiskey that Grant drinks, and I'll send every general in the field a barrel of it"; Lincoln himself specifically denied that he ever said any such thing (although he did get a good chuckle out of the story). Such quotations belong to the realm of folklore, which, while certainly connected with the new language and literature mentioned above, can and should fill a separate volume.

CIVIL WAR QUOTATIONS

CHARLES FRANCIS ADAMS

Born 18 August 1807 in Boston, Massachusetts. Father of Charles Francis Adams, Jr., and Henry Brooks Adams. Before the Civil War, Charles Francis Adams was a politician. During the war, he was President Lincoln's minister to England. In his late years, he prepared for publication the diary of his father, John Quincy Adams, the 6th president of the United States. Charles Francis Adams died 21 November 1886 in Boston.

1   This is the 4th of July. Eighty-six years ago our ancestors staked themselves in a contest of a far more dangerous and desperate character. The only fault they committed was in omitting to make it more general and complete. Had they then consented to follow Thomas Jefferson to the full extent of his first draught of the Declaration, they would have added little to the seven years severity of their struggle and would have entirely saved the present trials from their children.

— 4 July 1862, letter to Charles Francis Adams, Jr.

2   The privileged classes all over Europe rejoice in the thoughts of the ruin of the great experiment of popular government.

— 31 July 1863, letter to Charles Francis Adams, Jr.

3   No more wanton and wicked struggle was ever initiated by profligate and desperate men than this against a government which had only been too lenient and generous to them.

— 24 August 1863, letter to Charles Francis Adams, Jr.

4   It would be superfluous in me to point out to your Lordship that this is war.

— 5 September 1863, note to Lord Russell, concerning the construction of two ironclad Confederate rams at Liverpool

5   The thinner ranks of the rebel armies show no signs of recuperation. Their paper money is dear at the price of old rags, for it does not pay for the making. And the heart that upheld them is gone. This stage of the disease cannot last any great length of time.

— 10 February 1865, letter to Charles Francis Adams, Jr.

CHARLES FRANCIS ADAMS, JR.

Born 27 May 1835 in Boston, Massachusetts. Son of Charles Francis Adams and brother of Henry Brooks Adams. Charles Francis Adams, Jr., joined the Union cavalry and rose from first lieutenant (28 December 1861) through captain (1 December 1862) and lieutenant colonel (8 September 1864) to colonel (14 March 1865) before being breveted a brigadier general near the end of the war. After the war, he became a lawyer and historian. Died 20 March 1915 in Washington, D.C.

6   For years our family has talked of slavery and of the South, and been most prominent in the contest of words, and now that it has come to blows, does it become us to stand aloof from the conflict?
    — 10 June 1861, letter to his father

7   Scott's campaign is wholly destroyed and he must now go to work and reconstruct it. While our army is demoralised, theirs is in the same degree consolidated.
    — 23 July 1861, letter to his father, after the Union loss at 1st Bull Run

8   Go to work at once in England with all your energy and force your way into magazines and periodicals there and in America, so that you can make yourself heard. For there is going to be difficulty about this blockade and much bad feeling....Touch England through her pocket and help your country that way.
    — 23 August 1861, letter to Henry Adams

9   The President is not equal to the crisis; that we cannot now help. The Secretary of War is corrupt and the Secretary of the Navy is incompetent; that we can help and ought to.
    — 5 November 1861, letter to Henry Adams

10   This war is killing slavery. Not by any legal quibble of contrabands or doubtful theory of confiscation, but by stimulating free trade....The whole system of cotton growing—all its machinery from the slave to the hoe in his hand—is awkward, cumbrous, expensive and behind the age....If fair competition in the growth of cotton be once established a new system of economy and agriculture must inevitably be introduced here in which the slave and his hoe will make room for the free laborer and the plough.
    — 2 April 1862, letter from Port Royal Island, South Carolina, to Henry Adams

11 The army is a great place to learn philosophy, I find, and in it you not only get careless of danger, but indifferent as to what disposition is made of you.

— 28 June 1862, letter to his father

12 I do my best for my horses and am sorry for them; but all war is cruel and it is my business to bring every man I can into the presence of the enemy, and so make war short. So I have but one rule, a horse must go until he can't be spurred any further, and then the rider must get another horse as soon as he can seize on one.

— 12 May 1863, letter to his mother

13 I do believe Jackson had genius and in that respect stands alone in the annals of this most stupid and uninspired of struggles. Certainly his death excited throughout this army a deep regret which was lost only in a sense of intense relief. Today I am sure, as Americans, this army takes a pride in "Stonewall" second only to that of the Virginians and confederates. To have fought against him is next to having fought under him.

— 23 July 1863, letter to his father

14 The feeling about Grant is peculiar—a little jealousy, a little dislike, a little envy, a little want of confidence—...and only brilliant success will dissipate the elements. If he succeeds, the war is over.

— 1 May 1864, letter to his father

15 In the hands of a General who gave them success, there is no force on earth which could resist this Army.

— 1 May 1864, letter to his father

16 War is cruel in all its parts—a horrid blessing sent on mankind in a shape curiously like a curse; and in all wars the purest form of squalid misery to which God's image is anywhere reduced has ever been found in the depots of prisoners.

— 8 January 1865, letter to his mother

17 This inaugural strikes me in its grand simplicity and directness as being for all time the historical keynote of this war.

— 7 March 1865, letter to his father, concerning President Lincoln's 2nd Inaugural Address

HENRY BROOKS ADAMS

Born 16 February 1838 in Boston, Massachusetts. Son of Charles Francis Adams and brother of Charles Francis Adams, Jr. Henry served as his father's private

secretary in London from 1861 to 1868. Later Henry was an educator, editor, writer, and historian. Died 27 March 1918 in Washington, D.C.

18 I have no doubt that barring a few lives and legs and arms lost, they'll all like it and be the better for it. And as for the lives and legs, if they estimate theirs as low as I do mine, the loss won't amount to much. Pain is the only thing I should fear, but after all, one's health is just as likely to be benefitted as to be hurt by a campaign, bullets and all.
> — 26 July 1861, letter to Charles Francis Adams, Jr.

19 Here we are dying by inches. Every day our authority, prestige and influence sink lower in this country.
> — 25 October 1861, letter from England to Charles Francis Adams, Jr.

20 I firmly believe that before many centuries more, science will be the masters of man. The engines he will have invented will be beyond his strength to control. Some day science may have the existence of mankind in its power, and the human race commit suicide by blowing up the world.
> — 11 April 1862, letter to Charles Francis Adams, Jr., concerning military inventions, such as ironclads

21 I wanted to hug the army of the Potomac. I wanted to get the whole of the army of Vicksburg drunk at my expense. I wanted to fight some small man and lick him.
> — 23 July 1863, letter to Charles Francis Adams, Jr., after the Union success at Vicksburg

22 The courage of the rebs has been marvellous, but human nature has its limits and unless the sun shines a little, the devil himself would lose heart in such a case.
> — 30 September 1864, letter to Charles Francis Adams, Jr., after the Union's successful Atlanta campaign

LOUISA MAY ALCOTT

Born 29 November 1832 in Germantown, Pennsylvania. For a brief period during late 1862 and early 1863, she was a Union nurse at a Washington, D.C., hospital. Later she became a famous writer of books, including Hospital Sketches *(1863) and* Little Women *(1868-69). Died 6 March 1888 in Boston.*

23 I've often longed to see a war, and now I have my wish. I long to be a man; but as I can't fight, I will content myself with working for those who can.
> — April 1861, journal

24 Sewing and knitting for "our boys" all the time. It seems as if a few energetic women could carry on the war better than the men do it so far.
— October 1861, journal

25 The first thing I met was a regiment of the vilest odors that ever assaulted the human nose, and took it by storm....I must bear it. I did, armed with lavender water, with which I so besprinkled myself and premises, that...I was soon known among my patients as "the nurse with the bottle."
— late 1862, letter published in *Hospital Sketches* (1863)

26 John Suhre a Virginian blacksmith is the prince of patients....He is about thirty, I think, tall & handsome, mortally wounded & dying royally, without reproach, repining or remorse. Mrs. Ropes & myself love him & feel indignant that such a man should be so early lost, for though he might never distinguish himself before the world, his influence & example cannot be without effect, for real goodness is never wasted.
— January 1863, journal

EDWARD PORTER ALEXANDER

Born 26 May 1835 in Washington, Georgia. Known as Porter Alexander. West Point class of 1857. After resigning as a second lieutenant from the United States Army (1 May 1861), he entered Confederate service as a captain (3 June 1861) and later won promotions to colonel (December 1862) and brigadier general (26 February 1864). After the war, he taught engineering, engaged in the railroad business, and held several public offices. Died 28 April 1910 in Savannah, Georgia.

27 A chicken could not live in that field when we open on it.
— 13 December 1862, comment to James Longstreet at Marye's Heights

CHARLES ANDERSON

Anderson was a Union soldier.

28 Yesterday morning was the first time we had to carry our meat, for the maggots always carried it till then. We had to have an extra guard to keep them from packing it clear off.
— 26 August 1861, letter to sister

ROBERT ANDERSON

Born 14 June 1805 near Louisville, Kentucky. West Point class of 1825. Before the war, he rose to the rank of major and in November 1860 took command of the Federal garrison at Charleston harbor, South Carolina. On 14 April 1861, he surrendered Fort Sumter to Beauregard. He was promoted to brigadier general (15 May 1861) but was forced by ill health to retire (27 October 1863). On 3 February 1865 he was breveted a major general, and on 14 April 1865 he returned to the newly recaptured Fort Sumter to raise the Stars and Stripes. Died 26 October 1871 in Charleston, South Carolina.

29   I have the honor to acknowledge the receipt of your communication demanding the evacuation of this fort, and to say, in reply thereto, that it is a demand with which I regret that my sense of honor, and of my obligations to my Government, prevent my compliance. Thanking you for the fair, manly, and courteous terms proposed, and for the high compliment paid me, I am, general, very respectfully, your obedient servant, Robert Anderson.

> — 11 April 1861, reply to Beauregard's demand that Anderson evacuate Fort Sumter

30   I shall await the first shot, and if you do not batter us to pieces, we shall be starved out in a few days.

> — 11 April 1861, remark to the Confederate officers who had delivered Beauregard's demand for the evacuation of Fort Sumter (A.R. Chisolm's version)

31   If we never meet in this world again, God grant that we may meet in the next.

> — 12 April 1861, remark to the Confederate officers who had just informed him that they would open fire on his fort in one hour

32   Gentlemen, this is a very awkward business.

> — 13 April 1861, remark to Beauregard's emissaries when he learned that he had surrendered to an unauthorized person, Louis T. Wigfall

JOHN ALBION ANDREW

Born 31 May 1818 in Windham, Maine. Republican governor of Massachusetts (1860-66). Died 30 October 1867 in Boston.

33   A poor document but a mighty act.

> — 22 September 1862, letter to Albert Gallatin Brown, concerning the Emancipation Proclamation

ELIZA FRANCES ANDREWS

Born 10 August 1840 in Washington, Georgia. Known as Fanny Andrews. A young diarist during the Civil War, she later became a well-known poet, novelist, and essayist. Died 21 January 1931 in Rome, Georgia.

34 Father Hamilton said that at one time the prisoners died at the rate of a hundred and fifty a day, and he saw some of them die on the ground without a rag to lie on or a garment to cover them. Dysentery was the most fatal disease, and as they lay on the ground in their own excrements, the smell was so horrible that the good father says he was often obliged to rush from their presence to get a breath of pure air. It is dreadful. My heart aches for the poor wretches, Yankees though they are, and I am afraid God will suffer some terrible retribution to fall upon us for letting such things happen. If the Yankees ever should come to southwest Georgia and go to Anderson and see the graves there, God have mercy on the land!
    — 27 January 1865, diary entry concerning the Andersonville prison

ANONYMOUS (NORTH AND SOUTH)

35 May the hand of the devil strike you down before long—You are destroying the country.
    Damn you—every breath you take.
    — 20 February 1861, letter to President-elect Lincoln, signed "Hand of God against you"; writer unknown but representative of many people North and South

36 A rich man's war and a poor man's fight.
    — common saying; both sides allowed wealthy draftees to hire substitutes, and Southerners who owned twenty (later fifteen) or more slaves were exempt; North Carolina's Governor Zebulon Vance was among the earliest associated with the saying

37 Here's your mule.
    — nonsense slang expression used by soldiers, North and South

ANONYMOUS (NORTHERN CIVILIANS)

38 Remember Ellsworth!
    — 1861, patriotic slogan in memory of Elmer Ellsworth, the Union's first casualty

39 I used to be glad to prepare private soldiers. They were worth a five-dollar bill apiece. But, Lord bless you, a colonel pays a hundred, and a brigadier

general two hundred. There's lots of them now, and I have cut the acquaintance of everything below a major. I might, as a great favor, do a captain, but he must pay a major's price. I insist upon that! Such windfalls don't come every day. There won't be another such killing for a century.

> — late June 1862, comment from an embalmer to the noncombatant George Alfred Townsend

40   Look at Pharoah's army going to the Red Sea.

> — 27 June 1863, comment by a woman as Hood's Confederate troops passed through Chambersburg, Pennsylvania

41   We know that with every explosion, and the scream of each shell, human beings were hurried, through excruciating pain, into another world, and that many more were torn, and mangled, and lying in torment worse than death, and no one able to extend relief.

> — 3 July 1863, from *The Diary of a Lady of Gettysburg, Pennsylvania*

42   Dear friend the Peapple is in for making Peas yeas Peas they wand and thay pray that you will make it thay all say before the Lextion for you there was Bills posted up evrewhere that you would make a change in the cabnet and would make Peas the tok is about Peas but we cant see it and have not seen it. they say this cruel Ware has bin going long a nuf there is Thousands of Widdows Thousands and Thousands of orphans were there Fathers has Left there Happie Homes now slain up on the Field of Battle for the Love of his country.

> — 16 January 1865, letter to President Lincoln

43   Anything to preserve the Union! (Alternate version: Preserve the Union—at any cost!)

> — common saying, especially early in the war

44   On to Richmond!

> — common saying among civilians and soldiers; a shortened version of "Forward to Richmond!" (see *New York Tribune*, June 1861)

45   These cookies are expressly for the sick soldiers, and if anybody else eats them, *I hope they will choke him!*

> — note attached to a box of cookies sent to the Chicago Sanitary Commission

46   We won't fight to free the nigger.

> — slogan of antiwar Democrats

47   You are not *my* husband nor son; but you are the husband or son of some woman who undoubtedly loves you as I love mine. I have made these

garments for you with a heart that aches for your sufferings, and with a longing to come to you to assist in taking care of you.

> — note sent with items to the Chicago Sanitary Commission

ANONYMOUS (NORTHERN MILITARY)

48 Give those South Carolina villians h—l and we will support you.

> — 10 April 1861, letter to President Lincoln by a member of the New York National Guard

49 I know I'm going home. I've had enough of fighting to last my lifetime.

> — July 1861, comment by a straggler as he joined the Federal retreat from 1st Bull Run (21 July 1861)

50 Frémont and the Union!

> — 25 October 1861, war cry by troops during action at Springfield, Missouri.

51 All quiet on the Potomac.

> — 1861, common saying early in the war, ridiculing McClellan's policy of delay; probably generated by McClellan's telegrams stating that "all is quiet tonight"; Ethel Lynn Beers used this common saying as the basis of her poem "The Picket Guard"

52 John Brown's body lies a-mould'ring in the grave,
His soul is marching on.
Glory! Glory Hallelujah!
Glory! Glory Hallelujah!
Glory! Glory Hallelujah!
His soul is marching on.

    . . .

They'll hang Jeff Davis on a sour apple tree,
As they go marching on.

> — 1861, "John Brown's Body," originally a humorous song aimed at a Massachusetts sergeant named John Brown, punning his name with that of the abolitionist martyr John Brown

53 Boys, for God's sake stop firing! You are killing your friends!

> — 6 April 1862, appeal by a Union officer to Confederates just before they shot him dead at the Hornets' Nest, Shiloh

54 This durn fight ain't got any rear!

> — 6 April 1862, comment by a wounded soldier who was ordered to the rear by his captain at the Hornets' Nest, Shiloh

55 Yes, by God, and I'm trying to get back to it just as fast as I can!
— 25 May 1862, reply by a Wisconsin soldier when Gen. Nathaniel P. Banks, at Winchester, shouted to fleeing Federals, "Stop, men! Don't you love your country?"

56 The General has one fault. He thinks everybody's made of cast iron like himself.
— 1 July 1862, comment on Philip Kearny by one of his men

57 Rally, boys, rally! Die like men; don't run like dogs!
— 17 September 1862, exhortation by a soldier to fellow Federals fleeing at Antietam

58 Don't be skeered, gen'men! Only de debble can pick yo' bones. Ain't no shark go' find his way into dis here iron coffin.
— 29 December 1862, comment by the black cabin cook on the U.S.S. *Monitor* as it was sinking

59 Now I lay me down to sleep
In mud that's many fathoms deep;
If I'm not here when you awake,
Just hunt me up with an oyster rake.
— January 1863, facetious prayer while on Burnside's infamous Mud March

60 Fredericksburg! Fredericksburg!
— 3 July 1863, battle cry of soldiers during Pickett's Charge at Gettysburg

61 Sometimes we have to double-quick; / This Dixie mud is mighty slick. / The soldier's fare is very rough, / The bread is hard, and beef is tough, / That's the way they put us through, / I tell you what, it's hard to do. / But we'll obey duty's call, / To conquer Dixie, that is all!
— 1863, song sung by the 8th Kentucky

62 He looks as if he meant it.
— spring 1864, comment from one private to another after Grant's first inspection of the Army of the Potomac

63 General, I dodged a shell once, and if I hadn't, it would have taken my head off. I believe in dodging.
— 9 May 1864, retort by a soldier to Major General John Sedgwick, who had just told the soldier that the enemy "couldn't hit an elephant at this distance"

64   We could blow that damn fort out of existence if we could run a mine shaft under it.

> — June 1864, Union soldier's remark overheard by Henry Pleasants of the 48th Pennsylvania, who passed the idea to his superiors; the result was the Crater (30 July 1864), a Union disaster

65   I'd follow Uncle Billy to hell.

> — July 1864, comment by a soldier about William T. Sherman

66   Vote as you shoot.

> — 1864, Republican party campaign slogan among Union troops

67   Oh, hell, we've got twenty-seven major generals up at camp. What we want is hardtack.

> — January 1865, complaint voiced by soldiers at the Savannah port when a ship pulled in with Major General John G. Foster

68   Hail, Columbia, happy land, / If I don't burn you, I'll be damned!

> — February 1865, song sung by Sherman's men as they marched toward Columbia, South Carolina

69   Well, good-bye, boys. This means death.

> — 1 April 1865, soldier's comment when told that he and his fellows would attack Petersburg the next day

70   You're the man I've been looking for for the last four years.

> — April 1865, comment by a soldier to Captain A.J. Ricks as the latter rode through the Union army with news of Lee's surrender

71   All in the three years.

> — common saying, especially when something went wrong, meaning "All the same to the average soldier"

72   All ye sick men, all ye sick men, / Get your calomel, get your calomel, / Get your calomel, get your calomel.

> — soldiers' words to the bugle sick call

73   Are you all dead? Are you all dead? / No, thank the Lord, there's a few left yet, / There's a few—left—yet!

> — soldiers' words to the bugle sick call

74   A damned goggle-eyed old snapping turtle.

> — a description of General Meade by his own men

75   Dan, Dan, Dan Butterfield, Butterfield, / Dan, Dan, Dan Butterfield, Butterfield.

> — soldiers' words to a special brigade bugle call used in Daniel Butterfield's command

76　Dear General Bragg, here's to your health, / With Secesh script to swell your wealth; / Your coat of arms, when Fortune deals, / We trust will bear a pair of heels. / Then shoot, boys, shoot! The foe is put to rout, / And Bragg a Boo and Morgan, too, / Have started on for Dixie. / Hey, ho! we've laid them low, / Se-cessh are blue as in-di-go.

> — "Bragg a Boo," song satirizing the Confederate general Braxton Bragg; credited by one soldier to E.W. Locke

77　Dr. Jones says, Dr. Jones says: / Come and get your quin, quin, quin, quinine, / Come and get your quinine, / Q-u-i-n-i-n-e!

> — soldiers' words to the bugle sick call

78　Fall in, ye poor devils, as fast as ye can, / And when ye get tired I'll rest you again.

> — soldiers' words to the bugle call to fall in after a rest

79　　Go the the stable, as quick as you're able,
　　　　And groom off your horses, and give them some corn;
　　　For if you don't do it the captain will know it,
　　　　And then you will rue it, as sure as you're born.

> — soldiers' words to the bugle stable call

80　　Half a mile, half a mile,
　　　Half a mile onward,
　　　Right through the Georgia troops
　　　Broke the two hundred.
　　　"Forward the Mule Brigade!
　　　Charge for the Rebs!" they neighed.
　　　Straight for the Georgia troops
　　　Broke the two hundred.

　　　. . .

　　　Mules to the right of them,
　　　Mules to the left of them,
　　　Mules behind them
　　　Pawed, neighed, and thundered.
　　　Breaking their own confines,
　　　Breaking through Longstreet's lines
　　　Into the Georgia troops,
　　　Stormed the two hundred.

> — "Charge of the Mule Brigade," a soldiers' parody of Tennyson's "Charge of the Light Brigade"; based on an 1863 incident in which two hundred Union mules accidentally helped repulse a Rebel attack

81　I can't wake 'em up, I can't wake 'em up, I can't wake
　　'em up in the morning,
　　I can't wake 'em up, I can't wake 'em up, I can't wake
　　'em up at all.
　　The corporal's worse than the private, the sergeant's
　　worse than the corporal,
　　The lieutenant's worse than the sergeant, and the
　　captain's worst of all.
　　I can't wake 'em up, I can't wake 'em up, I can't wake
　　'em up in the morning,
　　I can't wake 'em up, I can't wake 'em up, I can't wake
　　'em up at all.
　　　　— soldiers' words to the reveille bugle call (other versions also exist)

82　I fights mit Sigel.
　　　　— common saying among German-American volunteers under
　　　　German-born General Franz Sigel

83　Old Rosy is our man. / Old Rosy is our man. / He'll show his deeds,
where'er he leads. / Old Rosy is our man.
　　　　— song sung by western soldiers about William S. Rosecrans

84　Our Father who art in Washington,
　　Uncle Abraham be they Name,
　　Thy will be done at the South as at the North
　　Give us this day our dailey rations,
　　Of crackers salt horse and Pork,
　　[For]Give us our short comeings,
　　As we forgive our Quarter Master,
　　For thine is the power,
　　The soldiers and the Nigers,
　　For the space of 2 Years.
　　　　— parody of the Lord's Prayer; this version recorded by Henry J.H.
　　　　Thompson, a Connecticut soldier

85　Soldier's letter, nary red, / Hardtack and no soft bread, / Postmaster,
please put it through, / I've nary cent, but six months due.
　　　　— comical verse on the envelope of a soldier's letter

86　Soupy, soupy, soupy, without any bean,
　　Porky, porky, porky, without any lean,
　　Coffee, coffee, coffee, without any cream.
　　　　— soldiers' words to the bugle mess call

87   'Tis the song and sigh of the hungry,
Hard crackers, hard crackers, come again no more!
Many days have you lingered upon your stomachs sore,
O hard crackers, come again no more!
> — soldiers' parody of the song "Hard Times Come Again No More";
> attributed to the 1st Iowa; after being served with cornmeal mush,
> they changed the words:

It is the dying wail of the starving,
Hard crackers, hard crackers, come again once more;
You were old and very wormy, but we pass your failings o'er.
O hard crackers, come again once more!

88   'Tis the song of the soldier, weary, hungry, and faint,
   Hardtack, hardtack, come again no more;
Many days have I chewed you and uttered no complaint,
   O Greenbacks, come again once more.
> — soldiers' parody of the song "Hard Times Come Again No More"

89   We are the boys of Potomac's ranks,
Hurrah! Hurrah!
We are the boys of Potomac's ranks,
We ran with McDowell, retreated with Banks,
And we'll all drink stone blind—Johnny, fill up the bowl.
> — sung to the tune of "When Johnny Comes Marching Home," sung
> by soldiers in the Army of the Potomac

90 With their backs to the field and their feet to the foe.
> — soldiers' description of an honorable death

91 Whoever saw a dead cavalryman?
> — common saying among infantrymen

92 Who wouldn't be a soldier?
> — common saying meaning "Who cares?"

93 Zou! Zou! Zou!
> — war cry of Zouave troops

ANONYMOUS (SOUTHERN CIVILIANS)

94 A lady's thimble will hold all the blood that will be shed.
> — common saying just before the war started

95 You stand on the hearts of widows and orphans and childless mothers to be, and the voice of their wailing goes up to God this day.... The wail of lost souls slain in faith makes mournful music to live and die by.
> — [30 December 1861?], letter to President Lincoln, signed "One who loves our country North & South"

96 A tin can on a shingle!
> — 9 March 1862, description of the U.S.S. *Monitor* by a Confederate spectator

97 Them as wants to fight, let 'em fight—I don't.
> — 10 April 1863, statement by a Texas Unionist, recorded by Arthur Fremantle

98 I just wanted to see de man what made old massa run.
> — 7 September 1864, comment by former slave as Sherman entered Atlanta

99 Every life that is now lost in this war is murder; murder, sir....You have conquered us, and it is best to submit and make wise use of the future.
> — 19 February 1865, comment by a citizen of Columbia, South Carolina, to George Ward Nichols, a Union captain

100 I know I am free, for I have seen Father Abraham and felt him.
> — 3 April 1865, comment by former slave as Lincoln entered Richmond

101 Better a widow than married to a craven.
> — popular home-front motto among women

102 Forward to Washington! (alternate version: On to Washington!)
> — common saying among civilians and soldiers; a response to the North's "Forward/On to Richmond!" (see *New York Tribune*, June 1861; and anonymous [Northern civilians], "On to Richmond")

103 The Yankees cannot do us any more harm than our own soldiers have done.
> — common saying

ANONYMOUS (SOUTHERN MILITARY)

104 From home and friends we all must go, / To meet a strong but dastard foe. / Look away, look away, look away to Richmond town; / And ere again those friends we see / We vow to die or all be free; / Look away, look away, look away to Richmond town.
> — 1861, soldiers' words to the tune of the song "Dixie's Land"

105 Soldier boy, O soldier boy, a soldier boy for me, / If ever I get married, a soldier's wife I'll be.

> — 1861, "Song of the Mississippi Volunteers," written by Confederate soldiers

106 It was reported that they were retreating, but I guess they were retreating after us.

> — 23 March 1862, soldier's remark to Stonewall Jackson at Newtown, near Kernstown

107 Do the generals expect us to be killed and want us to wear our burial shrouds?

> — April 1862, comment by 2nd Texas troops when issued undyed white uniforms just before Shiloh (6 April 1862)

108 It's a hornets' nest in there.

> — 6 April 1862, soldiers' description of a Federal defense line at Shiloh

109 You have slain all my men and cattle, and you may take the battery and be damned.

> — 7 April 1862, dying words from a chief of artillery to Union troops at Shiloh

110 The Yankee host with blood-stained hands / Came Southward to divide our lands / This narrow & contracted spot / Is all this Yankee scoundrel got.

> — 10 July 1862, diary entry by an unknown Confederate soldier

111 Better take that flag down. We're awful fond of charging breastworks.

> — 10 September 1862, attributed comment by a Confederate soldier to a woman with a Union flag pinned to her dress at Frederick, Maryland (see also 27 June 1863)

112 General, you aren't wounded; you are only bruised!

> — 17 September 1862, stretcher bearer's announcement to Maxcy Gregg at Antietam

113 Yes, and here we lie.

> — 17 September 1862, a wounded, captured Mississippian's reply to Norman J. Hall of the 7th Michigan, who had said, "You fought and stood well," after Antietam

114 Yes, auntie, the Yankees gave us the devil, and they'll give us hell next.

> — 17 September 1862, a soldier's response to a slave woman who, after Antietam, had asked "Did you have a hard fight today?"

115   Boys, you can fight as well as we can, but Old Jackson is always one day ahead of you.
> — September 1862, a prisoner of war's comment to the Union officer Henry M. Pearson, praising Stonewall Jackson

116   If you want to smell hell—
If you want to have fun—
If you want to catch the devil—
Jine the Cavalry!
> — c. 1862, song in the cavalry division, Army of Northern Virginia

117   Man that is born of woman and enlists in Jackson's Army, has but few days to live, short rations and much hard work, sleeps but little and marches many miles.
> — 1862, common saying among Stonewall Jackson's men, reported by John Stone, 2nd Maryland, in a letter home

118   Oh, how do you like the army, / The brass-mounted army, / The high-falutin' army, / Where eagle buttons rule?
> — 1862, "The Brass-mounted Army," song

119   Burnside stuck in the mud.
This way to Richmond.
Yanks, if you can't place your pontoons, we will send help.
> — January 1863, Rebel signs taunting Burnside's men during the Mud March

120   We've given 'em h-ll on the Mississippi, h-ll on the Sabine, and h-ll in various other places.
> — 2 April 1863, boast to Arthur Fremantle by a Confederate captain from Texas

121   Yankees, we leave you, not because we cannot take Washington, but because it is not worth taking; and besides, the climate is not agreeable. A man should be amphibious to inhabit it.
> — April 1863, note left by Confederates who had withdrawn from their siege of the Federals at Washington, North Carolina

122   Kill me! Will someone kill me? I am in such anguish that it will be a mercy to do it—I have got to die—kill me—don't let me suffer!
> — 16 May 1863, plea to nearby Federals by a Confederate wounded in the head at Champion's Hill, Mississippi; the man died a few hours later

123 Take care, madam, for Hood's boys are great at storming breastworks when the Yankee colors is on them. (Alternate version: These old rebs are hell on breastworks.)

> — 27 June 1863, attributed comment by a soldier to a woman holding a Union flag on her bosom at Chambersburg, Pennsylvania (see also 10 September 1862)

124 If you can't feed us, you had better surrender us, horrible as the idea is, than suffer this noble army to disgrace themselves by desertion.

> — late June 1863, note signed "Many Soldiers" to their commander, John C. Pemberton, at Vicksburg

125 Run, old hare. If I was an old hare, I'd run too.

> — 3 July 1863, comment by a soldier when he saw a rabbit run to the rear of the Confederate forces at Gettysburg

126 Home, boys, home! Remember, home is over beyond those hills!

> — 3 July 1863, battle cry by a lieutenant during Pickett's Charge, Gettysburg

127 We'll follow you, Marse George. We'll follow you.

> — 3 July 1863, chant by George E. Pickett's men during their charge at Gettysburg

128 It's hotter here than it was in front.

> — 3 July 1863, comment by prisoners when directed to the rear at Gettysburg

129 We will fight them, sir, till hell freezes, and then, sir, we'll fight them on the ice.

> — July 1863, boast by an officer to Fitzgerald Ross while retreating from Gettysburg

130 I would charge hell itself for that old man.

> — 6 May 1864, Texas soldier's remark concerning Robert E. Lee

131 It's all a damned mess! And our two armies ain't nothing but howling mobs!

> — May 1864, comment by a captured Confederate private at the Wilderness

132 Where is Grant a-going to elbow us again?

> — 12 June 1864, question by a Confederate picket at Barker's Mill on the Chickahominy River, shouted to the nearby Federal lines; Grant had repeatedly edged around Lee's right flank during the recent campaign

133 You damned Yankee sons of bitches have killed our old Gen. Polk.
— 14 June 1864, note left by a Rebel infantryman for Union soldiers at Pine Mountain

134 About enough for another killin'.
— July 1864, Confederate soldier's reply to a Federal's question, "How many men have you fellows got left?"

135 Take the white man! Kill the nigger!
— 30 July 1864, attributed battle cry of soldiers at the Crater

136 Old Imboden's gone up the spout, And Old Jube Early's about played out.
— 22 September 1864, refrain of a song sung by a soldier after the Confederate defeat at Fisher's Hill

137 If, as it has often been remarked that "War is the result of a nation's sins"—then the sins of this nation must have been very great, and the atonement is truly one of the most painful mortality.
— 20 October 1864, introduction to the autograph album of Confederate prisoners of war at Johnson's Island, Lake Erie

138 And now I'm going Southward,
    For my heart is full of woe,
I'm going back to Georgia
    To find my "Uncle Joe."
You may sing about your dearest maid,
    And sing of Rosalie,
But the gallant Hood of Texas
    Played hell in Tennessee.
— December 1864, song sung by John B. Hood's troops to the tune of "The Yellow Rose of Texas"; "Uncle Joe" was Joseph E. Johnston

139 You go to hell. I've been there.
— December 1864, reply by one of Hood's infantrymen when, falling back from severe fighting at Nashville, he was ordered by a staff officer (a breed known to the rank and file as a "yaller dog") to halt and face the enemy

140 I'm running 'cause I can't fly!
— early April 1865, comment by a boy soldier among Lee's troops as Lee retreated toward Appomattox

141 My shoes are gone; my clothes are almost gone. I'm weary, I'm sick, I'm hungry. My family have been killed or scattered. And I have suffered all

this for my country. I love my country....But if this war is ever over, I'll be damned if I ever love another country!

> — early April 1865, comment by a straggler from James Longstreet's army during the retreat to Appomattox

142 You've got me, and a hell of a git you got!

> — early April 1865, comment by an exhausted, footsore soldier as he was captured by a Federal

143 We don't want to surrender any ammunition! We've been saving ammunition all this war! Hope we were not saving it for a surrender!

> — 9 April 1865, soldier's comment at Appomattox

144 I love you just as well as ever, General Lee!

> — 9 April 1865, soldier's comment after Lee's surrender to Grant

145 Good-bye, general. God bless you. We'll go home, make three more crops, and try them again.

> — 12 April 1865, soldier's comment to Bryan Grimes when the latter announced Lee's surrender

146 You got on sich a nice new-niform, you got sich nice boots on, you ridin' sich a nice hoss, an' you look like yer bowels wuz so reglar.

> — April 1865, attributed comment by a soldier to a Federal at the end of the war

147 Come all you wagon dogs, rejoice—
I will sing you a song,
If you'll join in the chorus—bow wow wow;
When we go to leave this world,
We will go above with sheets unfurled—bow wow wow.

> — song sung by Terry's Texas Rangers to "wagon dogs," shirkers who hung back with the wagon train; attributed to a cavalryman

148 General Lee to the rear!

> — chant by soldiers who wanted to protect Lee during battle; voiced on multiple occasions, e.g., 12 May 1864 at Spotsylvania

149 He's hell on retreat!

> — common saying among his own troops about Braxton Bragg, noted for his controversial command decisions

150 I'm feeling for a furlough.

> — punch line, in a widely circulated story, from a soldier who was waving his arms on either side of a tree (hoping to get a slight wound) and was asked what he was doing

151 It's no use killing these fellows; a half dozen take the place of every one we kill.

> — common saying about Union troops

152 The race is not to them that's got / The longest legs to run / Nor the battle to that people / That shoots the biggest gun.

> — doggerel from the "Texas Bible"

LEWIS ADDISON ARMISTEAD

Born 18 February 1817 in New Bern, North Carolina. Dismissed from West Point for breaking a plate over the head of a fellow cadet, Jubal A. Early. Armistead entered the army in 1839 and resigned as a captain on 26 May 1861. During the Civil War, he became a Confederate major (16 March 1861), colonel (23 September 1861), and brigadier general (1 April 1862). Mortally wounded at Gettysburg on 3 July 1863, he died 2 days later in Union hands.

153 Never mind me. We want men with guns in their hands.

> — 3 July 1863, reply to a soldier who pointed out that since Armistead was exposing himself to enemy fire, the soldier should be allowed to do the same

154 Give them the cold steel!

> — 3 July 1863, battle cry during Pickett's Charge at Gettysburg

155 Tell General Hancock that I know I did my country a great wrong when I took up arms against her, for which I am sorry, but for which I cannot live to atone.

> — 3 July 1863, comment to Lieutenant Mitchell, Hancock's aide-de-camp, after Armistead was mortally wounded at Gettysburg

AUGUSTA DAILY CONSTITUTIONALIST

The Augusta Daily Constitutionalist *was a newspaper in Augusta, Georgia.*

156 Atlanta is this great strategic point....The approaches to the Gate City—every one of them—must be made a second Thermopylae.

> — 1 May 1864

CIVIL WAR QUOTATIONS

JAMES L. AUTREY

Autrey was a Confederate colonel and the military governor of Vicksburg, Mississippi.

157 Mississippians don't know, and refuse to learn, how to surrender.
> — 18 May 1862, reply to Union forces asking for the surrender of Vicksburg

ISSAC ERWIN AVERY

Born 1828. A North Carolina resident who became a Confederate captain (16 May 1861), lieutenant colonel (1 June 1862), and colonel (11 June 1862). Wounded at Gettsyburg on 2 July 1863, he died the next day.

158 Tell my father that I died with my face to the enemy. (Alternate version: Tell my father I fell with my face to the enemy.)
> — 2 July 1863, final words before his death at Gettysburg

CHARLES BABBOTT

Babbott was a Union private.

159 Short and Sweet just like a rosted maget.
> — 1 January 1863, letter to his father, characterizing a letter the soldier had received

SULLIVAN BALLOU

Ballou, a 32-year-old Providence lawyer and former Speaker of the Rhode Island House of Representatives, was a major with the 2nd Rhode Island when he was killed in action 21 July 1861 at 1st Bull Run.

160 The indications are very strong that we shall move in a few days—perhaps tomorrow. Lest I should not be able to write again, I feel impelled to write a few lines that may fall under your eye when I shall be no more....If it is necessary that I should fall on the battle field for my Country, I am ready.
> — 14 July 1861, letter to his wife

161 I have no misgivings about, or lack of confidence in the cause in which I am engaged, and my courage does not halt or falter. I know how strongly American Civilization now leans on the triumph of the Government, and how great a debt we owe to those who went before us through the blood and

sufferings of the Revolution. And I am willing—perfectly willing—to lay down all my joys in this life to help maintain this Government, and to pay that debt.

— 14 July 1861, letter to his wife

162 I cannot describe to you my feelings on this calm Summer Sabbath night, when two-thousand men are sleeping around me, many of them enjoying perhaps the last sleep before that of death.

— 14 July 1861, letter to his wife

163 A pure love of my Country and of the principles I have so often advocated before the people—another name of Honor that I love more than I fear death, has called upon me and I have obeyed.

— 14 July 1861, letter to his wife

164 Sarah my love for you is deathless, it seems to bind me with mighty cables that nothing but Omnipotence could break; and yet my love of Country comes over me like a strong wind and burns me unresistibly on with all these chains to the battle field.

— 14 July 1861, letter to his wife

165 The memories of the blissful moments I have spent with you come creeping over me....Never forget how much I love you, and when my last breath escapes me on the battle field, it will whisper your name.... But, O Sarah! if the dead can come back to this earth and flit unseen around those they loved, I shall always be near you; in the gladest days and in the darkest nights...*always, always,* and if there be a soft breeze upon your cheek, it shall be my breath, as the cool air fans your throbbing temple, it shall be my spirit passing by. Sarah do not mourn me dead; think I am gone and wait for thee, for we shall meet again.

— 14 July 1861, letter to his wife

BALTIMORE AMERICAN AND COMMERCIAL ADVERTISER

The Baltimore American and Commercial Advertiser *was a newspaper in Baltimore, Maryland.*

166 Never was a greater hope placed upon apparently more insignificant means, but never was a great hope more triumphantly fulfilled.

— 12 March 1862, item on the U.S.S. *Monitor* (the reporter was Edward Fulton)

NATHANIEL PRENTICE (PRENTISS) BANKS

Born 30 January 1816 in Waltham, Massachusetts. Politician who, on 16 May 1861, was appointed a Union major general of volunteers. After the war, he was a United States congressman (1865-73, 1875-79, 1889-91) and a United States marshall (1879-88). Died 1 September 1894 in Waltham.

167 I will not retreat. We have more to fear from the opinions of our friends than the bayonets of our enemies.
— 23 May 1862, comment at Strasburg

168 Stop, men! Don't you love your country?
— 25 May 1862, query to fleeing Federals at Winchester; a Wisconsin soldier replied, "Yes, by God, and I'm trying to get back to it just as fast as I can!"

ROBERT W. BANKS

Banks was a Confederate private.

169 If I ever lose my patriotism, and the "secesh" spirit dies out, then you may know the "Commissary" is at fault. Corn meal mixed with water and tough beef three times a day will knock the "Brave Volunteer" under quicker than Yankee bullets.
— 22 October 1862, letter home

WILLIAM BARKSDALE

Born 21 August 1821 in Rutherford County, Tennessee. Lawyer, journalist, and politcian. During the war, he became a Confederate colonel (May 1861) and brigadier general (12 August 1862). Wounded 2 July 1863 at Gettysburg, he died the following day.

170 Tell my wife I am shot, but we fought like hell.
— 2 July 1863, dying words to a Federal surgeon at Gettysburg

FRANCIS CHANNING BARLOW

Born 19 October 1834 in Brooklyn, New York. Lawyer who, during the Civil War, became a private (19 April 1861) and first lieutenant (1 May 1861) in the New York state militia, and then a Union army lieutenant colonel (9 November 1861), colonel (14 April 1862), brigadier general (19 September 1862), and major general (25 May 1865). After the war, he returned to law practice and, while attorney general of New York (1871-73), began the prosecution of the Tweed ring, a faction of Tammany Hall politicians. Died 11 January 1896 in New York City.

171   Make your peace with God and mount, gentlemen; I have a hot place picked out for some of you today.

> — 12 May 1864, remark to his men at the Mule Shoe, Spotsylvania

PHINEAS TAYLOR BARNUM

Born 5 July 1810 in Bethel, Connecticut. Showman and entrepreneur who transformed the amusement business by the use of massive publicity. In the 1840s, he created Barnum's American Museum of freaks and oddities. In the 1870s, he turned to circuses, including The Barnum and Bailey Greatest Show on Earth. Died 7 April 1891 in Bridgeport, Connecticut.

172   The late events which have occurred in this vicinity, concluding with the arrest of Schnabel, have rendered secessionists so scarce, I cannot find one for exhibition in my museum.

> — 30 August 1861, letter to President Lincoln

JOSEPH JACKSON BARTLETT

Born 21 November 1834 in Binghamton, New York. Lawyer who, during the Civil War, became a Union major (21 May 1861), colonel (21 September 1861), and brigadier general (4 October 1862, expired 4 March 1863, reappointed 30 March 1863). Later he was brevetted a major general. After the war, he resumed his law career and served as a diplomat and deputy pension commissioner. Died 14 January 1893 in Baltimore, Maryland.

173   If sheep attack you, you are obliged to fight.

> — 23 May 1864, tongue-in-cheek remark to Union soldiers who had killed and eaten some sheep

CLARA BARTON

Born 25 December 1821 in North Oxford, Massachusetts. Her full name was Clarissa Harlowe Barton. Before the Civil War, she was a teacher and copyist. During the war, she was a Union nurse. In 1881 Barton founded the American

Red Cross, and in later years she authored many books. Died 12 April 1912 in Glen Echo, Maryland.

174 If *it must be*, let it come, and when there is no longer a soldier's arm to raise the Stars and Stripes above our Capitol, may God give me strength to mine.
> — 25 April 1861, letter home

175 I may be compelled to *face* danger, but *never fear it*, and while our soldiers can stand and *fight*, I can stand and feed and nurse them.
> — 1861, letter to her father

176 I greatly fear that the few privileged, elegantly dressed ladies who ride over and sit in their carriages to witness "splendid services" and "inspect the Army of the Potomac" and come away "delighted," learn very little of what lies there under canvas.
> — 16 December 1861, letter to the Ladies Relief Committee of Worcester

177 My business is stanching blood and feeding fainting men; my post the open field between the bullet and the hospital.
> — 24 June 1863, letter to T.W. Meighan

178 I make gruel—not speeches.
> — 24 June 1863, letter to T.W. Meighan

FRANCIS S. BARTOW

Bartow was a colonel with the 8th Georgia.

179 They have killed me; but boys, *never* give it up.
> — 21 July 1861, attributed dying words at 1st Bull Run

JANE B. BEALE

Beale was a widow with 9 children in Fredericksburg, Virginia

180 Necessity has no law and I do not admire naked martyrdom, so we abuse the Yankees to our heart's content, but buy their goods still.
> — 11 July 1862, journal

PIERRE GUSTAVE TOUTANT BEAUREGARD

Born 28 May 1818 in St. Bernard Parish, near New Orleans, Louisiana. West Point class of 1838. Before the Civil War, he rose to brevet major, briefly served as superintendent of West Point (23-28 January 1861), and resigned as a captain

(20 February 1861). During the war, he became a Confederate brigadier general (1 March 1861) and full general (31 August 1861, to rank from 21 July). After the war, he was a railroad executive and supervisor of the Louisiana state lottery. Died 20 February 1893 in New Orleans.

181 I am ordered by the Government of the Confederate States to demand the evacuation of Fort Sumter....The flag which you have upheld so long and with so much fortitude, under the most trying circumstances, may be saluted by you on taking it down.
> — 11 April 1861, message to Robert Anderson

182 My troops are not only willing, but are anxious, to meet the enemies of our country under all circumstances.
> — 3 June 1861, letter to Jefferson Davis

183 A reckless and unprincipled tyrant has invaded your soil....All rules of civilized warfare are abandoned, and they proclaim by their acts, if not on their banners, that their war-cry is "Beauty and booty."
> — 5 June 1861, proclamation to the people of Virginia

184 Let tomorrow be their Waterloo.
> — 19 July 1861, comment to his men before 1st Bull Run

185 Hail, Elzey! thou Blücher of the day.
> — 21 July 1861, praise to Arnold Elzey at 1st Bull Run

186 Oh, my country! I would readily have sacrificed my life and those of all the brave men around me to save your honor and to maintain your independence from the degrading yoke which those ruthless invaders had come to impose and render perpetual, and the day's issue has assured me that such emotions must also have animated all under my command.
> — 26 August 1861, report on 1st Bull Run

187 We must give up some minor points, and concentrate our forces, to save the most important ones, or we will lose all of them in succession.
> — 4 February 1862, letter to Roger A. Pryor

188 You have bravely fought the invaders of your soil for two days in his own position. Fought your superior in numbers, in arms, in all the appliances of war. Your success has been signal. His losses have been immense, outnumbering yours in all save the personal worth of the slain.
> — 16 April 1862, address to his troops at Corinth, Mississippi

189 The true maxims of war require us never to abandon our communications, but act on those of the enemy without exposing our own.
> — 18 March 1864, message to James Longstreet

BARNARD ELLIOTT BEE

Born 8 February 1824 in Charleston, South Carolina. West Point class of 1845. He resigned from the United States Army as a captain (3 March 1861) and entered Confederate service, earning quick promotions up to brigadier general (17 June 1861). He was credited with giving Thomas J. Jackson the nickname of "Stonewall" at 1st Bull Run. Bee was mortally wounded in that battle and died the following day, 22 July 1861.

190   There is Jackson standing like a stone wall. Let us determine to die here, and we will conquer. (Alternate version: There is Jackson standing like a stone wall. Rally behind the Virginians.)

> — 21 July 1861, exhortation to his men; Bee's meaning has been debated, some saying that he was praising Jackson's tenacity under fire, others that Bee was complaining about Jackson's reluctance to help

HENRY WARD BEECHER

Born 24 June 1813 in Litchfield, Connecticut. Minister, abolitionist, and brother of Harriet Beecher Stowe. Died 8 March 1887 in New York City.

191   A thoughtful mind, when it sees a nation's flag, sees not the flag only, but the nation itself; and whatever may be its symbols, its insignia, he reads chiefly in the flag the government, the principles, the truths, the history which belongs to the nation that sets it forth.

> — 1861, "The National Flag"

192   This is the common people's war. They furnish the men, the money, and its enthusiasm and patriotism....But we are like to be ruined by an administration that will not tell the truth, that spends precious time at President-making.

> — 10 July 1862, article in *The Independent*, a weekly

193   Our armies have been managed as if they were a body of nurses in a foundling hospital, watching at every step lest they tread on a baby....It is war that we are making—war first, war second, war wholly! It is not Politics. It is not Constitution-making....It is War, absolute, terrible, and immeasurable War!

> — 24 July 1862, article in *The Independent*

194   Certainly neither Mr. Lincoln nor his Cabinet have proved leaders. Fear was stronger than Faith!

> — 7 August 1862, article in *The Independent*

195 At present, the North is beaten....Let it be known that the Nation wasted away by an incurable consumption of Central Imbecility.
— 11 September 1862, article in *The Independent*

196 On this solemn and joyful day we again lift to the breeze our father's flag, now again the banner of the United States.... As long as the sun endures, or the stars, may it wave over a nation neither enslaved nor enslaving.
— 14 April 1865, oration at flag-raising ceremonies, Fort Sumter

ETHEL LYNN BEERS

Born 13 January 1827 in Goshen, New York. Her original name was Ethelinda Eliot; she split her first name to form two names, and obtained her permanent surname by marrying William H. Beers. She was a poet, best known for the poem given below. Died 11 October 1879 in Orange, New Jersey.

197 "All quiet along the Potomac," they say, / "Except here and there a stray picket / Is shot, as he walks on his beat, to and fro, / By rifleman hid in the thicket."... / "All quiet along the Potomac to-night," / No sound save the rush of the river; / While soft falls the dew on the face of the dead, / The picket's off duty forever.
— 30 November 1861, "The Picket Guard," poem published in *Harper's Weekly*, later better known as "All Quiet Along the Potomac To-night" (see "All quiet on the Potomac" under anonymous [Northern civilians], 1861); the poem became a popular song

JUDAH PHILIP BENJAMIN

Born 6 August 1811 in Christiansted, St. Croix, Danish West Indies (now the Virgin Islands). As a child, he moved with his family to the American South. Before the Civil War, he was a lawyer and politician. During the war, he became the Confederate attorney general (25 February 1861), secretary of war (17 September 1861), and secretary of state (18 March 1862). After the war, he practiced law in England. Died 6 May 1884 in Paris, France.

198 It is not men we lack, but muskets.
— 25 October 1861, letter to Albert S. Johnston

199 The law does not require any approval by the President, but he entirely approves my order to hang every bridge-burner you can catch and convict.
— 10 December 1861, message to William H. Carroll

200   The Department can only trust to the skill and prudence of our generals and the indomitable spirit of our people to maintain a struggle in which the disparity of numbers, already fearful, becomes still more threatening from the impossibility of adding to our stock of arms.

— 25 January 1862, letter to Joseph E. Johnston

201   The men in many cases really will not go home. A number of them who came here with their bounty and furloughs are going back to you at once. They came here, had a frolic with their bounty money, spent it all, and have agreed to go straight back to camp, receiving their commutation for transportation instead of furlough.

— 3 February 1862, letter from Richmond, Virginia, to Joseph E. Johnston

202   It is of no use to re-enforce him; he is not going to fight.

— 1864, comment to Jefferson Davis about Joseph E. Johnston

J. KELLY BENNETTE

Bennette was the 8th Virginia Cavalry's medical orderly.

203   I don't know anything of this General L. except what he shows in his face but it cannot be a change for the worse for I take it that there are few meaner men unhung than this Robert Ransom.

— 20 August 1864, diary entry when Lunsford Lomax replaced Ransom as chief of Jubal Early's cavalry

DANIEL DAVIDSON BIDWELL

Born 1819 in New York. Before the Civil War, he was a Buffalo, New York, police official. During the war, he became a Union colonel (21 October 1861) and brigadier general (11 August 1864). Killed in action 19 October 1864 at Cedar Creek, Virginia.

204   Tell them I died at my post doing my duty.

— 19 October 1864, statement to a surgeon after Bidwell was mortally wounded at Cedar Creek

JAMES M. BINFORD

Binford was a private with the 21st Virginia.

205   I must say, I have had enough of the glory of war. I am sick of seeing dead men and men's limbs torn from their bodies....When the war ends, if I am alive, no one will return to peaceful avocations more willingly than I.
— 13 August 1862, letter to his sisters

HORACE BINNEY

Born 4 January 1780 in Philadelphia, Pennsylvania. Lawyer who, during the Civil War, wrote pamphlets defending President Lincoln's suspension of the writ of habeas corpus. Died 12 August 1875 in Philadelphia.

206   The assault upon Fort Sumter started us all to our feet, as one man; all political division ceased among us from that very moment....There is among us but one thought, one object, one end, one symbol—the Stars and Stripes.
— 27 May 1861, letter to Sir J.T. Coleridge

CHARLES MINOR BLACKFORD

Born 17 October 1833 in Fredericksburg, Virginia. Before the Civil War, he was a lawyer. During the war, he rose quickly from corporal to first lieutenant to captain (1861). After the war, he returned to the law. Died 10 March 1903 in Lynchburg, Virginia.

207   No victory has ever been won without bringing about a fight.
— 21 June 1863, letter to his wife, concerning Joseph E. Johnston's reluctance to test his troops

208   Never in my life have I seen so many ugly women as I have seen since coming to this place. It may be that the pretty ones do not show themselves but the ugly ones parade around everywhere.
— 30 June 1863, letter from near Chambersburg, Pennsylvania, to his wife

209   Men, women and children are alike all afflicted with a yankee twang that grates against my nerves and ear-drums most terribly.
— 30 June 1863, letter from near Chambersburg, Pennsylvania, to his wife

210 They vastly outnumbered us, and though our men made a charge which will be the theme of the poet, painter and historian of all ages, they could not maintain the enemy's lines much less capture them.
> — 4 July 1863, letter to his wife, after Gettysburg

211 It is hard to maintain one's patriotism on ashcake and water.
> — 10 August 1864, letter to his wife

212 Our men are deserting quite freely. It looks very blue to them, and the fact that Sherman marched from Atlanta to Savannah without seeing an armed Confederate soldier is well calculated to make them despondent.
> — 24 March 1865, letter to his wife

GERTRUDE, VICTOR GUS., AND KATIE BLOEDE

The Bloedes were children from Brooklyn.

213 You have added glory to the sky & splendor to the sun, & there are but few men who have ever done that before, either by words or acts....The foul blot of many years on our own glorious flag, you have erased with one stroke of your pen.
> — 4 January 1863, letter to President Lincoln, concerning the Emancipation Proclamation

GEORGE HENRY BOKER

Born 6 October 1823 in Philadelphia, Pennsylvania. Writer and diplomat. Died 2 January 1890 in Philadelphia.

214 What are you waiting for, tardy George?
> — January 1862, "Tardy George," satirical poem about George B. McClellan

215 And there, while thread will hang to thread, / Oh, let that ensign fly! / The noblest constellation set / Against the Northern sky.
> — 1862, "The *Cumberland*," poem about the U.S.S. *Cumberland*, sunk by the Confederate ironclad *Virginia* (formerly the U.S.S.*Merrimack*)

JOHN WILKES BOOTH

Born 26 April 1838 in Bel Air, Maryland. Actor who, on 14 April 1865, shot President Lincoln. Booth himself was shot and killed on 26 April 1865 near Bowling Green, Virginia.

216 This man's appearance, his pedigree, his coarse low jokes and anecdotes, his vulgar similes and his frivolity, are a disgrace to the seat he holds.
> — early 1865, attributed comment on President Lincoln

217 I have too great a soul to die like a criminal.
> — early 1865, attributed comment

218 Sic semper tyrannis!
> — 14 April 1865, Virginia's state motto (Latin for "Thus always to tyrants"), shouted by Booth after shooting President Lincoln; some heard it as "The South is avenged!" or "The South shall be free!"

219 Tell mother I die for my country.
> — 26 April 1865, statement after being shot

220 Useless, useless.
> — 26 April 1865, dying words

BOSTON SUNDAY HERALD

The Boston Sunday Herald *was a periodical in Boston, Massachusetts.*

221 There are shoddy lawyers, shoddy doctors, shoddy preachers, and shoddy teachers,...and, worse than all, there are shoddy newspapers whose especial business it is to puff up all the shoddy in the world and endeavor to make the people believe that it is the genuine article.
> — 15 February 1863

JOSEPH BOYD

Boyd was a Confederate private.

222 I advise you, and as strongly as ever, to not come to war. I tell you you will repent it if you do, I do believe. You have no idea of what it is to be a soldier.
> — 12 April 1862, letter to his brother

BRAXTON BRAGG

Born 22 March 1817 in Warrenton, North Carolina. West Point class of 1837. He left the army in 1856 to be a Louisiana planter. During the Civil War, he became a Confederate brigadier general (7 March 1861), major general (12 September 1861), and full general (12 April 1862). After the war, he was a civil engineer. Died 27 September 1876 in Galveston, Texas.

223   Our strength consists in the enemy's weakness.
> — 22 October 1861, letter to Jefferson Davis, referring to the North's lack of resolve in using its superior resources

224   Universal suffrage, furloughs, and whiskey have ruined us.
> — 1862, comment after Shiloh (April 1862)

225   The great changes of command and commanders here has well nigh overburdened me, but I hope yet to mark the enemy before I break down.
> — 22 July 1862, letter from Tupelo, Mississippi, to his wife

226   This campaign must be won by marching, not fighting.
> — September 1862, statement made in Kentucky

WILLIAM H. BREARLEY

Brearley was a Union private.

227   If you ever go into battle, have your canteen full. I was so dry at one time I could have drank out of a mud puddle—without stopping to ask questions.
> — 26 September 1862, letter to his father

228   I had a bullett strike me on the top of the head just as I was going to fire and a piece of Shell struck my foot—a ball hit my finger and another hit my thumb I concluded they ment me.
> — 26 September 1862, letter to his father

JOHN CABELL BRECKINRIDGE

Born 15 January 1821 near Lexington, Kentucky. Lawyer and politician who served as vice president of the United States (1857-61) and, in 1860, ran for president as the nominee of a Southern faction of the Democratic party. During the Civil War, he became a Confederate brigadier general (2 November 1861), won promotion to major general (14 April 1862), and served as secretary of war during the last few months of the Confederacy. After the war, he returned to the practice of law. Died 17 May 1875 in Lexington.

229 My poor Orphans! My poor Orphan Brigade! They have cut it to pieces.
— 2 January 1863, comment after Stones River

JOHN BRIGHT

Born 16 November 1811 in Rochdale, Lancashire, England. British politician. Died 27 March 1889 in Rochdale.

230 In a few years, a very few years, the twenty millions of freemen in the North will be thirty millions, or even fifty millions, a population equal to or exceeding that of this Kingdom. When that time comes, I pray that it may not be said amongst them that, in the darkest hour of their country's trials, England, the land of their fathers, looked on with icy coldness and saw unmoved the perils and calamities of their children.
— 4 December 1861, speech on the American Civil War

231 My opinion is that the Northern States will manage somehow to muddle through.
— 1862, attributed comment

NOAH BROOKS

Born 24 October 1830 in Castine, Maine. Journalist who, in December 1862, began to cover Washington, D.C., for the Sacramento Daily Union. *After the war, he was a writer and editor for various newspapers. Died 16 August 1903 in Pasadena, California.*

232 There comes a line of stretchers with men who have left arms, legs, hands, feet, and much blood upon the fatal field of Fredericksburg. Rebel guns have maimed these men for life, and those who went forth full of vigor, hope, and ambition, their hearts beating high with visions of glory and prowess, have returned again—broken, decrepit, useless, and disfigured by the enginery of war against which they manfully surged in solid columns again and again.
— 19 December 1862, news dispatch to the *Sacramento Daily Union*

233 Our men, burning to advance, are held in check and are wasting in numbers and being soured and made malcontent by inactivity and idleness....They will not do anything without McClellan, but will they do anything with him?
— 14 January 1863, news dispatch to the *Sacramento Daily Union*

ORVILLE HICKMAN BROWNING

Born 10 February 1806 in Harrison County, Kentucky. Lawyer and politician who helped organize the Republican party. He was a longtime friend of Abraham Lincoln. Died 10 August 1881 in Quincy, Illinois.

234 Be of good cheer. You have your future in your own hands, and the power to make your name one of the most justly revered and illustrious in the annals of the American race.
— 19 August 1861, letter to President Lincoln

WILLIAM GANNAWAY BROWNLOW

Born 29 August 1805 in Wythe County, Georgia. Nicknamed Parson. Pro-Union Southern journalist and politician. Died 29 April 1877 in Knoxville, Tennessee.

235 Grape for the rebel masses, and hemp for their leaders!
— 15 March 1862, speech in Knoxville

SIMON BOLIVAR BUCKNER

Born 1 April 1823 in Hart County, Kentucky. West Point class of 1844. He left the army in 1855 to enter business. During the Civil War, he became a Confederate brigadier general (14 September 1861), major general (16 August 1862), and lieutenant general (20 September 1864). After the war, he returned to business and in 1887 was elected governor of Kentucky. Died 8 January 1914 near Munfordville, Kentucky.

236 The distribution of the forces under my command incident to an unexpected change of commanders and the overwhelming force under your command compel me, notwithstanding the brilliant success of the Confederate arms yesterday, to accept the ungenerous and unchivalrous terms which you propose.
— 16 February 1862, note surrendering Fort Donelson to Ulysses S. Grant

237 Utter a shout of defiance against the Northern tyranny and proclaim that, under the guidance of heaven, Kentucky shall prove worthy of her ancient fame.
— 24 September 1862, proclamation to the people of Kentucky

CIVIL WAR QUOTATIONS

BUFFALO EXPRESS

The Buffalo Express *was a newspaper in Buffalo, New York.*

238 God—Grant—Victory.
— slogan during the Civil War

ORVILLE C. BUMPASS

Bumpass was a Confederate private.

239 The state of the morals is quite as low as the soil, almost all the women are given to whoredom & the ugliest, sallowfaced, shaggy headed, bare footed dirty wretches you ever saw.
— 22 October 1864, letter from northern Alabama to his wife

HIRAM BURNHAM

Born c. 1814 in Maine. Before the Civil War, he was a lumberman and politician. During the war, he became a Union lieutenant colonel (July 1861), colonel (December 1861), and brigadier general (April 1864). Killed in action 29 September 1864 at Fort Harrison, Virginia.

240 When we reached the fort my command was in perfect order, and as my men faced about I read in their faces the stern determination to suffer death in any form rather than give up an inch of ground.
— 7 May 1862, report on Williamsburg

241 Every man was in his place, and we poured a volley into them which thinned their ranks terribly. Blinded and dismayed they still pressed on, firing wildly at random. Again our forces poured into them, sending death and destruction into their midst. They wavered, they faltered, they halted. We saw our advantage. Sending forth cheer on cheer we steadily advanced and poured into them until the rout was complete.
— 7 May 1862, report on Williamsburg

JOHN H. BURNHAM

Burnham was a Union officer, rising to the rank of lieutenant colonel on 26 December 1862.

242 The pockets of all our dead were emptied. In some instances, they cut the pockets out of the clothing, not stopping to examine them on the field.

The shoes, too, were taken from all our dead bodies. This I think is a very plain indication of the state of the leather market in the Confederacy.

— 4 October 1862, letter to "Mother and Family," concerning the aftermath of Antietam

JOHN L. BURNS

Born 5 September 1793 in Burlington, New Jersey (some sources give 1789 in Pennsylvania). A veteran of the War of 1812, he later became a Gettysburg, Pennsylvania, cobbler. In 1863 he joined the Federal soldiers during the battles at Gettysburg. Eventually he was wounded 3 times, was briefly held prisoner, and won the title of "The Old Hero of Gettysburg." Died 4 February 1872 in Bonneauville, Pennsylvania, and buried in Gettysburg.

243　They fit terribly,—the Rebs couldn't make anything of them fellers.

— 1 July 1863, comment to Franklin A. Haskell, complimenting the Union soldiers at Gettysburg

AMBROSE EVERETT BURNSIDE

Born 23 May 1824 in Liberty, Indiana. West Point class of 1847. He left the army in 1853 to manufacture firearms. During the Civil War, he became a Union colonel (2 May 1861), brigadier general (6 August 1861), and major general (18 March 1862). From November 1862 to January 1863, he commanded the Army of the Potomac. After the war, he was the governor of Rhode Island (1866-68) and a United States senator (1875-81). Died 13 September 1881 in Bristol, Rhode Island.

244　The mission of our joint expedition is not to invade any of your rights, but to assert the authority of the United States, and thus to close with you the desolating war brought upon your State by comparatively a few bad men in your midst.

— 16 February 1862, proclamation to the people of North Carolina

245　After the occupation of this island by our troops a few irregularities occurred in the way of destruction of property, such as burning fences, taking furniture and wood from houses, killing stock, etc., but in no case has personal violence or indignities been offered....I have ordered payment for these damages to be made to those who seem well disposed to our Government and have taken the oath of allegiance.

— 20 February 1862, letter to Lorenzo Thomas, concerning Roanoke Island

246 Thank God, the day is ours!

— 14 March 1862, attributed comment on seeing the Federal flag within enemy lines, near New Bern, North Carolina

247 Whoever, after the issue of this order, shall, within the limits to which the Union Arms may extend in this Department, utter one word against the Government of these United States, will be at once arrested and closely confined.

— 28 April 1862, General Order No. 28, Department of North Carolina

HORACE BUSHNELL

Born 14 April 1802 in Bantam, Connecticut. Theologian. Died 17 February 1876 in Hartford, Connecticut.

248 Adversity kills only where there is a weakness to be killed.

— late July 1861, sermon after the Union defeat at 1st Bull Run; the quotation comes from Proverbs (24:10): "If thou faint in the day of adversity, thy strength is small"

249 We want no newspaper government, and least of all a newspaper army....Let the government govern, and the army fight, and let both have their own counsel, disturbed and thrown out of balance by no gusty conceit or irresponsible and fanatical clamor.

— late July 1861, sermon after the Union defeat at 1st Bull Run

BENJAMIN FRANKLIN BUTLER

Born 5 November 1818 in Deerfield, New Hampshire. Before the Civil War, he was a lawyer and politician. During the war, he became a brigadier general in the Massachusetts militia (17 April 1861) and major general of Union volunteers (16 May 1861). From May to December 1862, he was the military governor in New Orleans. After the war, he served as a United States congressman (1867-75, 1877-79) and the governor of Massachusetts (1883-84). In 1884 he unsuccessfully ran for president of the United States on the Greenback and Anti-Monopolist ticket. Died 11 January 1893 in Washington, D.C.

250 He who does his duty to the Union, does his duty to the state; and he who does his duty to the state, does his duty to the Union.

— 16 May 1861, response to a serenade in Washington, D.C.

251 Many things in a man's life may be worse than death. So, to a government, there may be many things, such as dishonor and disintegration, worse than the shedding of blood.

— 16 May 1861, response to a serenade in Washington, D.C.

252 I shall hold these Negroes as contraband of war, since they are engaged in the construction of your battery and are claimed as your property.

— 24 May 1861, reply to a Confederate officer who had requested the return of three escaped slaves

253 It has come to the knowledge of the Commanding General, that notwithstanding all his efforts to prevent the introduction of intoxicating liquors into the island and among his command, to be used as a beverage, we are still followed by this curse of the army.... All intoxicating liquors kept for sale or to be used as a beverage will be seized and destroyed, or confiscated to hospital uses.

— 28 March 1862, General Order No. 7, Ship Island

254 This outrage will be punished in such manner as in my judgment will caution both the perpetrators and abettors of the act, so that they shall fear the *stripes* if they do not now reverence the stars of our banner.

— 29 April 1862, letter to Edwin M. Stanton, referring to William B. Mumford's desecration of the United States flag in New Orleans (Mumford was executed on 7 June 1862)

255 I am a friend to Southern rights now, but I came here to put down Southern wrongs.

— 1 May 1862, comment to Pierre Soulé, spokesman for New Orleans city officials; so recorded by Butler himself, though others have the quotation as "I was always a friend of Southern rights but an enemy of Southern wrongs"

256 This hunger does not pinch the wealthy and influential, the leaders of the rebellion, who have gotten up this war, and are now endeavoring to prosecute it without regard to the starving poor, the workingman, his wife and child. Unmindful of their suffering fellow-citizens at home, they have caused or suffered provisions to be carried out of the city for Confederate service since the occupation by the United States forces.

— 9 May 1862, General Order No. 25, New Orleans

257 There having been outrages committed at and near Kennerville, such as killing chickens, robbing sugar houses, insulting women, and disgracing the flag and the country. You will detail a picked sergeant and six men of

tried fidelity and honesty, to be stationed at Kennerville as a guard for the inhabitants.

— 14 May 1862, message to J.W. Phelps

258 As the officers and soldiers of the United States have been subject to repeated insults from the women (calling themselves ladies) of New Orleans in return for the most scrupulous non-interference and courtesy on our part, it is ordered that hereafter when any female shall by word, gesture, or movement insult or show contempt for any officer or soldier of the United States she shall be regarded and held liable to be treated as a woman of the town plying her avocation.

— 15 May 1862, General Order No. 28, the "Woman Order"

259 The Negro here by long habit and training has acquired a great horror of fire-arms, sometimes ludicrous in the extreme when the weapon is in his own hand.

— 25 May 1862, letter from New Orleans to Stanton

260 We are threatened with a Guerilla War which is claimed will be interminable. I take leave to suggest that it can be terminated in a few days. A reward of a $1000 for each Guerilla head, and freedom to the Negro who should bring it in, would bring that uncivilized system of war fare to a sudden termination by an equally uncivilized remedy. "Fire set to fight fire."

— 3 July 1862, letter from New Orleans to Stanton

261 I hold that rebellion is treason, and that treason, persisted in, is death, and any punishment short of that due a traitor gives so much clear gain to him from the clemency of the government.

— 24 December 1862, published farewell address to the people of New Orleans

262 I saw that this Rebellion was a war of the aristocrats against the middling men, of the rich against the poor....I therefore felt no hesitation in taking the substance of the wealthy, who had caused the war, to feed the innocent poor, who had suffered by the war.

— 24 December 1862, published farewell address to the people of New Orleans

263 There is but one thing that at this hour stands between you and your government—and that is slavery.

The institution, cursed by God, which has taken its last refuge here, in His providence will be rooted out as the tares from the wheat, although the wheat be torn up with it.

— 24 December 1862, published farewell address to the people of New Orleans

264 I never will ask the color of the man who exposes his life to protect mine upon the same battle-field in defence of the honor of my country.
— 28 February 1863, letter to Salmon P. Chase

265 The colored man fills an equal space in ranks while he lives, and an equal grave when he falls.
— 5 December 1863, General Order No. 46, recommending equal pay for black soldiers

266 Competent officers make good soldiers; efficient officers can prevent outrage and plunder on the part of their men.
— 16 January 1864, General Order No. 10

267 Smith has gone out, and will be relieved, and will not be employed by Grant again during the campaign. He intrigued to get me out and behold the result.
— 18 July 1864, letter to his wife, concerning William F. Smith

268 You will lose less men in a defence however protracted and deadly than you will in a retreat.
— 29 July 1864, message to Robert S. Foster at Deep Bottom, Virginia

SARAH H. BUTLER

Mrs. Butler was the wife of Benjamin F. Butler.

269 Never has anything been more deserved. Their insolence is beyond endurance, and must be checked.
— 15 May 1862, letter to Harriet H. Heard, concerning the "Woman Order" (see Benjamin F. Butler, 15 May 1862)

270 About a dozen ladies have called on me to express their feeling for the Union, but apparently in fear lest their coming should be known. They say the town ought to have been shelled, that leniency is not understood by this bragging, cutthroat people, and that they deny being whipped, because they have not yet suffered.
— 15 May 1862, letter to Harriet H. Heard concerning the women of New Orleans

271 Mr. Butler gets letters almost daily, that he will be poisoned or assassinated, and that leagues are formed, sworn to accomplish it.
— 15 May 1862, letter to Harriet H. Heard

GEORGE WASHINGTON CABLE

Born 12 October 1844 in New Orleans. Author and reformer (an advocate of prison reform and civil rights for blacks). During the Civil War, he spent two years in the 4th Mississippi Cavalry. His war experiences are reflected in his novel The Cavalier *(1901). Died 31 January 1925 in St. Petersburg, Florida.*

272 So, Jim, take care of yourself, be a good soldier, study army regulations, *read your bible, say your prayers without fear of comment,* write to us often, keep up your spirits, don't fall in love nor the enemy's hands.
— 26 November 1864, letter to his brother

273 These are the "Times that try men's souls," and my constant prayer is that when ours are tried they may go through the ordeal as gold thro' the refiner's fire.
— 16 April 1865, letter to his mother

EDWARD RICHARD SPRIGG CANBY

Born August 1817 in Kentucky. West Point class of 1839. A career soldier, he was a major (since 3 March 1855) when the Civil War began. During the war, he became a Union colonel (14 May 1861), brigadier general of volunteers (31 March 1862), and major general of volunteers (7 May 1864). After the war, he stayed in the army and was killed in the line of duty by Modoc Indians on 11 April 1873 in northern California.

274 The people of the Territory, with few exceptions, I believe, are loyal, but they are apathetic in disposition, and will adopt any measures that may be necessary for the defense of their Territory with great tardiness, looking with greater concern to their private, and often petty interests, and delaying or defeating the objects of the Government by their personal or political quarrels.
— 16 August 1861, letter to the assistant adjutant general of the Western Department, concerning the New Mexico Territory

JAMES CARRIE

Carrie was an English-born schoolmaster who joined the Union forces as a private with the 18th Missouri. He was killed on 6 April 1862 at Shiloh.

275 I trust I am prepared to offer myself a bloody sacrifice on the altar of my adopted country, if need be.
— 3 February 1862, letter to his wife

276 Soldiering is a good deal like going to school, we have to put up with a good many rules, that looked hard to us at first, but of which we now see the necessity. We had to be broke in like oxen to work. Now we begin to work pretty well.

— 7 March 1862, letter to his wife

ADRIAN CARRUTH

Carruth was a Confederate private from Mississippi.

277 Buzzards would not eat it at any season of the year.

— 4 March 1863, letter to his sister, regarding military beef

JOSHUA LAWRENCE CHAMBERLAIN

Born 8 September 1828 in Brewer, Maine. College teacher who, during the Civil War, became a Union lieutenant colonel (8 August 1862), colonel (20 May 1863), brigadier general (18 June 1864), and brevet major general (29 March 1865). After the war, he was governor of Maine, president of Bowdoin College, a businessman, and a writer. In 1893 he was awarded the Congressional Medal of Honor for his action at Little Round Top, Gettysburg. Died 24 February 1914 in Portland, Maine.

278 The edge of the fight rolled backward and forward like a wave.

— 6 July 1863, report on Gettysburg

279 An officer fired his pistol at my head with one hand, while he handed me his sword with the other.

— 6 July 1863, report on Gettysburg

280 I am willing to fight men in arms, but not *babes in arms*.

— 14 December 1864, letter to his sister, after his men had burned out women and children near Petersburg in retaliation for the actions of Confederate bushwhackers against Union soldiers

281 I owe the Country three years of service. It is a time when every man should stand by his guns.

— 12 February 1865, letter to his father

282 But there is no promise of life in peace, & no decree of death in war.

— 12 February 1865, letter to his father

283 Don't let anybody stop me except the enemy.

— 31 March 1865, comment to Gouverneur K. Warren, at White Oak Road near Five Forks, Virginia

CHARLESTON DAILY COURIER

The Charleston Daily Courier *was a newspaper in Charleston, South Carolina.*

284 It has become a trite remark among the troops, that "all a Yankee is now worth is his shoes"; and it is said...that some of our regiments have become so expert in securing these coveted articles, that they can make a charge and strip every dead Yankee's feet they pass without coming to a halt.
— 3 September 1862

CHARLESTON MERCURY

The Charleston Mercury *was a newspaper in Charleston, South Carolina*

285 King Lincoln—Rail Splitter Abraham—Imperator!
— 9 March 1861, dateline 5 March 1861, Washington, D.C., after Lincoln's first inauguration

286 When the Government of the North shall have fled into Pennsylvania, when the public buildings in Washington shall have been razed to the ground, so as to forbid the hope of their ever again becoming the nest of Yankee despotism, then, at last, may we expect to see the hope of success vanish from the Northern mind, and reap the fruit of our bloody and long continued trials.
— 6 September 1862

287 It is impossible for an invasion to have been more foolish and disastrous.
— 30 July 1863, after Gettysburg

288 Blackguard and buffoon as he is, he has pursued his end with an energy as untiring as an Indian and a singleness of purpose that might almost be called patriotic.
— 10 January 1865, concerning Abraham Lincoln

JAMES CHESNUT, JR.

Born 18 January 1815 in Camden, South Carolina. Before the war, he was a lawyer and politician. He began the war as a Confederate colonel and served under Beauregard at Fort Sumter. Later he was an aide to Jefferson Davis and became a brigadier general (23 April 1864). After the war, Chesnut was active in overthrowing Reconstruction politicians in his state. Died 1 February 1885 at his plantation near Camden.

289   By authority of Brigadier-General Beauregard, commanding the Provisional Forces of the Confederate States, we have the honor to notify you that he will open the fire of his batteries on Fort Sumter in one hour from this time.

> — 12 April 1861, 3:20 A.M., note to Major Robert Anderson, Union commander of Fort Sumter; Chesnut dictated the message to Captain Stephen D. Lee

290   The success of our cause depends not merely on the ability and fidelity, but to a great extent also on the harmony and hearty co-operation, of those who are chief and chosen instruments in the direction of our affairs. Any extended distrust in the crisis of our fate will bring dire calamities upon us. We must heed not the universal babbling of some nor the deliberate malice of many.

> — 9 November 1861, letter to Jefferson Davis

MARY BOYKIN MILLER CHESNUT

Born 31 March 1823 in Statesburg, South Carolina. Wife of James Chesnut, Jr. She is the most celebrated diarist of the Confederacy. In the 1880s, she rewrote her Civil War-period diary (which she usually called a "journal"), making multiple versions of many portions of it and leaving the work unfinished and untitled at her death. An 1880s version was published in 1905 as A Diary from Dixie *(edited by Isabella D. Martin and Myrta Lockett Avary); however, it was marred by an excessively heavy editorial hand. A 1981 edition,* Mary Chesnut's Civil War *(edited by C. Vann Woodward), more clearly represents Chesnut's own 1880s material. Most of the familiar Chesnut diary quotations—long assumed to have been written in the 1860s—were actually created in the 1880s. Of her original, Civil War-period, diary, only certain sections of 1861 and 1865 are extant; they were published in 1984 as* The Private Mary Chesnut *(by C. Vann Woodward and Elisabeth Muhlenfeld). The quotations below are labeled to indicate whether they belong to the "original" or "1880s" version. Mary Chesnut died 22 November 1886 in Camden, South Carolina.*

291   Our mobs are gentlemen. The men who make the row in the northern cities are here hoeing cotton.

> — 5 March 1861, diary (original)

292   The cry to day is *war*.

> — 6 March 1861, diary (original)

293 I wonder if it be a sin to think slavery a curse to any land. Sumner said not one word of this hated institution which is not true. Men & women are punished when their masters & mistresses are brutes & not when they do wrong....God forgive *us*, but ours is a *monstrous* system & wrong & iniquity.
— 18 March 1861, diary (original)

294 Not by one word or look can we detect any change in the demeanor of these negro servants....Are they stolidly stupid or wiser than we are, silent and strong, biding their time?
— 13 April 1861, diary (1880s)

295 Trescot says this victory will be our ruin. It lulls us into a fool's paradise of conceit at our superior valor. And the shameful farce of their flight will wake every inch of their manhood.
— 24 July 1861, diary (1880s), concerning 1st Bull Run

296 Time and tide wait for no man, and there was a tide in our affairs which might have led to Washington, and we did not take it and so lost our fortune, this round.
— 1 August 1861, diary (1880s)

297 I think *these* times make all women feel their humiliation in the affairs of the world. With men it is on to the field—"glory, honour, praise, &c, power." Women can only stop at home—& every paper reminds us that women are to be *violated*—ravished & all manner of humiliation. How are the daughters of Eve punished.
— 29 August 1861, diary (original)

298 Seward's little bell reigns supreme.
— 29 August 1861, diary (1880s); for "Seward's little bell," see William Henry Seward, 1861

299 New Orleans gone—and with it the Confederacy. Are we not cut in two? That Mississippi ruins us if lost. The Confederacy done to death by the politicians.
— 27 April 1862, diary (1880s)

300 There are people who still believe negroes to be property. Like Noah's neighbors, who insisted that the Deluge would only be a little shower, after all.
— 29 April 1862, dairy (1880s)

301 Hope springs eternal in the Southern breast.
— 24 May 1862, diary (1880s)

302   Since Vicksburg they have not a word to say against Grant's habits. He has the disagreeable habit of not retreating before irresistible veterans.
>   — 1 January 1864, diary (1880s)

303   We are going to be wiped off the face of the earth.
>   — 21 September 1864, diary (1880s)

304   These stories of our defeats in the Valley fall like blows upon a dead body. Since Atlanta I have felt as if all were dead within me, forever.
>   — 29 September 1864, diary (1880s)

305   Through the deep waters we wade.
>   — 1 December 1864, diary (1880s)

306   Shame—disgrace—misery....The grand smash has come.
>   — 23 February 1865, dairy (original)

CINCINNATI COMMERCIAL

The Cincinnati Commercial *was a newspaper in Cincinnati, Ohio.*

307   The painful intelligence reaches us...that Gen. William T. Sherman, late commander of the Department of the Cumberland, is insane. It appears that he was at the time while commanding in Kentucky, stark mad.
>   — 11 December 1861

308   The city of Fredericksburg was a trap, and we had plunged into it. The policy of permitting us to "occupy and possess" it under commanding batteries, was clear enough. The blunder stood revealed.
>   — 17 December 1862

CINCINNATI GAZETTE

The Cincinnati Gazette *was a newspaper in Cincinnati, Ohio.*

309   To arms! The time for playing war has passed. The enemy is approaching our doors.
>   — September 1862

ACHILLES V. CLARK

Clark was a sergeant with the Confederate 20th Tennessee when he wrote the letter below.

310 The poor deluded negroes would run up to our men fall upon their knees and with uplifted hands scream for mercy but they were ordered to their feet and then shot down. The white men fared but little better....I with several others tried to stop the butchery and at one time had partially succeeded but General Forrest ordered them shot down like dogs, and the carnage continued.

— April 1864, letter to his sisters, after the massacre at Fort Pillow

HOWELL COBB

Born 17 September 1815 in Jefferson City, Georgia. Before the war, he was a lawyer and politician. While Speaker of the Provisional Congress, he joined the Confederate army as a colonel (15 July 1861). Later he won promotions to brigadier general (13 February 1862) and major general (9 September 1863). After the war, he practiced law. Died 9 October 1868 in New York City.

311 You cannot make soldiers of slaves, nor slaves of soldiers....If slaves will make good soldiers our whole theory of slavery is wrong—but they won't make soldiers.

— 8 January 1865, letter to James A. Seddon

WILLIAM H. CODY

Cody was a Confederate private.

312 If we do strike them Yankees again, they will get wone of the worst whippings they ever had for the most of the boys are mighty anxious to get a lick at them for some blankets.

— 18 October 1864, letter to his sister

ROBERT COLBY

Colby was a civilan from New York City.

313 You need more dignity.

— 18 May 1861, letter to President Lincoln

IDELEA COLLENS

Collens was a Confederate civilian.

314 Receive, then, from your mothers and sisters, from those whose affections greet you, these colors woven by our feeble but reliant hands; and when this bright flag shall float before you on the battlefield, let it not only inspire you with the brave and patriotic ambition of a soldier aspiring to his own and his country's honor and glory, but also may it be a sign that cherished ones appeal to you to save them from a fanatical and heartless foe.

— late April 1861 (reported in the *New Orleans Daily Crescent* on 29 April 1861), speech as she presented a flag to the DeSoto Rifles of Louisiana

ROSCOE CONKLING

Born 30 October 1829 in Albany, New York. Lawyer and politician who served as a United States congressman (1859-63 and 1865-67) and senator (1867-81) from New York. Died 18 April 1888 in New York City.

315 War is not a question of valor, but a question of money....It is not regulated by the laws of honor, but by the laws of trade. I understand the practical problem to be solved in crushing the rebellion of despotism against representative government is who can throw the most projectiles? Who can afford the most iron or lead?

— early August 1861, comment after the Union loss at 1st Bull Run

JAMES AUSTIN CONNOLLY

Born 8 March 1840 in Newark, New Jersey. Lawyer who became a Union major (6 September 1862) and brevet lieutenant colonel (13 March 1865). After the war, he returned to law and entered politics. Died 15 December 1914 in Springfield, Illinois.

316 We are *somewhat* whipped but will get over it. The rebs were too numerous for us, they didn't have enough desertions.

— 22 September 1863, letter to his wife, after Chickamauga

317 After all a little spice of danger, every day, is an excellent thing; it drives away the blues and gives to the soldier's life that dash of romance which makes pictures on the memory that never fade.

— 9 December 1863, letter to his wife

318 I am out of money, we are all out of money, but we don't need money down here—don't need *anything* but men, muskets, ammunition, hard tack, bacon, and *letters from home.*

> — 20 June 1864, letter to his wife during the Atlanta camapign

319 Soldiers may *be* gentlemen but they can't *live* like gentlemen and do soldier's duty.

> — 19 January 1865, letter to his wife

CHAUNCEY COOKE

Cooke was a private with the 25th Wisconsin.

320 Not many minutes after coming into camp, every fence and movable thing in sight is pulled down to make the fires. God pity this south land when we are done with it.

> — 3 May 1864, diary

JOHN ROGERS COOKE

Born 9 June 1833 in Jefferson Barracks, Maryland. He entered the United States Army in 1855 but resigned on 30 May 1861. During the Civil War, he became a Confederate first lieutenant (1861), major (February 1862), colonel (April 1862), and brigadier general (1 November 1862). After the war, he was a merchant. Died 10 April 1891 in Richmond, Virginia.

321 We will stay here...if we must all go to hell together.

> — 17 September 1862, statement to a messenger for James Longstreet at Antietam

322 Tell General Longstreet to send me some ammunition. I have not a cartridge in my command, but will hold my position at the point of the bayonet.

> — 17 September 1862, statement to a messenger for Longstreet at Antietam

DOUGLAS HANCOCK COOPER

Born 1 November 1815, probably in Amite County, Mississippi. Before the Civil War, he was a United States Indian agent. During the war, he raised an Indian unit for the Confederate army and became a colonel (1861) and a brigadier general (2 May 1863). After the war, he pressed Indian claims against the United States. Died 29 April 1879 in Old Fort Washita, Indian Territory.

323 There seems to be a disposition to keep the Indians at home. This seems to me a bad policy. They are unfit for garrison duty, and would be a terror to the Yankees.
> — 25 July 1861, letter to Jefferson Davis

SAMUEL COOPER

Born 12 June 1798 in Hackensack, New Jersey. West Point class of 1815. From 1852 to 1861, he was the adjutant general of the United States Army. He resigned that post (7 March 1861), became a Confederate brigadier general (16 March 1861) with the joint roles of adjutant and inspector general, and was promoted to full general (31 August 1861, to rank from 16 May). After the war, he was a farmer. Died 3 December 1876 in Cameron, near Alexandria, Virginia.

324 If an invasion of Kansas is rendered necessary..., it will be a question for you to determine, after fully considering the consequences as affecting the neutrality of the Cherokees, which should not be disregarded if it is possible by diplomacy to prevent it; the great object of your command being not only to conciliate the Indian nations, but to obtain their active co-operation with us in prosecuting the war.
> — 26 June 1861, letter to Ben McCulloch

RACHEL BOWMAN CORMANY

Born 12 April 1836 in Carlisle Hill, Ontario, Canada. Wife of Samuel Eckerman Cormany. She died 18 February 1899 in Johnstown, Pennsylvania.

325 Just a week this morning the rebels turned up in our devoted town again....They demanded 500,000 dollers in default of which the town would be burned—They were told that it was imposible to raise that amount—The reb's then came down to 100,000 in gold which was just as imposible. when they were informed of the imposibility they deliberately went from house to house & fired it. The whole heart of the town is burned. they gave us no time for people to get any thing out.
> — 6 August 1864, diary entry concerning the Confederate soldiers'
> burning of Chambersburg, Pennsylvania, on 30 July 1864

SAMUEL ECKERMAN CORMANY

Born 24 May 1838 near Chambersburg, Pennsylvania. Before the Civil War, he was a store clerk. In September 1862, he enlisted as a private with the 16th Pennsylvania Cavalry. He rose to sergeant (July 1863), second lieutenant (May 1864), and first lieutenant and adjutant (11 December 1864). After the war, he was a Christian preacher. Died 20 April 1921 in Pennsylvania.

326 I had a fine chat with some of the rebel Ladies—I do admire their pluck—what a pity their minds didn't run in a different Channel—a better channel. So the efforts of such animated feelings would not be so hopelessly wasted on a waning cause tottering on its last legs.
　　— 15 July 1863, diary

327 I said "Boys drop that Rebel Flag" We fired—The flag fell. Another reb picked it up—another little volley and it dropped again—another picked it up, and stepped behind a lone tree—held it out, i.e., The flagpole resting on the ground—The arm extending from the tree—held the pole erect. Again our little group fired "for that arm" and the flag fell.
　　— 16 July 1863, diary entry concerning the battle of Shepherdstown

328 Oh! to be fully well, & stronger, so as to be able to fully enjoy this wild adventurous work of crushing the Southern Cause. Sending the ragged half fed Johnies home—and straightening things up so we could go home too to stay.
　　— 6 April 1865, diary entry during the pursuit of Lee's army to Appomattox

JOHN MURRAY CORSE

Born 27 April 1835 in Pittsburgh, Pennsylvania. Attended West Point for a couple of years but left early and became a lawyer and politician. During the war, he joined the Union army as a major (13 July 1861) and later won promotions to lieutenant colonel (21 May 1862), colonel (29 March 1863), brigadier general (11 August 1863), and major general (5 October 1864). After the war, he worked in railroad and bridge construction and engaged in Massachusetts politics. Died 27 April 1893 in Winchester, Massachusetts.

329 When I think of the noble that fall and the ignoble that remain to enjoy the boon obtained at such a cost, I am filled with murmurings.
　　— September 1864, letter to William Ennis, brother of the slain Thomas J. Ennis

330 Your communication demanding surrender of my command I acknowledge receipt of, and respectfully reply that we are prepared for the "needless effusion of blood" whenever it is agreeable to you.

> — 5 October 1864, written reply to Samuel French, the Confederate major general who had asked Corse to surrender to avoid the "needless effusion of blood" at Allatoona

331 C.R.S.E.H.E.R.

> — 5 October 1864, flag signal sent to William T. Sherman from Allatoona, meaning "Corse [is] here"

332 I am short a cheek-bone and an ear, but am able to whip all h—l yet!

> — 6 October 1864, message from Allatoona to Captain L.M. Dayton, Sherman's aide-de-camp

ORRIN J. CRANE

Crane, at the age of 28, entered the Union army on 13 June 1861 with the 7th Ohio. He won promotions from captain to major (25 May 1862) and lieutenant colonel (2 March 1863). Killed in action 27 November 1863 at Ringgold, Georgia.

333 So terrific was the fire of our men that the enemy fell like grass before the mower.

> — 25 September 1862, report on Antietam

JOHN JORDAN CRITTENDEN

Born 10 September 1787 in Woodford County, Kentucky Before the war, he was a lawyer and politician, serving several terms in the United States Senate. In December 1860 he offered a series of compromise resolutions in the Senate in an effort to avoid war. Died 26 July 1863 in Frankfort, Kentucky.

334 Rather bear the wrongs you have than fly to others which you know not of.

> — 2 March 1861, speech to Senate, encouraging a compromise to avoid disunion; a paraphrase of Shakespeare's "And makes us rather bear those ills we have/Than fly to others that we know not of" (*Hamlet*, act 3, scene 1)

LEMUEL L. CROCKER

Crocker was a lieutenant with the 118th Pennsylvania when the incident below took place. Later he became a captain before resigning on 26 February 1864.

335 Shell and be damned!
> — 1 October 1862, spoken reply to an orderly from the corps commander, Fitz-John Porter, who had threatened to shell Crocker if he did not stop recovering wounded soldiers from the field after a battle at Shepherdstown, West Virginia

EDWARD EPHRAM CROSS

Born 22 April 1832 in Lancaster, New Hampshire. When the Civil War began, he was in the Mexican army. He returned to his home state and became a Union colonel (22 October 1861). After recovering from wounds in several battles, he was finally mortally wounded on 2 July 1863 at Gettysburg, Pennsylvania.

336 You have never disgraced your state; I hope you won't this time. If any man runs I want the file closers to shoot him; if they don't, I shall myself. That's all I have to say.
> — 17 September 1862, warning to his troops at Antietam

337 Too late, General. This is my last battle.
> — 2 July 1863, comment to Winfield Scott Hancock, who had just hinted at a promotion for Cross, mortally wounded just a few minutes later at Gettysburg

338 I think the boys will miss me.
> — 2 July 1863, dying words at Gettysburg

KATE CUMMING

Born 1835 in Edinburgh, Scotland. She moved to Alabama as a youth with her family. During the Civil War, she was a Confederate nurse. After the war, she was a teacher. Died 5 June 1909 in Birmingham, Alabama

339 Seeing an enemy wounded and helpless is a different thing from seeing him in health and power. The first time I saw one in this condition every feeling of enmity vanished at once.
> — 13 April 1862, diary

340 A stream of blood ran from the table into a tub in which was the arm. It had been taken off at the socket, and the hand, which but a short time before grasped the musket and battled for the right, was hanging over the

edge of the tub, a lifeless thing. I often wish I could become as callous as many seem to be, for there is no end to these horrors.

— 24 April 1862, diary

HENRY H. CURRAN

When he fought at Fredericksburg, Curran was a lieutenant with the 146th New York. Later he rose to major in the same regiment. Killed in action at the Wilderness, Virginia, 5 May 1864.

341 The slaughter is terrible—the result disastrous. Until we have good generals it is useless to fight battles.

— December 1862, observation after Fredericksburg

ANDREW GREGG CURTIN

Born 22 April 1817 in Bellefonte, Pennsylvania. Lawyer who served as the governor of Pennsylvania (1861-67) and a United States congressman (1881-87). Died 7 October 1894 in Bellefonte.

342 It was not a battle; it was a butchery.

— December 1862, remark to President Lincoln, after Fredericksburg

SAMUEL RYAN CURTIS

Born 3 February 1805 in Clinton County, New York. West Point class of 1831. After a year of garrison duty, he resigned and turned to engineering, law, and politics. During the Civil War, he became a Union colonel (1861), brigadier general (to rank from 17 May 1861), and major general (21 March 1862). Died 26 December 1866 in Council Bluffs, Iowa.

343 I have given free papers to negroes who were mustered by their rebel masters to blockade my way to my supplies. These negro prisoners were the most efficient foes I had to encounter; they are now throwing down their axes and rushing in for free papers.

— 31 July 1862, letter from Arkansas to Henry W. Halleck

344 Society is terribly mutilated, and masters and slaves are afraid of famine.

— 31 July 1862, letter from Arkansas to Halleck

345 Decisive and active measures are scattering and scaring the bands out of the States.

— 23 October 1862, message from St. Louis, Missouri, to Benjamin Loan

346 The wealthy secesh rebels must be made to suffer. They support the poor scamps that hide in the brush.

— 23 October 1862, message from St. Louis, Missouri, to Benjamin Loan

GEORGE ARMSTRONG CUSTER

Born 5 December 1839 in New Rumley, Ohio. West Point class of 1861. Appointed a second lieutenant soon after graduation, he later rose to captain in the Regulars (5 June 1862) and, in the volunteer army, brigadier general (29 June 1863) and major general (15 April 1865). After the war, he was a famous frontier army officer. Killed by Indians 25 June 1876 at the Little Bighorn River.

347 At night, when it is too dark to shoot or be shot at, both come out of hiding-places, holler at each other, calling names and bragging what they intend to do. Then, when daylight appears, the party which sees the other first, fires, and that puts a stop till night comes, when the same thing is repeated.

— 11 March 1862, letter to Ann Reed

348 I have more confidence in General McClellan than in any man living. I would forsake everything and follow him to the ends of the earth. I would lay down my life for him.

— 17 March 1862, letter to his parents

349 Oh, could you but have seen some of the charges that were made! While thinking of them I cannot but exclaim "Glorious War!"

— 12 October 1863, letter to Annette Humphrey, after Brandy Station

350 Where in hell is the rear?

— June 1864, query during battle at Trevilian Station

351 While I am still as strongly wedded to the "noble profession of arms" as I ever have been and hope ever to be, I frequently discover myself acting as umpire between my patriotism and my desire to be and remain with my darling.

— 1 July 1864, letter to his wife

352 This is the bulliest day since Christ was born.

— 19 September 1864, comment to Charles W. Deane at Winchester

353 By God, Phil! We've cleaned them out of their guns and got ours back!

— 19 October 1864, exclamation to Sheridan at Cedar Creek

354 I respectfully present to you the small writing-table on which the conditions for the surrender of the Confederate Army of Northern Virginia were written by Lieutenant General Grant—and permit me to say, Madam, that there is scarcely an individual in our service who has contributed more to bring this about than your very gallant husband.
— 10 April 1865, letter to his wife

JOHN B. CUZNER

Cuzner was a soldier with the 16th Connecticut.

355 Mother wanted to come down and see me she wrote and asked me what I thought of it but the camp is no place for Women there is so much vulgar talk I thought I had got toughened to it, but last night one of the boys got tight and his swearing made my hair stand straight up.
— 28 August 1863, letter to Ellen Vandorn

CHARLES ANDERSON DANA

Born 8 August 1819 in Hinsdale, New Hampshire. After a long tenure as a journalist with the New York Tribune, *he served as an assistant secretary of war (1863-65). Later he returned to journalism. Died 17 October 1897 in Glen Cove, Long Island, New York.*

356 The mania for sudden fortunes made in cotton, raging in a vast population of Jews and Yankees scattered throughout this whole country,...has to an alarming extent corrupted and demoralized the army. Every colonel, captain, or quartermaster is in secret partnership with some operator in cotton; every soldier dreams of adding a bale of cotton to his monthly pay.
— 21 January 1863, letter from Memphis, Tennessee, to Secretary of War Stanton

357 The storming of the ridge by our troops was one of the greatest miracles in military history. No man who climbs the ascent by any of the roads that wind along its front can believe that 18,000 men were moved up its broken and crumbling face unless it was his fortune to witness the deed....Neither Grant nor Thomas intended it. Their orders were to carry the rifle-pits along the base of the ridge and capture their occupants, but when this was accomplished the unaccountable spirit of the troops bore them bodily up those impracticable steeps, over the bristling rifle-pits on the crest and the thirty cannon enfilading every gully. The order to storm appears to have been

given simultaneously by Generals Sheridan and Wood, because the men were not to be held back, dangerous as the attempt appeared to military prudence.

— 26 November 1863, report to Stanton on the Union victory at Missionary Ridge

JEFFERSON COLUMBUS DAVIS

Born 2 March 1828 in Clark County, Indiana. When the Civil War began, he was already a first lieutenant in the army. During the war, he became a Union captain (14 May 1861), colonel (1 August 1861), and brigadier general (18 December 1861). On 29 September 1862, after an argument, he shot and mortally wounded a superior officer, William Nelson. Davis was never tried for the cold-blooded murder. After the war, he remained in the army. Died 30 November 1879 in Chicago

358 A force of sufficient strength to give the enemy a successful battle in his rear would settle all trouble about here.

— 13 September 1861, message to John C. Frémont, concerning action at Booneville, Missouri.

359 Forward harness and wagons; can't do anything with mules without them.

— 18 September 1861, message to John C. Frémont

JEFFERSON FINIS DAVIS

Born 3 June 1808 in Christian County, Kentucky. West Point class of 1828. In 1835 he left the army to become a Mississippi planter. Later he entered politics, serving as a congressman, a senator, and, under President Pierce, the secretary of war. During the Civil War, Davis was the president of the Confederate States of America. After the war, he traveled abroad and wrote The Rise and Fall of the Confederate Government *(1881). Died 6 December 1889 in New Orleans, Louisiana.*

360 The right solemnly proclaimed at the birth of the States, and which has been affirmed and reaffirmed in the bills of rights of the states subsequently admitted into the Union of 1789, undeniably recognizes in the people the power to resume the authority delegated for the purposes of government. Thus the sovereign states here represented proceeded to form this Confederacy; and it is by the abuse of language that their act has been denominated revolution.

— 18 February 1861, Inaugural Address as provisional president of the Confederacy

361 All we ask is to be let alone.

— 18 February 1861, attributed remark, not in the printed version of his Inaugural Address

362 We are without machinery, without means, and threatened by a powerful opposition; but I do not despond, and will not shrink from the task imposed upon me.

— February 1861, letter to his wife

363 The *creature* has been exalted above its *creators*; the *principals* have been made subordinate to the *agent* appointed by themselves.

— 29 April 1861, speech to Confederate Congress

364 In moral and social condition they had been elevated from brutal savages into docile, intelligent, and civilized agricultural laborers, and supplied not only with bodily comforts but with careful religious instruction. Under the supervision of a superior race their labor had been so directed as not only to allow a gradual and marked amelioration of their own condition, but to convert hundreds of thousands of square miles of the wilderness into cultivated lands covered with a prosperous people.

— 29 April 1861, speech to Confederate Congress

365 Enough was done for glory, and the measure of duty was full.

— 4 August 1861, letter to Beauregard after 1st Bull Run

366 The tyranny of an unbridled majority, the most odious and least responsible form of despotisim, has denied us both the right and remedy.

— 22 February 1862, Inaugural Address as president of the permanent Confederate government

367 Tender consideration for worthless and incompetent officers is but another name for cruelty toward the brave men who fall sacrifices to these defects of their leaders.

— 8 October 1862, message to Congress

368 Now, therefore, I, Jefferson Davis, President of the Confederate States of America, and in their name, do pronounce and declare the said Benjamin F. Butler to be a felon, deserving of capital punishment. I do order that he shall no longer be considered or treated simply as a public enemy of the Confederate States of America, but as an outlaw and common enemy of mankind, and that, in the event of his capture, the officer in command of the capturing force do cause him to be immediately executed by hanging.

— 23 December 1862, proclamation

369 In the course of this war our eyes have often been turned abroad. We have expected sometimes recognition, and sometimes intervention, at the hands of foreign nations; and we had a right to expect it. Never before in the history of the world have people so long a time maintained their ground, and shown themselves capable of maintaining their national existence, without securing the recognition of commercial nations. I know not why this has been so, but this I say: "Put not your trust in princes" and rest not your hopes on foreign nations. This war is ours; we must fight it ourselves. And I feel some pride in knowing that, so far, we have done it without the good will of anybody.

— 26 December 1862, speech to the Mississippi state legislature

370 Were you capable of stooping to it, you could easily surround yourself with those who would fill the press with your laudations, and seek to exalt you for what you had not done rather than detract from the achievements which will make you and your army the subject of history and object of the world's admiration for generations to come....To ask me to substitute you by some one in my judgment more fit to command, or who would possess more of the confidence of the army or of the reflecting men in the country is to demand for me an impossibility.

— 11 August 1863, letter to Robert E. Lee

371 It must be a rare occurrence if a battle is fought without many errors and failures, but for which more important results would have been obtained, and the exposure of these diminishes the credit due, impairs the public confidence, undermines the morale of the Army, and works evil to the cause for which brave men have died, and for which others have the same sacrifice to make.

— 3 October 1863, letter to Braxton Bragg

372 I tried with all my power to avert this war. I saw it coming, and for twelve years I worked night and day to prevent it, but I could not. The North was mad and blind; it would not let us govern ourselves, and so the war came, and now it must go on till the last man of this generation falls in his tracks, and his children seize his musket and fight his battle, unless you acknowledge our right to self-government. We are not fighting for slavery. We are fighting for independence and that, or extermination, we will have.

— 17 July 1864, statement to James F. Jaquess and James R. Gilmore, unofficial peace envoys from the North

373 If the Confederacy falls, there should be written on its tombstone, "Died of a theory."

— late 1864, comment while arguing in favor of a bill to turn slaves into soldiers

374 I have been laboring without much progress to advance the raising of negro troops.
                    — 1 April 1865, letter to Lee

375 Relieved from the necessity of guarding cities and particular points, important but not vital to our defense, with an army free to move from point to point and strike in detail the detachments and garrisons of the enemy, operating on the interior of our own country, where supplies are more accessible, and where the foe will be far removed from his own base and cut off from all succor in case of reverse, nothing is now needed to render our triumph certain but the exhibition of our own unquenchable resolve....Let us meet the foe with fresh defiance, with unconquered and unconquerable hearts.
                    — 4 April 1865, his last message to the people of the Confederacy

376 I certainly have no special regard for Mr. Lincoln; but there are a great many men of whose end I would much rather have heard than his. I fear it will be disastrous for our people, and I regret it deeply.
                    — 19 April 1865, comment to Stephen Mallory on hearing of Lincoln's death

MRS. L.E. DAVIS

Mrs. Davis was a Confederate civilian.

377 I wish you would have all the big leguslater men and big men about towns ordered in to confederate serviz. they any no serviz to us at home.
                    — 22 August 1864, letter to Jefferson Davis

F.W. DELANG

Delang was a doctor from Indiana.

378 None but you can overcome this Storm and you are the only Pilot to lead the Ship into the Harbor.
                    — 14 September 1864, letter to President Lincoln

GEORGE S. DENISON

Denison was a Treasury Department investigator in New Orleans during Benjamin F. Butler's military rule there in 1862.

379 A brother of Gen. Butler is here, who is called Colonel Butler, though he occupies no position in the army. Government officers, citizens, and rebels,

generally believe him to be the partner or agent of Gen'l. Butler. He does a heavy business, and by various practices has made between one and two million dollars since the capture of the city. Governor Shepley, and especially Colonel French (Provost Marshal), are supposed to be interested, but these officers I believe to be entirely under control of Gen'l. Butler, who knows everything, controls everything, and should be held responsible for everything.

> — 10 October 1862, letter to Salmon P. Chase, concerning Benjamin F. Butler's rule in New Orleans

380 I believe the present military authorities are so corrupt that they will take all means to make money....Many officers and soldiers want to go home, not wishing to risk their lives to make fortunes for others.

> — 10 October 1862, letter to Salmon P. Chase, concerning Benjamin F. Butler's rule in New Orleans

381 I know of but one fault to be found with Gen. Butler. He has (in my opinion) been altogether too willing to permit his friends to make fortunes.

> — 27 October 1862, letter to Salmon P. Chase

JOHN ADAMS DIX

Born 24 July 1798 in Boscawen, New Hampshire. At the age of fourteen, he entered the army. In 1828, as a captain, he resigned to pursue law and politics. From January to March 1861, he was the United States secretary of the treasury. During the Civil War, he served as a Union major general (commissioned 16 May 1861). After the war, he was minister to France and governor of New York. Died 21 April 1879 in New York City.

382 If anyone attempts to haul down the American flag, shoot him on the spot.

> — 29 January 1861, telegram to W. Hemphill Jones, a treasury official in New Orleans; known as the American Flag Dispatch

STEPHEN ARNOLD DOUGLAS

Born 23 April 1813 in Brandon, Vermont. Lawyer and politician. He was the Democratic nominee for president in 1860. Died 3 June 1861 in Springfield, Illinois.

383 Every man must be for the United States or against it. There can be no neutrals in this war, only patriots—or traitors.

> — 1 May 1861, speech in Chicago

FREDERICK DOUGLASS

Born into slavery in Tuckahoe, near Easton, Talbot County, Maryland. His birthdate is uncertain, but he later settled on 14 February 1817. His original name was Frederick Augustus Washington Bailey; after he escaped from slavery in 1838, he adopted the surname Douglass. He settled in the North and became an orator, journalist, abolitionist, and civil-rights leader. Died 20 February 1895 in Washington, D.C.

384 The contest must now be decided, and decided forever, which of the two, Freedom or Slavery, shall give law to this Republic. Let the conflict come.
— March 1861, *Douglass' Monthly*

385 Abolition may be postponed, but it cannot be prevented. If it comes not from enlightenment, moral conviction and civilization, it will come from the fears of tyrants no longer able to hold down their rising slaves.
— April 1861, "The Future of the Abolition Cause," *Douglass' Monthly*

386 Fire must be met with water, darkness with light, and war for the destruction of liberty must be met with war for the destruction of slavery.
— May 1861, "How to End the War," *Douglass' Monthly*

387 Freedom for all, or chains for all.
— May 1861, caption in the *Douglass' Monthly*

388 It is not merely a war for slavery, but it is a war for slavery dominion.
— May 1861, "The Fall of Sumter," *Douglass' Monthly*

389 The Negro is the key of the situation—the pivot upon which the whole rebellion turns.
— September 1861, *Douglass' Monthly*

390 We would tell him that this is no time to fight with one hand, when both are needed; that this is no time to fight with your white hand, and allow your black to remain tied.
— September 1861, *Douglass' Monthly*, a statement aimed at President Lincoln

391 We are striking the guilty rebels with our soft, white hand, when we should be striking with the iron hand of the black man.
— 14 January 1862. speech

392 The destiny of the colored American...is the destiny of America.
— 12 February 1862, speech at Emancipation League, Boston, Massachusetts

393 I have implored the imperiled nation to unchain against her foes, her powerful black hand.

> — 2 March 1863, "Men of Color, to Arms," an article

394 Liberty won by white men would lose half its luster. "Who would be free themselves must strike the first blow." "Better even die free, than live slaves."

> — 2 March 1863, "Men of Color, to Arms"

395 I urge you to fly to arms, and smite with death the power that would bury the government and your liberty in the same hopeless grave.

> — 2 March 1863, "Men of Color, to Arms"

396 The day dawns; the morning star is bright upon the horizon! The iron gate of our prison stands half open. One gallant rush from the North will fling it wide open, while four millions of our brothers and sisters shall march out into liberty.

> — 2 March 1863, "Men of Color, to Arms"

397 The relation subsisting between the white and colored people of this country is the great, paramount, imperative, and all-consuming question for this age and nation to solve.

> — May 1863, speech at the Church of the Puritans, New York City

398 That every slave who escapes from the Rebel States is a loss to the Rebellion and a gain to the Loyal Cause I need not stop to argue[;] the proposition is self evident. The negro is the stomach of the rebellion.

> — 29 August 1864, letter to President Lincoln

SAMUEL FRANCIS DU PONT

Born 27 September 1803 on Bergen Point (now called Bayonne), New Jersey. He became a navy midshipman in 1815, and when the Civil War broke out, he was a captain. During the war, he rose to Union rear admiral (July 1862). Died 23 June 1865 in Philadelphia, Pennsylvania.

399 My hand and heart are in it.

> — June 1861, remark to William H. Seward, proclaiming loyalty to the United States

400 We seem to have an ebb tide in the Navy now.

> — 26 January 1863, letter to his wife, referring to recent defeats

401 Success is not in my hands; to do my duty is.

> — 10 March 1863, letter to his wife

402 The monitors are not intended to lose life except by sinking as a general rule. They are iron coffins; once perforated they go down.

> — 25 April 1863, letter to his wife

403 A silly faith in monitors...led to a great blunder.

> — c. 29 April 1863, letter to William Wister McKean, after the poor showing of ironclads at Charleston

404 I did not lie and call a defeat a reconnaissance.

> — 11 May 1863, letter to Henry Winter Davis, after the Charleston failure

405 It is service during war but not war service.

> — 11 June 1864, letter to Charles H. Davis when offered command of the Pacific Squadron

JUBAL ANDERSON EARLY

Born 3 November 1816 in Franklin County, Virginia. West Point class of 1837. He resigned from the army in 1838 to become a lawyer and politician. He began his participation in the war as a Confederate colonel and later won promotions to brigadier general (21 July 1861), major general (23 April 1863, retroactive to 17 January), and lieutenant general (31 May 1864). After the war, he resumed his law practice. Died 2 March 1894 in Lynchburg, Virginia.

406 All the companies here are well mounted, and would make fine companies if there were arms for them.

> — 8 June 1861, letter from Lynchburg, Virginia, to Robert S. Garnett

407 Chaplain, I have known you for the past thirty years, and all that time you have been trying to get to Heaven, and now that the opportunity is offered, you are fleeing from it.

> — 13 December 1862, remark to a fleeing chaplain at Fredericksburg

408 I not only wish them all dead but I wish them all in Hell.

> — 15 December 1862, comment to Wade Hampton, after Robert E. Lee had chided Early for wishing Federals all dead

409 Damn it, holler them across.

> — May 1864, order to his men when they said they were out of ammunition at an engagement near Richmond

410 Major, we haven't taken Washington, but we've scared Abe Lincoln like hell!

> — 12 July 1864, comment to Major Henry Kyd Douglas after the Confederate raid on Washington, D.C.

411 The laurel is a running vine.

> — October 1864, comment on hearing of the flight of Thomas L. Rosser's Laurel Brigade at Tom's Brook (9 October)

412 The Yankees got whipped; we got scared.

> — October 1864, comment after the battle at Cedar Creek

DANIEL EDWARDS

Edwards was a civilian from Allegany County, New York.

413 I am 65 years old am able to do a fair days work (not the hardest kind of work) day after day—am willing to go to the army, or rather into some fort or garison....Avery Coon is a stout man of about my age—will go too.... We have faith in God and dry Powder.

> — 28 March 1864, letter to President Lincoln

E.J. ELLIS

Ellis was a captain with the 16th Louisiana.

414 The fact is I would like first rate to get such a wound....Oh! wouldn't it be nice to get a 30 days leave and go home and be petted like a baby, and get delicacies to eat...and then if I ever run for a little office I could limp and complain of the "old wound."

> — 15 February 1863, letter to his mother

ARNOLD ELZEY

Born 18 December 1816 in Somerset County, Maryland. His full name was Arnold Elzey Jones. West Point class of 1837. He resigned from the United States Army as a captain (25 April 1861) and soon joined the Confederate army as a lieutenant colonel. Elzey quickly went through that rank and full colonel to brigadier general (21 July 1861), finally reaching major general (4 December 1862). After the war, he was a farmer. Died 21 February 1871 in Baltimore, Maryland.

415 Now for a yellow sash or six feet of ground.

> — 21 July 1861, comment to Bradley Johnson as Elzey went into battle at 1st Bull Run, expecting either promotion (referring to the sword belt sash of a general) or death in the aftermath

RALPH WALDO EMERSON

Born 25 May 1803 in Boston, Massachusetts. Poet, lecturer, and essayist. The leading member of a group of New England idealists known as the Transcendentalists. Died 27 April 1882 in Concord, Massachusetts.

416   Sometimes gunpowder smells good.
> — April 1861, comment at a navy yard, expressing relief that the war had begun

417   Grief and pride ruled the hour.
> — 20 April 1861, letter to his daughter Edith, describing the departure of Union soldiers

418   The country is cheerful and jocund in the belief that it has a government at last. The men in search of a party, parties in search of a principle, interests and dispositions that could not fuse for want of some base—all joyfully unite in this great Northern party on the basis of Freedom.
> — 3 May 1861, journal

419   The war goes on educating us to a trust in the simplicities, and to see the bankruptcy of all narrow views.
> — 5 August 1861, journal

420   Far better that this grinding should go on, bad and worse, than we should be driven by any impatience into a hasty peace restoring the old rottenness.
> — 1 January 1862, journal

421   I do not wish to abdicate so extreme a privilege as the use of the sword or the bullet. For the peace of the man who has forsworn the use of the bullet seems to me not quite peace.
> — 1 January 1862, journal

422   It is, as I said, a war of Instincts.
> — 1 January 1862, journal

423   Emancipation is the demand of civilization. That is a principle; everything else is an intrigue.
> — 31 January 1862, speech to a gathering in Washington, D.C.

424   The war is welcome to the Southerner; a chivalrous sport to him, like hunting, and suits his semi-civilized condition.
> — 31 January 1862, speech to a gathering in Washington, D.C.

425   War, the searcher of character, the test of men, has tried already so many reputations, has pricked so many bladders....Scott, McDowell, McClellan, Frémont, Banks, Butler, and I know not how many more, are brought

up, each in turn, dragged up irresistibly to the anthropometer, measured and weighed, and the result proclaimed to the Universe.
— March 1862, journal

426 The man McClellan ebbed like a sea.
— June 1862, journal

427 Why are people so sensitive about the reputation of General McClellan? There is always something rotten about a sensitive reputation. Besides, is not General McClellan an American citizen? And is it not the first attribute and distinction of an American to be abused and slandered as long as he is heard of?
— July 1862, journal

428 George Francis Train said in a public speech in New York, "Slavery is a divine institution." "So is hell," exclaimed an old man in the crowd.
— October 1862, journal

429 The war was and is an immense mischief, but brought with it the immense benefit of drawing a line, and rallying the Free States to fix it impassably.
— November 1862, "The President's Proclamation," in *The Atlantic Monthly*

430 The war is our sole and doleful instructor. All our bright young men go into it, to be misused and sacrificed hitherto by incapable leaders.
— 8 December 1862, letter to Thomas Carlyle

431 Pay ransom to the owner.
And fill the bag to the brim.
Who is the owner? The slave is the owner,
And ever was. Pay him.
— 1 January 1863, "Boston Hymn," poem read at a Boston celebration of the Emancipation Proclamation

432 So nigh is grandeur to our dust, / So near is God to man, / When Duty whispers low, *Thou must,* / The youth replies, *I can.*
— 1863, "Voluntaries," poem after the death of Robert Gould Shaw (July 1863)

433 War disorganizes, but it is to reorganize.
— 1863, "The Man of Letters" (a revised version of "The Scholar," a lecture delivered 22 July 1863)

434 War ennobles the age. We do not often have a moment of grandeur in these hurried, slipshod lives, but the behavior of the young men has taught

us much. We will not again disparage America, now that we have seen what men it will bear.

— 1863, "The Man of Letters"

435   The times are dark but heroic.

— 1863, "The Man of Letters"

436   When our young officers come back from the army, on a forty days' furlough, they find apathy and opposition in the cities.

— October 1863, journal

437   I shall always respect War hereafter. The cost of life, the dreary havoc of comfort and time, are overpaid by the Vistas it opens of Eternal Life, Eternal Law, reconstructing and uplifting Society.

— 26 September 1864, letter to Thomas Carlyle

438   The War at last appoints the generals, in spite of parties and Presidents. Every one of us had his pet, at the start, but none of us appointed Grant, Sherman, Sheridan, and Farragut,—none but themselves.

— September 1864, journal

439   Rarely has a man so fitted to the event.

— 19 April 1865, funeral oration for Abraham Lincoln

JOHN ERICSSON

Born 31 July 1803 in Sweden. An inventor and military engineer. In 1826 he moved to England and in 1839 to the United States. In 1861 he designed the first ironclad with a revolving turret, the U.S.S. Monitor *(launched in early 1862). Died 8 March 1889 in New York City.*

440   The impregnable and aggressive character of this structure will admonish the leaders of the Southern Rebellion that the batteries on the banks of their rivers will no longer present barriers to the entrance of the Union forces.

The iron-clad intruder will thus prove a severe monitor to those leaders....I propose to name the new battery *Monitor*.

— 20 January 1862, letter to Gustavus V. Fox, assistant secretary of the navy

441   A single shot will sink a ship, while a hundred rounds cannot silence a fort.

— 1863, comment regarding the bombardment of Charleston, South Carolina

A.N. ERSKINE

Erskine was a soldier with the 4th Texas.

442 Yesterday evening we (the Texas Brigade) was in one of the hardest fought battles ever known....I never had a clear conception of the horrors of war untill that night and the [next] morning. On going round on that battlefield with a candle searching for my friends I could hear on all sides the dreadful groans of the wounded and their heart piercing cries for water and assistance. Friends and foes togather....I am satisfied not to make another such charge. For I hope dear Ann that this big battle will have some influence in terminating this war. I assure you I am heartily sick of soldiering.
— 28 June 1862, letter after the battle of Gaines's Mill

THOMAS EVANS

Thomas was a Union soldier.

443 Darkness was upon us, and Jackson was on us, and fear was on us.
— May 1863, diary entry on Chancellorsville

EDWARD EVERETT

Born 11 April 1794 in Dorchester, Massachusetts. Orator, educator, and statesman. At the 19 November 1863 dedication of the Gettysburg national cemetery, he was the principal speaker. Died 15 January 1865 in Boston, Massachusetts.

444 I should be glad, if I came as near to the central idea of the occasion, in two hours, as you did in two minutes.
— 20 November 1863, letter to President Lincoln, concerning their respective speeches at Gettysburg

RICHARD STODDERT EWELL

Born 8 February 1817 in Georgetown, D.C. West Point class of 1840. He resigned as a captain in the United States Army (7 May 1861) to join the Virginia forces as a lieutenant colonel and soon became a colonel in the Confederate army. He won promotions to brigadier general (17 June 1861) and major general (23 January 1862) before losing a leg at Groveton (August 1862). As a lieutenant general, he returned to duty (23 May 1863) with a wooden leg. Ewell was captured at Sayler's Creek (6 April 1865) and imprisoned in Fort Warren,

Massachusetts, till 19 August. After the war, he lived on a farm near Spring Hill, Tennessee, where he died on 25 January 1872.

445   We will breakfast together here, and dine together in hell.
— 21 July 1861, comment to John B. Gordon at 1st Bull Run

446   I tell you, sir, women would make a grand brigade—if it was not for snakes and spiders! They don't mind bullets—women are not afraid of bullets; but one big black-snake would put a whole army to flight.
— 21 July 1861, comment to John B. Gordon at 1st Bull Run

447   We transport here...only necessary cooking utensils in bags (not chests), axes, picks, spades, and tent-flies, and the lawful amount of officers' baggage and subsistence stores (80 to 100 pounds), horseshoes, etc. The road to glory cannot be followed with much baggage.
— 14 May 1862, letter to L. O'B. Branch

448   I never saw one of Jackson's couriers approach without expecting an order to assault the North Pole!
— 1862, comment during the Shenandoah Valley campaign (May-June)

449   Old Jackson is no fool; he knows how to keep his own counsel, and does curious things; but he has method in his madness; he has disappointed me entirely.
— 9 June 1862, remark to Thomas T. Munford, after Port Republic

450   By God, he'll never see the backs of my men. Their pants are out at the rear and the sight would paralyze this western bully.
— 1862, attributed comment when he heard of Union General John Pope's boast that his western troops had "always seen the backs of our enemies" (14 July 1862)

451   Some 100,000 human beings have been massacred in every conceivable form of horror, with three times as many wounded, all because a set of fanatical abolitionists and unprincipled politicians backed by women in petticoats and pants and children.
— August 1862, letter to a kinswoman

452   Suppose that ball had struck you; we would have had the trouble of carrying you off the field, sir. You see how much better fixed for a fight I am than you are. It don't hurt a bit to be shot in a wooden leg.
— 1 July 1863, comment to John B. Gordon after a Minié bullet had struck Ewell in his peg leg

DAVID GLASGOW FARRAGUT

Born 5 July 1801 in Campbell's Station, Tennessee. Foster brother of David D. Porter. Farragut was commissioned a midshipman in 1810, and later he became a lieutenant (1822), commander (1844), and captain (1855). During the Civil War, he was promoted to a Union rear admiral (16 July 1862) and vice admiral (23 December 1864). After the war, he became the first American full admiral (25 July 1866). Died 14 August 1870 in Portsmouth, New Hampshire.

453 Fighting is nothing to the evil of the river—getting on shore, running afoul of one another, losing anchors, etc.
— 1862, letter

454 I have now obtained what I have been looking for all my life—a flag—and having obtained it, all that is necessary to complete the scene is victory. If I die in the attempt, it will be only what every officer has to expect.
— 1862, letter to his wife

455 I think the best protection against the enemy's fire is a well-directed fire from our own guns.
— March 1863, order for the attack on Port Hudson

456 I want none of this Nelson business i. ..y squadron about not seeing signals.
— March 1863, reprimand to Lieutenant W.S. Schley for failing to obey a signal promptly during the attack on Port Hudson

457 I can only plead my zeal to serve my country, and the chances of war.
— March 1863, report to Gideon Welles after the attack on Port Hudson

458 Don't flinch from the fire, boys! There's a hotter fire than that waiting for those who don't do their duty! Give that rascally tug a shot!
— 24 April 1863, command to his crew as a Confederate tug pushed a fire ship alongside Farragut's vessel

459 I have him under my control. The minute he opens, I silence him.
— 6 June 1863, signal message to Nathaniel P. Banks

460 Damn the torpedoes! Full speed ahead! (alternate version: Damn the torpedoes! Four bells, Captain Drayton, go ahead!)
— 5 August 1864, order as his ship entered a minefield during the battle of Mobile Bay

461 Remember also that one of the requisite studies for an officer is *man*. Where your analytical geometry will serve you once, a knowledge of men

will serve you daily. As a commander, to get the right man in the right place is one of the questions of success or defeat.

— 13 October 1864, letter to his son

462   As to being prepared for defeat, I certainly am not. Any man who is prepared for defeat would be half defeated before he commenced. I hope for success; shall do all in my power to secure it and trust to God for the rest.

— 1864, letter to his wife

EDWIN H. FAY

Fay enlisted with the Minden Rangers, a Confederate cavalry company, as a private in April 1862. By the time of his letter below, he had risen to the rank of sergeant.

463   I expect to murder every Yankee I ever meet when I can do so with impunity if I live a hundred years and peace is made in six months. Peace will never be made between me and any Yankee if I can kill him without too great risk.

— 10 July 1863, letter to his wife

RICHARD S. FAY, JR.

Before the Civil War, Fay was treasurer of a corporation in which Benjamin F. Butler had a controlling interest. During the war, Fay was Butler's broker for various business dealings.

464   When I first arrived, my friends were in doubt whether I was an idiot or a secessionist, because I did not believe that our armies could overrun Virginia unopposed, and because I asserted that the Southern army was better manned and officered than ours, because their farmers and their gentry composed it, instead of the offscourings of streets and lanes and the stable keepers and bar keepers New York sends us. Today, the feeling is as exaggerated the other way, and the hopelessness of the attempt to conquer "Dixie" is commonly spoken of.

—27 July 1861, letter to Benjamin F. Butler

WINFIELD SCOTT FEATHERSTON

Born 8 August 1820 near Murfreesboro, Tennessee. Lawyer and politician who became a Confederate colonel (spring 1861) and brigadier general (4 March

1862). After the war, he returned to the law and to state politics in Mississippi. Died 28 May 1891 in Holly Springs, Mississippi.

465 Charge, Mississippians, charge! Drive them into the Potomac or into eternity!
— 21 October 1861, command to his men at Ball's Bluff

ALBINUS R. FELL

Fell was a Federal cavalryman.

466 When a person is sick in camp they might as well dig a hole and put him in as to take him to one of the informal hells called hospitals.
— 19 January 1862, letter to his wife

MILLARD FILLMORE

Born 7 January 1800 in Cayuga County, New York. Lawyer and politician who served as the thirteenth president of the United States (1850-53). Died 8 March 1874 in Buffalo, New York.

467 I can in some measure appreciate the difficulties with which the administration of the Government is now embarrassed by this unholy rebellion; for I heard the threatening thunder, and viewed the gathering storm at a distance in 1850; and...I approve most cordially of the firm stand which you have taken in Support of the constitution, *as it is*, against insane abolitionism on one side and rebellious secessionism on the other, and hope and trust that you will remain firm.
— 16 December 1861, letter to President Lincoln

WILBUR FISK

Born 7 June 1839 in Sharon, Vermont. From 1861 to 1865, he was a private in Company E of the 2nd Vermont Volunteers. During that time, he regularly contributed letters to The Green Mountain Freeman, *a Vermont newspaper, signing himself as "Anti-Rebel." After the war, he was a a farmer and preacher. Died 12 March 1914 in Geneva, Kansas.*

468 The boys think it *their* duty to put down rebellion and nothing more, and they view the abolition of slavery in the present time as saddling so much additional labor upon them before the present great work is accomplished. Negro prejudice is as strong here as anywhere.
— 20 May 1862, letter to *The Green Mountain Freeman*

469 If a man wants to see human suffering and human depravity in their grossest phases he need not go to the Kingdom of Dahomey, nor cross the Arabian Desert to find it. Let him go to the Convalescent Camp, and he can see enough to sicken his soul forevermore, unless his heart is harder than adamant.

> — February 1863, letter to *The Green Mountain Freeman*

470 Their bodies were swollen, black, and hideously unnatural. Their eyes glared from their sockets, their tongues protruded from their mouths, and in almost every case, clots of blood and mangled flesh showed how they had died, and rendered a sight ghastly beyond description. My God, could it be possible that such were lively and active like other people so shortly previous, with friends, parents, brothers and sisters to lament their loss. It certainly was so, but it was hard to realize it.

> — 13 July 1863, letter to *The Green Mountain Freeman*, a description of the casualties at Gettysburg

471 I have seen men shot down by scores and hundreds in the field of battle, and have stood within an arm's reach of comrades that were shot dead; but I believe I never have witnessed that from which any soul shrunk with such horror, as to see those two soldiers shot dead in cold blood at the iron decree of military law.

> — 20 December 1863, letter to *The Green Mountain Freeman*, a reaction to an execution

NATHAN BEDFORD FORREST

Born 13 July 1821 in Bedford County, Tennessee. Before the war, he rose from poverty to become a wealthy businessman. In June 1861 he joined the Tennessee Mounted Rifles as a private, but he was soon commissioned a lieutenant colonel and authorized to raise his own cavalry unit. He began his series of famous raids by attacking at Murfreesboro (13 July 1862), won promotions to brigadier general (21 July 1862) and major general (4 December 1863), led the infamous Fort Pillow massacre (12 April 1864), and became a lieutenant general (28 February 1865). After the war, Forrest returned to business pursuits and associated himself with the Ku Klux Klan. Died 29 October 1877 in Memphis, Tennessee.

472 Parson! For God's sake, pray. Nothing but God Almighty can save that fort!

> — 14 February 1862, comment to David C. Kelley, a minister-turned-soldier, at Fort Donelson

473   Boys, these people are talking about surrendering, and I am going out of this place before they do or bust hell wide open.
> — February 1862, comment to his men after his superiors had decided to surrender Fort Donelson

474   I will charge under my own orders.
> — 6 April 1862, statement at Shiloh to Major General Cheatham, who had refused to order a charge

475   Come on, boys, if you want a heap of fun and to kill some Yankees.
> — May 1862, recruiting ad

476   I didn't come here to make half a job of it. I'm going to have them all.
> — 13 July 1862, remark at Murfreesboro

477   I must demand an unconditional surrender of your force as prisoners of war or I will have every man put to the sword.
> — 13 July 1862, message to Union Colonel John G. Parkhurst at Murfreesboro

478   I just took the short cut and got there first with the most men.
> — summer 1862, comment to John Hunt Morgan, concerning a successful operation in middle Tennessee; on future occasions, Forrest reiterated this sentence in variant forms

479   Charge them both ways!
> — 31 December 1862, attributed order to his men when trapped between two enemy forces at Parker's Crossroads (this story is probably a legend)

480   I will be in my coffin before I will fight again under your command.
> — 3 February 1863, statement to Major General Joseph Wheeler

481   Whenever you see anything blue, shoot at it, and do all you can to keep up the scare. (Alternate version: Shoot at everything blue and keep up the skeer.)
> — 30 April 1863, order to his men at Hog Mountain, near Sand Mountain

482   I am glad to have you for a pilot, but I am not going to make breastworks of you.
> — 1 May 1863, remark to Emma Sansom, his guide near Gadsden, Alabama

483   No damned man shall kill me and live! (Alternate version: I am mortally wounded and will kill the man who shot me.)
> — 13 June 1863, statement to J. Lee Bullock, after Forrest was shot by one of his own lieutenants, Andrew W. Gould

484 I demand the unconditional surrender of this garrison, promising you that you shall be treated as prisoners of war....Should my demand be refused, I cannot be responsible for the fate of your command.
> — 12 April 1864, note to Union Major Lionel F. Booth at Fort Pillow

485 Men, if you will do as I say I will always lead you to victory.
> — 12 April 1864, speech to his men after Fort Pillow

486 Get 'em scared, and then keep the scare on 'em. (Alternate version: Get 'em skeered, and then keep the skeer on 'em.)
> — 11 June 1864, order to John W. Morton, Jr., in pursuit of Federals after Brice's Cross Roads

487 We'll whip 'em in five minutes.
> — 14 July 1864, comment to Abraham Buford at Harrisburg

488 Men, you may all do as you damn please, but I'm a-going home.
> — 3 May 1865, remark to Charles Clark and Isham G. Harris, who wanted to continue the war

489 Any man who is in favor of a further prosecution of this war is a fit subject for a lunatic asylum, and ought to be sent there immediately.
> — 3 May 1865, remark to Charles Clark and Isham G. Harris

490 Men, we have surrendered. We have made our last fight.
> — 4 May 1865, attributed speech to his troops at Meridian

491 Men, you have been good soldiers; a man who has been a good soldier can be a good citizen. I shall go back to my home upon the Mississippi River, there to begin life anew, and to you good old Confederates, I want to say that the latchstring of Bedford Forrest will always be on the outside of the door.
> — 4 May 1865, attributed speech to his troops at Meridian

492 I will share the fate of my men.
> — 9 May 1865, remark to Charles W. Anderson, after Forrest's decision to participate in the formal surrender with his troops instead of fleeing to Mexico

493 Civil War, such as you have just passed through, naturally engenders feelings of animosity, hatred, and revenge. It is our duty to divest ourselves of all such feelings, and, as far as in our power to do so, to cultivate friendly feelings toward those with whom we have so long contended.
> — 9 May 1865, farewell address to his men, written by his aide, Charles W. Anderson, with Forrest's guidance and approval, and printed over Forrest's name

494   I have never, on the field of battle, sent you where I was unwilling to go myself; nor would I now advise you to a course which I felt myself unwilling to pursue. You have been good soldiers; you can be good citizens. Obey the laws, preserve your honor, and the government to which you have surrendered can afford to be, and will be, magnanimous.
> — 9 May 1865, farewell address to his men

495   Forward, men, and mix with 'em.
> — frequent command

496   Shoot any man who won't fight.
> — frequent order

497   War means fighting, and fighting means killing. (Alternate version: War means fightin', and fightin' means killin'.)
> — frequent observation

GUSTAVUS VASA FOX

Born 13 June 1821 in Saugus, Massachusetts. Annapolis Naval Academy class of 1838. In 1856 he resigned as a lieutenant in the United States Navy and entered business. During the Civil War, he was the assistant secretary of the navy. In 1866 he helped negotiate the purchase of Alaska. In his later years he returned to business. Died 29 October 1883 in New York City.

498   It is a Bull Run to the Navy.
> — 27 March, 1862, letter to Flag Officer Louis M. Goldsborough, United States Navy, regarding the feeling excited by the escape of the Rebel steamer *Nashville* through the Union blockade

ARTHUR JAMES LYON FREMANTLE

Born November 1835. A British lieutenant colonel who toured America, especially the South, from April to July 1863, and published a diary of that period later that year. He became a full general in 1896. Died 25 September 1901 in Cowes, England.

499   In spite of their peculiar habits of hanging, shooting, &c., which seemed to be natural to people living in a wild and thinly populated country, there was much to like in my fellow travelers.
> — 28 April 1863, diary entry concerning Texas Confederates

500   The people who can't pay $300 naturally hate being forced to fight in order to liberate the very race who they are most anxious should be slaves. It is their direct interest not only that all slaves should remain slaves, but that

the free Northern Negroes who compete with them for labor should be sent to the South also.

— 14 July 1863, diary entry on Northerners

501 At the outbreak of the war it was found very difficult to raise infantry in Texas, as no Texan walks a yard if he can help it. Many mounted regiments were therefore organized, and afterwards dismounted.

— 1863, undated footnote to 3 May 1863 diary entry

502 I never can believe that in the nineteenth century the civilized world will be condemned to witness the destruction of such a gallant race.

— 1863, diary postscript on Confederates

JOHN CHARLES FRÉMONT

Born 21 January 1813 in Savannah, Georgia. Before the war, he was a famous western explorer, known as the Pathfinder. In 1856 he was the Republican party's first presidential candidate. Appointed a major general in the Union army (3 July 1861, to rank from 14 May), he briefly headed the Western Department in 1861 and the Mountain Department in 1862. In 1864 he led a third-party bid for the presidency but withdrew late in the race. After the war, he engaged in the railroad business and, in the late 1870s and early 1880s, served as territorial governor of Arizona. Died 13 July 1890 in New York City.

503 I am sorely pressed for want of arms. I have arranged with Adams Express Company to bring me everything with speed, and will buy arms to-day in New York.

— 30 July 1861, letter to President Lincoln

504 The property, real and personal, of all persons in the State of Missouri who shall take up arms against the United States, or who shall be directly proven to have taken an active part with their enemies in the field, is declared to be confiscated to the public use, and their slaves, if any they have, are hereby declared freemen.

— 30 August 1861, proclamation (later revoked by President Lincoln)

505 If upon reflection your better judgment still decides that I am wrong in the article respecting the liberation of slaves, I have to ask that you will openly direct me to make the correction. The implied censure will be received as a soldier always should the reprimand of his chief. If I were to retract of my own accord, it would imply that I myself thought it wrong, and that I had acted without the reflection which the gravity of the point demanded.

But I did not. I acted with full deliberation, and upon the certain conviction that it was a measure right and necessary, and I still think so.
— 8 September 1861, letter to President Lincoln

SAMUEL GIBBS FRENCH

Born 22 November 1818 in Gloucester County, New Jersey. West Point class of 1843. He resigned from the army in 1856 to become a Mississippi planter. At the beginning of the Civil War, he was the Mississippi state militia ordnance chief. Later he became a Confederate brigadier general (23 October 1861) and major general (to rank from 31 August 1862). After the war, he returned to planting. Died 20 April 1910 in Florala, Florida.

506 It appears to me that if the garrison was surprised, they were negligent; if not surprised, they did not offer a sufficient resistance.
— 22 April 1863, report on Battery Huger, Hill's Point, Virginia

EDWARD W. FULLER

Fuller was captain of the C.S.S. Queen of the West, *a Rebel ram*

507 There is that d— *Calhoun.* I would rather see the devil than that boat.
— April 1863, comment attributed to Fuller, who was referring to the U.S.S. *Calhoun*, which soon sank Fuller's *Queen of the West*

JAMES ABRAM GARFIELD

Born 19 November 1831 in Orange Township, Cuyahoga County, Ohio. Before the Civil War, he was a politician. During the war, he became a Union lieutenant colonel (21 August 1861), colonel (27 November 1861), brigadier general (11 January 1862), and major general (19 September 1863). On 5 December 1863 he resigned from the army to take a seat in the United States Congress. In 1880 he was elected president of the United States, but shortly after taking office in 1881 he was shot (2 July). Complications from the wound finally killed him on 19 September 1881 in Elberon, New Jersey.

508 Better lose a million men in battle than allow the government to be overthrown. The war will soon assume the shape of Slavery and Freedom. The world will so understand it, and I believe the final outcome will redound to the good of humanity.
— 14 April 1861, letter to J.H. Rhodes

509 A nation is not worthy to be saved if, in the hours of its fate, it will not gather up all its jewels of manhood and life, and go down into the conflict, however bloody and doubtful, resolved on measureless ruin or complete success.

> — 25 June 1864, speech to the United States House of Representatives

510 Fellow citizens! God reigns, and the government at Washington still lives!

> — 15 April 1865, speech in New York City, after the asassination of President Lincoln

RICHARD BROOKE GARNETT

Born 21 November 1817 in Essex County, Virginia. West Point class of 1841. At the outbreak of the Civil War, he resigned from the United States Army to become a Confederate major. On 14 November 1861, he was promoted to brigadier general. Killed in action 3 July 1863 at Gettysburg.

511 He is dead. Who can fill his place!

> — 11 May 1863, comment to Henry Kyd Douglas and Alexander S. Pendleton after the death of Stonewall Jackson

JOHN GIBBON

Born 20 April 1827 in Philadelphia, Pennsylvania. West Point class of 1847. He became Irvin McDowell's chief of artillery (1 October 1861), was promoted to brigadier general (2 May 1862) and major general (7 June 1864), and served as one of the commissioners who received the surrender of Lee's army at Appomattox. After the war, he remained in the army. Gibbon buried the massacre victims at Little Big Horn in 1876. Died 6 February 1896 in Baltimore, Maryland.

512 My men, do not leave your ranks to try to get shelter here. All these matters are in the hands of God, and nothing that you can do will make you safer in one place than another.

> — 3 July 1863, comment to his men who had taken shelter in an excavation at Gettysburg

JAMES SLOAN GIBBONS

Born 1 July 1810 in Wilmington, Delaware. Banker and abolitionist. Died 17 October 1892 in New York City.

513 We are coming, Father Abraham, three hundred thousand more, / From Mississippi's winding stream and from New England's shore.

> — 1862, "We Are Coming, Father Abraham, Three Hundred Thousand More," poem published in the *New York Evening Post* (16 July 1862), later a song; Abraham Lincoln had called for 300,000 more Union volunteers

ALFRED W. GILBERT

Gilbert was a Cincinnati engineer who entered the Union service in his 40s on 8 July 1861. He became a lieutenant colonel (27 July 1861), was mustered into the 39th Ohio (16 August 1861), and won promotion to colonel (8 July 1862) before resigning (1 October 1862)

514 The large and small balls bounced about just as if some of the great powers were playing a game of foot ball & the bombs burst over & around us until we really got to regard them more as if it was a pyrotechnic display, than if they were instruments of death, sent from a malignant & treacherous enemy.

> — 14 March 1862, letter to his wife, a description of the battle of New Madrid

J.G. GILCHRIST

Gilchrist was an Alabama secessionist.

515 Unless you sprinkle blood in the face of the people of Alabama, they will be back in the old Union in less than ten days.

> — early 1861, comment to Leroy P. Walker, Confederate secretary of war

PATRICK SARSFIELD GILMORE

Born 25 December 1829 in Ballygar, Ireland. He came to the United States in 1849 and became a composer and bandmaster. During the Civil War, he organized and trained the Massachusetts bands. Died 24 September 1892 in St. Louis, Missouri.

516   When Johnny comes marching home again, hurrah! hurrah! / We'll give him a hearty welcome then, hurrah! hurrah! / The men will cheer, the boys will shout, / The ladies they will all turn out, / And we'll all feel gay when Johnny comes marching home.
> — 1863, "When Johnny Comes Marching Home," song (originally published under the pseudonym Louis Lambert)

JAMES HENRY GOODING

Gooding was a member of the famous 54th Massachusetts Volunteer Infantry black regiment.

517   Now the main question is, Are we *Soldiers*, or are we *Labourers*?...The patient, trusting Descendants of Afric's Clime have dyed the ground with blood, in defense of the Union, and Democracy....Now your Excellency, we have done a Soldier's duty. Why can't we have a soldier's pay?...The Regt. do pray that they be assured their service will be fairly appreciated by paying them as American *Soldiers*, not as menial hirelings.
> — 28 September 1863, letter to President Lincoln, asking for equal pay with whites

JOHN BROWN GORDON

Born 6 February 1832 in Upson County, Georgia. Before the Civil War, he was a lawyer and superintendent of a coal mine. During the war, he became a Confederate captain (May 1861), major (c. 14 May 1861), colonel (28 April 1862), brigadier general (1 November 1862, unconfirmed; reappointed 11 May 1863 to rank from the 7th), and major general (14 May 1864). After the war, he engaged in law and politics. Died 9 January 1904 in Miami, Florida.

518   These men are going to stay here, General, till the sun goes down or victory is won!
> — 17 September 1862, statement to Robert E. Lee and D.H. Hill at Antietam

519   Suppose my back had been in a bow like yours? Don't you see that the bullet would have gone straight through my spine? Sit up or you'll be killed.
> — 12 May 1864, admonition to Thomas G. Jones after a bullet went through the back of Gordon's coat

G. MASON GRAHAM

Graham was chairman of the board of supervisors at the Louisiana Military Seminary in Alexandria, Louisiana.

520 Those of us who were *the last* to give up the Union, will be *the last* to give up the principle of *the right of a people to make their own government*—we will live to maintain it, or we will *die* in defense of it—[even though] our "cities, towns, yea people" *may* be destroyed.

> — 22 May 1861, letter to William T. Sherman, who had recently resigned as superintendent at Graham's seminary

JAMES A. GRAHAM

Graham was a Confederate captain from North Carolina.

521 I need not tell you that I dodge pretty often...for you can see that very plainly by the blots in this letter. Just count each blot a dodge and add in a few for I dont dodge for every shot.

> — 13 September 1864, letter to his mother

GORDON GRANGER

Born 6 November 1822 in Joy, New York. West Point class of 1845. In the Union army, he was promoted to captain (5 May 1861), colonel (2 September 1861), brigadier general (26 March 1862), and major general (17 September 1862). After the war, he was often on sick leave. Died 10 January 1876 in Santa Fe, New Mexico.

522 Why the hell does Rosecrans keep me here? There is the battle!

> — 20 September 1863, remark to Joseph S. Fullerton at Chickamauga

523 There's nothing in our front but ragtag, bobtail cavalry.

> — 20 September 1863, comment to a staff officer at Chickamauga

524 My men are fresh, and they are just the fellows for that work. They are raw troops, and they don't know any better than to charge up there.

> — 20 September 1863, statement to George H. Thomas at Chickamauga

525 Fix bayonets and go for them.

> — 20 September 1863, advice to John M. Brannan, who had asked what to do at Chickamauga

526   When those fellows get started all hell can't stop them.
> — 25 November 1863, comment to George H. Thomas as Union troops stormed up Missionary Ridge without orders

527   The battle is neither to the swift nor to the strong but to him that holds on to the end.
> — note to William S. Rosecrans

ULYSSES SIMPSON GRANT

Born 27 April 1822 in Point Pleasant, Ohio. His original name was Hiram Ulysses Grant. Through a clerical error, he was listed as Ulysses Simpson (his mother's maiden name) Grant at West Point; he kept the new version for the rest of his life. After graduating from West Point in 1843, he remained with the army and rose to captain before resigning in 1854. He then held a variety of minor jobs till the Civil War came. During the war, he became a colonel (17 June 1861), brigadier general of volunteers (31 July 1861, to rank from 17 May), major general of volunteers (16 February 1862), major general in the Regular Army (4 July 1863), lieutenant general in the Regular Army (2 March 1864), and commander in chief of all Federal forces (12 March 1864). In 1866 he was promoted to full general, and from 1869 to 1877 he was president of the United States. Died 23 July 1885 in Mount McGregor, New York.

528   There are but two parties now,—Traitors & Patriots and I want to be ranked with the latter, and I trust, the stronger party.
> — 21 April 1861, letter to his father

529   They are great fools in this section of the country and will never rest until they bring upon themselves all the horrors of war in its worst form.
> — 3 August 1861, letter from Mexico, Missouri, to his wife

530   We must cut our way out as we cut our way in.
> — 7 November 1861, comment at Belmont, after he had been told that he was surrounded

531   Yours of this date, proposing armistice and appointment of commissioners to settle terms of capitulation, is just received. No terms except unconditional and immediate surrender can be accepted. I propose to move immediately upon your works.
> — 16 February 1862, note to Simon Buckner, the Confederate commander at Fort Donelson

532   Fort Donelson will hereafter be marked in capitals on the maps of our united country.
> — 17 February 1862, General Order No. 2

533   I propose to attack at daylight and whip them.
> — 6 April 1862, remark to James B. McPherson at Shiloh

534   Yes, lick 'em tomorow, though.
> — 6 April 1862, response to William T. Sherman's question "We've had the devil's own day, haven't we?" after the first day at Shiloh

535   The Jews, as a class violating every regulation of trade established by the Treasury Department and also department orders, are hereby expelled from the department within twenty-four hours from the receipt of this order.
> — 17 December 1862, General Order No. 11, Department of the Tennessee (later revoked by President Lincoln)

536   It is a striking feature, so far as my observation goes, of the present volunteer army of the United States, that there is nothing which men are called upon to do, mechanical or professional, that accomplished adepts cannot be found for the duty required in almost every regiment.
> — 6 July 1863, report on Vicksburg

537   It's all right if it turns out all right. If not, someone will suffer.
> — 25 November 1863, remark at Missionary Ridge

538   You will find him him big enough for the purpose before we get through with him.
> — April 1864, comment to a staff officer who thought Philip Sheridan too small to lead Grant's cavalry

539   Wherever Lee goes, there you will go also.
> — 9 April 1864, letter to George Gordon Meade

540   Should my success be less than I desire and expect, the least I can say is, the fault is not with you.
> — 1 May 1864, letter to President Lincoln

541   When this army is defeated and when I am driven from this line, it will be when I have so few men left that they will not want any trains.
> — 6 May 1864, comment to a staff officer who had said that if they lost their position all their trains would be captured

542   Did Sheridan say that? He usually knows what he is talking about. Let him go ahead and do it.
> — 8 May 1864, comment to Meade when informed that Sheridan had boasted that, if left alone, he and his troopers could whip Jeb Stuart

543 I am now sending back to Belle Plain all my wagons for a fresh supply of provisions and ammunition, and propose to fight it out on this line if it takes all summer.
> — 11 May 1864, message from Spotsylvania to Henry Halleck

544 He was a gallant soldier and a Christian gentleman.
> — 21 May 1864, remark made when he stayed at the house where Stonewall Jackson had died

545 Lee's army is really whipped. The prisoners we now take show it, and the action of his army shows it unmistakably. A battle with them outside of intrenchments cannot be had.
> — 26 May 1864, letter to Halleck

546 If the enemy has left Maryland, as I suppose he has, he should have upon his heels veterans, militiamen, men on horseback, and everything that can be got to follow to eat out Virginia clear and clean as far as they go, so that crows flying over it for the balance of this season will have to carry their provender with them.
> — 14 July 1864, letter to Halleck

547 It was the saddest affair I have witnessed in the war.
> — 1 August 1864, letter to Halleck, concerning the Crater

548 They have robbed the Cradle and the grave equally to get their present force. Besides what they lose in frequent skirmishes and battles they are now losing from desertions and other causes at least one regiment per day. With this drain upon them the end is visible if we will be true to ourselves.
> — 16 August 1864, letter to Elihu Washburne

549 Where any of Mosby's men are caught hang them without trial.
> — 16 August 1864, message to Sheridan

550 If the war is to last another year, we want the Shenandoah Valley to remain a barren waste.
> — 26 August 1864, letter to Sheridan

551 I have just received your dispatch announcing the capture of Atlanta. In honor of your great victory, I have ordered a salute to be fired with *shotted* guns from every battery bearing upon the enemy. The salute will be fired within an hour, amid great rejoicing.
> — 4 September 1864, telegram to Sherman

552 You have accomplished the most gigantic undertaking given to any general in this war, and with a skill and ability that will be acknowledged in history as unsurpassed, if not unequalled.
> — 12 September 1864, letter to Sherman after the latter's capture of Atlanta

553 Everything looks like dissolution in the South. A few more days of success with Sherman will put us where we can crow loud.
> — 23 February 1865, letter to Elihu Washburne

554 I feel now like ending the matter....We will all act together as one army until it is seen what can be done with the enemy.
> — 29 March 1865, dispatch to Sheridan

555 The results of the last week must convince you of the hopelessness of further resistance on the part of the Army of Northern Virginia in this struggle. I feel that it is so, and regard it as my duty to shift from myself the responsibility of any further effusion of blood, by asking of you the surrender of that portion of the C.S. Army known as the Army of Northern Virginia.
> — 7 April 1865, note to Lee at Appomattox

556 The pain in my head seemed to leave me the moment I got Lee's letter.
> — 9 April 1865, comment to Horace Porter, referring to Lee's request for a meeting leading to his surrender

557 In accordance with the substance of my letter to you of the 8th inst., I propose to receive the surrender of the Army of Northern Virginia on the following terms, to wit: Rolls of all the officers and men to be made in duplicate, one copy to be given to an officer to be designated by me, the other to be retained by such officer or officers as you may designate. The officers to give their individual paroles not to take up arms against the Government of the United States until properly [exchanged], and each company or regimental commander to sign a like parole for the men of their commands. The arms, artillery, and public property to be parked, and stacked, and turned over to the officers appointed by me to receive them. This will not embrace the side-arms of the officers, nor their private horses or baggage. This done, each officer and man will be allowed to return to his home, not to be disturbed by the United States authorities so long as they observe their paroles, and the laws in force where they may reside.
> — 9 April 1865, surrender terms for Lee at Appomattox; the word *exchanged*, accidentally omitted by Grant, was inserted by Lee

558 I will not change the terms as now written, but I will instruct the officers I shall appoint to receive the paroles to let all the men who claim to

own a horse or mule take the animals home with them to work their little farms.

> — 9 April 1865, comment to Lee at Appomattox

559   The war is over, the rebels are our countrymen again, and the best sign of rejoicing after the victory will be to abstain from all demonstrations in the field.

> — 9 April 1865, request to his men as he rode away from the Appomattox meeting at which Lee had surrendered

HENRY GRAVES

Graves was a Confederate private.

560   I saw the body [of a man killed the previous day] this morning, and a horrible sight it was. Such sights do not affect me as they once did. I can not describe the change nor do I know when it took place, yet I know that there is a change for I look on the carcass of a man now with pretty much such feeling as I would do were it a horse or hog.

> — 16 June 1862, letter to his father

HORACE GREELEY

Born 3 February 1841 in Amherst, New Hampshire. Founder of the New York Tribune *in 1841 and an ardent abolitionist. Died 29 November 1872 in New York City.*

561   We think you are strangely and disastrously remiss in the discharge of your official and imperative duty with regard to the emancipating provisions of the new Confiscation Act....We think you are unduly influenced by the councils, the representations, the menaces of certain fossil politicians hailing from the Border Slave States.

> — 19 August 1862, "The Prayer of Twenty Millions," an open letter to President Lincoln, published in the *New York Tribune* 20 August 1862

562   The Rebels from the first have been eager to confiscate, imprison, scourage and kill; we have fought wolves with the devices of sheep.

> — 19 August 1862, "The Prayer of Twenty Millions"

WILLIAM BATCHELDER GREENE

Born 4 April 1819 in Haverhill, Massachusetts. Author, reformer, and Unitarian clergymen. Early in the Civil War, he was colonel of the 14th Massachusetts. He resigned from the service on 11 October 1862. Died 30 May 1878 in Weston-super-Mare, England.

563 You have had the kindness to offer me the command of a regiment to be composed of *transfugees* from the rebel army; that is, of men who, being prisoners of war in your hands, have voluntarily taken the oath of allegiance to the U.S., and have also voluntarily enlisted as soldiers of the Union.
— 16 March 1864, letter to Benjamin F. Butler

HENRY HAGADORN

Hagadorn was a Union private.

564 I must confess that I have seen but little of the wickedness and depravity of man until I joined the Army.
— 1863, diary

EDWARD EVERETT HALE

Born 3 April 1822 in Boston, Massachusetts. Author and Unitarian clergyman. Died 10 June 1909 in Roxbury, Massachusetts.

565 Behind all these men you have to do with, behind officers, and government, and people even, there is the country herself, your country, and...you belong to her as you belong to your own mother. Stand by her, boy, as you would stand by your mother.
— 1863, "The Man without a Country," story

566 He loved his country as no other man has loved her, but no man deserved less at her hands.
— 1863, epitaph for Philip Nolan, "The Man without a Country"

NORMAN J. HALL

Born c. 1837. West Point class of 1858. When the Civil War began, he was a second lieutenant. During the war, he rose to Union first lieutenant (14 May 1861), transferred to the volunteers, became colonel of the 7th Michigan (July 1862), was discharged from the volunteers because of disability (4 June 1864), returned to the Regular Army as a captain (to rank from 1 August 1863), and retired (22 February 1865). He won Regular Army brevets to captain (17

September 1862), major (13 December 1862), and lieutenant colonel (3 July 1863). Died 26 May 1867.

567 You fought and stood well. (Alternate version: You fought well and stood well.)

> — 17 September 1862, comment to a wounded Mississippi soldier captured at Antietam; the soldier replied, "Yes, and here we lie"

HENRY WAGER HALLECK

Born 16 January 1815 in Westernville, New York. West Point class of 1839. He resigned from the army as a captain in 1854 to become a lawyer. During the Civil War, he was commissioned a Union major general (19 August 1861) and was named the general in chief (11 July 1862). On 12 March 1864, Lincoln replaced Halleck with Grant, and Halleck's role was reduced to that of chief of staff. After the war, Halleck commanded military departments. Died 9 January 1872 in Louisville, Kentucky.

568 I am in the condition of a carpenter who is required to build a bridge with a dull ax, a broken saw, and rotten timber.

> — 6 January 1862, letter to President Lincoln, concerning unfit Union officers

569 Give me command in the West. I ask this in return for Forts Henry and Donelson.

> — 17 February 1862, telegram to George B. McClellan

570 A rumor has just reached me that since the taking of Fort Donelson General Grant has resumed his former bad habits. If so, it will account for his neglect of my often-repeated orders.

> — 4 March 1862, message to McClellan

571 Your going to Nashville without authority, and when your presence with your troops was of the utmost importance, was a matter of very serious complaint at Washington, so much so that I was advised to arrest you on your return.

> — 6 March 1862, message to Ulysses S. Grant

572 March where you please, provided you find the enemy and fight him.

> — early March 1862, message to Don Carlos Buell

573 The President is greatly dissatisfied with your delay, and sent for me several times to account for it. He has repeated to me time and again that there were imperative reasons why the enemy should be driven across the Tennessee River at the earliest possible moment.

> — 5 December 1862, message to William S. Rosecrans

574   We must live upon the enemy's country as much as possible and destroy his supplies. This is cruel warfare, but the enemy has brought it upon himself.
— April 1863, letter to Stephen A. Hurlbut

575   Call no council of war. It is proverbial that councils of war never fight. Do not let the enemy escape.
— 13 July 1863, telegram to George Gordon Meade after Gettysburg

CHARLES GRAHAM HALPINE

Born 20 November 1829 in Oldcastle, County Meath, Ireland. He immigrated to the United States in 1851 and became a writer. During the Civil War, he served as a private with the 69th New York state militia (20 April to 3 August 1861), became a Union major (5 September 1861), was temporarily assigned as a lieutenant colonel and assistant adjutant general on Major General David Hunter's staff (8 November 1862 to 1 July 1863), and resigned (31 July 1864) as a brevet brigadier general. After the war, he was an editor and politician. Died 3 August 1868 in New York City.

576   There is no romance to compare with the varying fluctuations of war in this ravaged but still beautiful Paradise.
— 29 May 1864, letter to "My Dearest Love," from the Shenandoah Valley

MURAT HALSTEAD

Born 2 September 1829 in Ross Township, Butler County, Ohio. Journalist for many years with the Cincinnati Commercial. *Died 2 July 1908 in Cincinnati, Ohio.*

577   How is it that Grant, who was behind at Fort Henry, drunk at Donelson, surprised at Shiloh, and driven back from Oxford, Mississippi, is still in command?
— 19 February 1863, letter to Salmon P. Chase

WILLIAM A. HAMBLIN

Hamblin was a private with the 4th Massachusetts Heavy Artillery.

578   In killing the President the South has lost their best friend....If the South will not learn what they have lost, they will be made to drink the dregs

of the cup that Lincoln would have spared them, and it is my desire that they should.

— 16 April 1865, letter to his wife

HANNIBAL HAMLIN

Born 27 August 1809 in Paris, Maine. Before the Civil War, he was a lawyer and politician. During the war, he was Lincoln's first vice president (1861-65). Hamlin served in the United States Senate from 1869 to 1881. Died 4 July 1891 in Bangor, Maine.

579 I desire to express my undissembled and sincere thanks for your Emancipation Proclamation. It will stand as the great act of the age.

— 25 September 1862, letter to President Lincoln

JAMES HENRY HAMMOND

Born 15 November 1807 in Newberry County, South Carolina. Lawyer, planter, and politician. Died 13 November 1864 on Beach Island, South Carolina.

580 Some malign influence seems to preside over your councils. Pardon me, is the majority always drunk?

— 9 April 1863, letter to Confederate Senator Robert M.T. Hunter

581 This miserable scheme of carrying on a war by Volunteers is utterly suicidal. The Chivalry go at the tap of the first drum and get badly cut up and physicked out the first campaign. Little remains for a second.

— 17 November 1861, letter to his son Harry

JAMES HAMNER

Hamner was a private with the 21st Tennessee Cavalry.

582 Tell Mr. Alford I am getting tired of the army, and would like to help him fish this summer, but fear I will have other fish to fry.

— 11 April 1863, letter to his mother

WADE HAMPTON

Born 28 March 1818 in Charleston, South Carolina. Before the Civil War, he was a planter and politician. During the war, he became a Confederate colonel (July 1861), brigadier general (23 May 1862), major general (3 September 1863), and lieutenant general (15 February 1865). After the war, he was

governor of South Carolina (1876-79) and a United States senator (1879-91). Died 11 April 1902 in Columbia, South Carolina.

583   I propose to fight.
>   — 11 June 1864, reply to Thomas Rosser's question, "General, what do you propose to do today?" at Trevilian Station

WINFIELD SCOTT HANCOCK

Born 14 February 1824 in Montgomery Square, near Norristown, Pennsylvania. West Point class of 1844. He began the war as a captain and later became a Union brigadier general of volunteers (23 September 1861), major general of volunteers (29 November 1862), and brigadier general of Regulars (12 August 1864). After the war, he remained in the army and rose to major general (1866). In 1880 he was the Democratic nominee for president of the United States, losing to another Civil War veteran, Republican James A. Garfield. Hancock died 9 February 1886 on Governors Island, New York.

584   Cross, this is the last time you'll fight without a star.
>   — 2 July 1863, remark to Colonel Edward E. Cross at Gettysburg, hinting at a promotion, but Cross was killed a few minutes later

585   Colonel, do you see those colors? Then take them!
>   — 2 July 1863, order to William Colvill at Gettysburg

586   There are times when a corps commander's life does not count.
>   — 3 July 1863, remark to an officer who had protested that Hancock should not expose himself to enemy fire at Gettysburg

587   I do not care to die. But I pray God I may never leave this field.
>   — 25 August 1864, comment to a colonel at Reams's Station, where Hancock's men had performed poorly

WILLIAM JOSEPH HARDEE

Born 12 October 1815 in Camden County, Georgia. West Point class of 1838. He rose to lieutenant colonel in the United States Army before resigning on 31 January 1861. During the Civil War, he became a Confederate colonel (16 March 1861), brigadier general (16 June 1861), major general (7 October 1861), and lieutenant general (10 October 1862). After the war, he was a planter. Died 6 November 1873 in Virginia.

588 Don't scatter your forces. There is one rule in our profession that should never be forgotten—it is to throw the masses of your troops on the fractions of the enemy.
> — 7 October 1862, advice to Braxton Bragg

HARPER'S WEEKLY

Harper's Weekly *was an important Northern periodical.*

589 Leaped to their feet, a thousand men, / Their voices echoing far and near; / "We go, we care not where or when; / Our country calls us, we are here!"
> — 27 April 1861

590 One of the first victims to the insane fury of the rioters was a negro cartman residing in Carmine Street. A mob of men and boys seized this unfortunate man on Monday evening, and having beaten him until he was in a state of insensibility, dragged him to Clarkson Street, and hung him from a branch of one of the trees that shade the sidewalk by St. John's Cemetery. The fiends did not stop here, however. Procuring long sticks, they tied rags and straw to the ends of them, and with these torches they danced around their victim, setting fire to his clothes, and burning him almost to a cinder.
> — 1 August 1863, a description of the New York City draft riots

CHARLES T. HASKELL, JR.

Charles T. Haskell, Jr., was a Confederate officer.

591 Tell Mother I died for her and my country.
> — 10 July 1863, dying words at Charleston, South Carolina

FRANKLIN ARETAS HASKELL

Born 13 July 1828 in Tunbridge, Vermont. Lawyer who, during the Civil War, became a first lieutenant (20 June 1861) and colonel (early 1864). Killed in action 3 June 1864 at Cold Harbor, Virginia.

592 Oh, the din and the roar, and these thirty thousand rebel wolf-cries! What a hell is there down that valley!
> — 16 July 1863, report on the 2 July 1863 fighting at Gettysburg

593   Where the long lines of the enemy's thousands so proudly advanced, see now how thick the silent men of gray are scattered. It is not an hour since those legions were sweeping along so grandly—now sixteen hundred of their fiery mass are strewn among the trampled grass, dead as the clods they load.
—— 16 July 1863, report on the 3 July 1863 fighting at Gettysburg

594   As long as patriotism is a virtue, and treason a crime, your deeds have made this crest, your resting place, hallowed ground.
—— 16 July 1863, report on the aftermath of the fighting at Gettysburg

NATHANIEL HAWTHORNE

Born 4 July 1804 in Salem, Massachusetts. His surname was originally Hathorne; he added the w. *A novelist whose books include* The Scarlet Letter *(1850) and* The House of the Seven Gables *(1851). He held government posts at the Boston customhouse (1839-41), the Salem customhouse (1846-49), and the Liverpool (England) consulship (1853-58). Died 19 May 1864 in Plymouth, New Hampshire.*

595   The regrettable thing is that I am too old to shoulder a musket myself, and the joyful thing is that Julian is too young.
—— May 1861, letter to Horatio Bridge; Julian was Hawthorne's son

596   I don't quite understand what we are fighting for, or what definite result can be expected. If we pummel the South ever so hard, they will love us never the better for it; and even if we subjugate them, our next step should be to cut them adrift. If we are fighting for the annihilation of slavery, to be sure, it may be a wise object, and offer a tangible result, and the only one which is consistent with a future reunion between North and South.
—— May 1861, letter to Horatio Bridge

597   It is the strangest and yet the fittest thing in the jumble of human vicissitudes, that he, out of so many millions, unlooked for, unselected by any intelligile process that could be based upon his genuine qualities, unknown to those who chose him, and unsuspected of what endowments may adapt him for his tremendous responsibility, should have found the way open for him to fling his lank personality into the chair of state.
—— March-April 1862, deleted material, concerning Abraham Lincoln, from "Chiefly about War Matters," published in the *Atlantic Monthly* (July 1862)

598   Undoubtedly thousands of warm-hearted, sympathetic, and impulsive persons have joined the Rebels, not from any real zeal for the course, but

because, between two conflicting loyalties, they chose that which necessarily lay nearest the heart.

— July 1862, "Chiefly about War Matters," in the *Atlantic Monthly*

599 When before, in all history, do we find a general in command of half a million of men, and in presence of an enemy inferior in numbers, and no better disciplined than his own troops, leaving it still debatable, after the better part of a year, whether he is a soldier or not?

— July 1862, "Chiefly about War Matters," in the *Atlantic Monthly*, the general referred to was McClellan

600 Everywhere some insignia of soldiership were to be seen—buttons, a red stripe down the trousers, a military cap; and sometimes, a round-shouldered bumpkin in the entire uniform.

— 15 August 1862, journal

CHARLES B. HAYDON

Haydon was an officer with the 2nd Michigan. From second lieutenant (22 September 1861), he earned promotions up to lieutenant colonel (30 July 1863) before dying of disease on 14 March 1864 in Cincinnati, Ohio.

601 Some men seem born to be shot.

— 9 April 1862, diary, after seeing a man killed by an isolated shell

602 A dead rebel soldier was today fished out of the well where we got what was supposed to be the best water.

— 14 June 1862, diary

ALEXANDER HAYS

Born 8 July 1819 in Franklin, Pennsylvania. West Point class of 1844. He resigned from the United States Army as a 2nd lieutenant in 1848 to join the California gold rush and to work as an engineer. From 25 April to 5 August 1861 he was a major in a three-month regiment of Pennsylvania volunteers. In the meantime, he was named a captain in the Regular Army (14 May 1861). However, he soon joined another volunteer regiment, the 63rd Pennsylvania, as a colonel (9 October 1861) and later rose to brigadier general (29 September 1862). Killed in action on 5 May 1864 at the Wilderness, Virginia. Posthumously promoted to major general.

603 Now, boys, look out; you will see some fun.

— 3 July 1863, comment at Gettysburg

604 We are tired of scientific leaders and regard strategy as it is called—a humbug. Next thing to cowardice. What we want is a leader who will go ahead.

> — 18 July 1863, letter to John B. McFadden on Meade's failure to pursue Lee after Gettysburg

WILLIAM SHAKESPEARE HAYS

Born 19 July 1837 in Louisville, Kentucky. Poet, composer, and songwriter. Died 23 July 1907 in Louisville.

605 On Shiloh's dark and bloody ground,
      the dead and wounded lay.
   Amongst them was a drummer boy,
      that beat the drum that day.

   . . .

   They wrote upon a simple board
      these words "This is a guide
   To those who mourn the drummer boy
      who prayed before he died."

> — 1862, "The Drummer Boy of Shiloh," song

CONSTANTINE A. HEGE

Hege was a private with the 48th North Carolina till he was captured by the Federals in the fall of 1863. After taking the oath of allegiance to the Union, he worked in Bethlehem, Pennsylvania, till the end of the war.

606 The human suffering, the loss of life and above all the loss of many a precious soul that is caused by war—would to God this war might end with the close of the year and we could all enjoy the blessing of a comfortable house and home one more time. I never knew how to value home until I came in the army.

> — 18 December 1862, letter to his parents

HARRY HIDDEN

Hidden was a lieutenant with the 1st New York Cavalry. Killed in action 9 March 1862 at Sangster's Station, Virginia.

607 Surrender! Never! I don't relish Libby Prison! Let's cut our way out!

> — 9 March 1862, command to his men at Sangster's Station

AMBROSE POWELL HILL

Born 9 November 1825 in Culpeper, Virginia. West Point class of 1847. He resigned from the United States Army as a 1st lieutenant (1 May 1861) and entered the Confederate forces as a colonel (9 May 1861). He won promotions to brigadier general (26 February 1862), major general (26 May 1862), and lieutenant general (May 1863). Killed in action 2 April 1865 near Petersburg, Virginia.

608   Damn you, if you will not follow me, I'll die alone!

         — 30 June 1862, angry remark shouted to his retreating troops at Frayser's Farm

609   Poor Kearny! He deserved a better death than that. (Alternate version: Poor Kearny! He deserved a better fate than to die in the mud.)

         — September 1862, comment on seeing his dead friend-enemy, shot in the seat of his pants and lying in the mud

610   I suppose I am to vegitate here all the winter under that crazy old Presbyterian fool. I am like the porcupine—all bristles, and all sticking out too, so I know we shall have a smash up before long.

         — 14 November 1862, letter to Jeb Stuart; the "fool" was Stonewall Jackson

611   Face the fire and go in where it is hottest!

         — 5 May 1864, order to an infantry captain

DANIEL HARVEY HILL

Born 12 July 1821 in York District, South Carolina. West Point class of 1842. In 1849 he resigned from the army to become an educator. During the Civil War, he was commissioned a Confederate colonel (11 May 1861), and later he won promotions to brigadier general (10 July 1861), major general (26 March 1862), and lieutenant general (11 July 1863, unconfirmed, so that he reverted to major general on 15 October 1863). After the war, he worked in journalism and then returned to education. Died 24 September 1889 in Charlotte, North Carolina.

612   The heroism shown at Seven Pines has had a most wonderful influence upon the subsequent battles around Richmond. After this decisive victory, under such disadvantageous circumstances, not a brigade in the ranks seemed to entertain the remotest doubt of our ultimate success over the besieging army of Yankees.

         — 1862, report on Fair Oaks (31 May and 1 June 1862)

613 The straggler is generally a thief and always a coward, lost to all sense of shame; he can only be kept in ranks by a strict and sanguinary discipline.
— November 1862, report after Antietam

614 The cavalry constitute the eyes and ears of the army. The safety of the entire command depends upon their vigilance and the faithfulness of their reports.
— 25 February 1863, address to his troops

615 The officers and men who permit themselves to be surprised deserve to die, and the commanding general will spare no effort to secure them their deserts.
— 25 February 1863, address to his troops

616 Many opportunities will be afforded to the cavalry to harass the enemy, cut off his supplies, drive in his pickets, etc. Those who have never been in battle will thus be enabled to enjoy the novel sensation of listening to the sound of hostile shot and shell, and those who have listened a great way off will be allowed to come some miles nearer, and compare the sensation caused by distant cannonade with that produced by the rattle of musketry.
— 25 February 1863, address to his troops

617 How much better it is thus to deserve the thanks of the country...than to skulk at home as the cowardly exempts do. Some of these poor dogs have hired substitutes, as though money could pay the service every man owes his country. Others claim to own twenty negroes....Others are warlike militia officers, and their regiments cannot dispense with such models of military skill and valor. And such noble regiments they have. Three field officers, four staff officers, ten captains, thirty lieutenants, and one private with a misery in his bowels. Some are pill and syringe gentlemen, and have done their share of killing at home. Some are kindly making shoes for the army, and generously giving them to the poor soldiers, only asking two months' pay. Some are too sweet and delicate for anything but fancy duty; the sight of blood is unpleasant, and the roar of cannon shocks their sensibilities.
— 24 April 1863, a general order

618 Promptness is the greatest of military virtues, evincing, as it does, zeal, energy, and discipline. The success of arms depends more upon celerity than any one thing else.
— 7 September 1863, circular

619 Shooters are more needed than tooters.
— endorsement disapproving an infantryman's request for a transfer to duty as a bandsman

JOHN H. HINES

Hines was a Confederate cavalryman from Kentucky.

620   I was glad to hear the opening of the battle because I wished to satisfy my curiosity for seeing a battle and I thought it would do one some good to see dead federals. But I had not seen many until the sight became sickening. I gave my canteen of water to a federal soldier who was badly wounded and felt glad I was able to relieve him. The same sight I thought an hour before I could glory in and even ride them down sick or well wherever I found them.
— 22 April 1862, letter to his family after Shiloh

HENRY HITCHCOCK

Born 3 July 1829 in Spring Hill, near Mobile, Alabama. Lawyer who, in 1863, joined the Union forces as an assistant adjutant general with the rank of major. He was William T. Sherman's legal advisor during the March to the Sea (late 1864). After the war, Hitchcock returned to his law practice. Died 18 March 1902 in St. Louis, Missouri.

621   He impresses me as a man of power more than any man I can remember. Not general intellectual power, not Websterian, but the sort of power which a flash of lightning suggests,—as clear, as intense, and as rapid.
— comment on Sherman

OLIVER WENDELL HOLMES

Born 29 August 1809 in Cambridge, Massachusetts. Essayist, poet, novelist, educator, and physician. Father of Oliver Wendell Holmes, Jr. Died 7 October 1894 in Boston.

622   Listen, young heroes! your country is calling! / Time strikes the hour for the brave and the true! / Now, while the foremost are fighting and falling, / Fill up the ranks that have opened for you!
— 1862, "Never or Now: An Appeal," poem

623   One flag, one land, one heart, one hand, / One Nation, evermore!
— 1862, "Voyage of the Good Ship Union," poem

OLIVER WENDELL HOLMES, JR.

Born 8 March 1841 in Boston, Massachusetts. Son of Oliver Wendell Holmes (preceding). Before the Civil War, he was a student at Harvard College. He became a first lieutenant in the 20th Massachusetts (July 1861) and rose to captain (spring 1862). In 1864 he was offered the rank of lieutenant colonel, but by then his regiment was decimated and he was tired of fighting, so he left the service as a captain on 17 July 1864. After the war, he was a lawyer and writer. In 1902 he became an associate justice of the United States Supreme Court. Died 6 March 1935 in Washington, D.C.

624　A bullet has a most villanous greasy slide through the air.
　　　— 2 June 1862, letter to his parents

625　War is an organized bore.
　　　— fall 1862, remark to visitors while he was recovering from a wound

626　The duties & thoughts of the field are of such a nature that one cannot at the same time keep home, parents and such thoughts as they suggest in his mind at the same time as a reality—Can hardly indeed remember their existence—and this too just after the intense yearning which immediately precedes a campaign.
　　　— 16 May 1864, letter to his parents

627　The straggling & marauding have become a great evil—Families are robbed and houses burned constantly by ruffians, chiefly, I suspect, noncombatants who move along the outskirts of the column.
　　　— 23 May 1864, diary

628　I started this thing a boy I am now a man and I have been coming to the conclusion for the last six months that my duty has changed—...I honestly think the duty of fighting has ceased for me—ceased because I have laboriously and with much suffering of mind and body earned the right...to decide for myself how I can best do my duty to myself to the country and, if you choose, to God.
　　　— 7 June 1864, letter to his mother

629　Get down, you damn(ed) fool, before you get shot!
　　　— 11 July 1864, warning to President Lincoln at Fort Stevens, Washington, D.C.; historical evidence suggests that a Union soldier may have shouted something like the above to Lincoln, but Holmes, who never claimed the quotation till some sixty years after the event, was probably not that soldier

THEOPHILUS HUNTER HOLMES

Born 13 November 1804 in Sampson County, North Carolina. West Point class of 1829. He resigned from the United States Army as a captain on 22 April 1861. During the Civil War, he became a Confederate brigadier general (5 June 1861), major general (7 October 1861), and lieutenant general (to rank from

10 October 1862). After the war, he was a farmer. Died 21 June 1880 near Fayetteville, North Carolina.

630 I am too much out of temper to write about the defeat, or I would give you an account of mismanagement and stupidity that would make you grieve for the course intrusted to such heads.

> — 18 October 1862, letter from Little Rock, Arkansas, to Thomas C. Hindman

JOHN BELL HOOD

Born 29 June 1831 in Owingsville, Kentucky. West Point class of 1853. He resigned from the United States Army as a first lieutenant (April 1861) and joined the Confederate forces at the same rank (April 1861). Later he won promotions to major (May 1861), colonel (October 1861), brigadier general (March 1862) and major general (October 1862). Wounded at Chickamauga (20 September 1863), he had his right leg amputated. Hood became a lieutenant general (February 1864, to rank from 20 September 1863) and then held the temporary rank of full general (18 July 1864 to 23 January 1865) while he commanded the Army of Tennessee. After the war, he was a businessman. Died 30 August 1879 in New Orleans, Louisiana.

631 Just look...at these dead and suffering men, every one of them as good as I am, and yet I am untouched.

> — 27 June 1862, comment to a staff officer, after Gaines's Mill

632 And now, sir, permit me to say that the unprecedented measure you propose transcends, in studied and ingenious cruelty, all acts ever before brought to my attention in the dark history of war. In the name of God and humanity I protest.

> — 9 September 1864, letter to William T. Sherman after the latter had demanded the evacuation of Atlanta

633 Sherman is weaker now than he will be in future, and I as strong as I can expect to be.

> — 22 September 1864, message to Braxton Bragg

JOSEPH HOOKER

Born 13 November 1814 in Hadley, Massachusetts. West Point class of 1837. He resigned from the United States Army in 1853 to become a farmer. During the Civil War, he was commissioned a Union brigadier general of volunteers (3 August 1861, to rank from 17 May), was promoted to major general of volunteers

(5 May 1862), was commissioned a brigadier general in the Regular Army (20 September 1862), replaced Burnside as head of the Army of the Potomac (26 January 1863), was in turn replaced by Meade (28 June 1863), and, for his action at Chattanooga (November 1863), won a brevet to major general in the Regular Army. He retired in 1868 after suffering a stroke. Died 31 October 1879 in Garden City, New York.

634 Every stalk of corn in the northern and greater part of the field was cut as closely as could have been done with a knife, and the slain lay in rows precisely as they had stood in their ranks a few moments before. It was never my fortune to witness a more bloody, dismal battle-field.
> — 8 November 1862, unfinished report on Antietam (September 1862)

635 The enemy is in my power, and God Almighty cannot deprive me of them. (Alternate version: God Almighty will not be able to prevent the destruction of the rebel army.)
> — 30 April 1863, comment just before Chancellorsville

636 It is with heartfelt satisfaction the commanding general announces to the army that the operations of the last three days have determined that our enemy must either ingloriously fly, or come out from behind his defenses and give us battle on our own ground, where certain destruction awaits him.
> — 30 April 1863, Gen. Order No. 47

637 The Rebel army...is now the legitimate property of the Army of the Potomac.
> — 30 April 1863, boast to William Swinton, a journalist

638 The Major General commanding trusts that a suspension in the attack today will embolden the enemy to attack him.
> — 1 May 1863, printed order to his generals, Chancellorsville

639 I have got Lee just where I want him; he must fight me on my own ground.
> — 1 May 1863, boast to Darius N. Couch, Chancellorsville

640 Profoundly loyal, and conscious of its strength, the Army of the Potomac will give or decline battle whenever its interest or honor may demand. It will also be the guardian of its own history and its own fame.
> — 6 May 1863, General Order No. 49

641 When...our true condition was revealed to them, their painful anxiety yielded to transports of joy which only soldiers can feel in the earliest moments of dawning victory.

— 4 February 1864, report of his November 1863 Chattanooga campaign

642 No one will consider the day as ended until the duties it brings have been discharged.

— 1 October 1864, General Order No. 71

643 Blows, not marches, are to kill the rebellion.

— 8 December 1864, letter to Benjamin F. Wade

HENRY HOTZE

Born 1834 in Zurich, Switzerland. As a child, he immigrated to the United States and settled in Mobile, Alabama. In 1861 he was a member of the Mobile Cadets, a company in the 3rd Alabama. In 1862 he went to London and established The Index, *a pro-Confederate newspaper. After the war, he worked as a journalist in Europe, where he died in the spring of 1887.*

644 It is marvellous with what wild-fire rapidity this tune of "Dixie" has spread over the whole South. Considered as an intolerable nuisance when first the streets re-echoed it from the repertoire of wandering minstrels, it now bids fair to become the musical symbol of a new nationality, and we shall be fortunate if it does not impose its very name on our country.

— 5 May 1861, *The Index*

SAMUEL HOUSTON

Born 2 March 1793 in Rockbridge County, Virginia. Known as Sam Houston. Before the Civil War, he was an Indian fighter with the United States Army, a lawyer, a United States congressman, the governor of Tennessee, a Texas pioneer, the president of the Republic of Texas, a United States senator, and the governor of the state of Texas. In March 1861 he left the governorship rather than take an oath of allegiance to the Confederacy. The city of Houston, Texas, is named after him. Died 26 July 1863 in Huntsville, Texas.

645 Let me tell you what is coming....Your fathers and husbands, your sons and brothers, will be herded at the point of the bayonet....You may, after the sacrifice of countless millions of treasure and of thousands of lives, as a bare possibility, win Southern independence...but I doubt it.

— Feb 1861, speech in Galveston, Texas

646 You have been transferred like sheep from the shambles. A government has been fastened upon you....You are to pay tribute to King Cotton.
> — 16 March 1861, proclamation to the people of Texas after a secession convention had ousted him from the governorship

647 My God, is it possible that all the people are gone mad?...The civil war now being inaugurated will be as horrible as his Satanic Majesty could desire.
> — 19 March 1861, according to Houston, his comment to armed Unionists who had offered to keep him in power by force

648 The hiss of the mob and the howls of their jackal leaders cannot deter me nor compel me to take the oath of allegiance to the so-called Confederate Government.
> — 31 March 1861, speech in Brenham, Texas

649 The soil of our beloved South will drink deep the precious blood of our sons.
> — 31 March 1861, speech in Brenham, Texas

650 Our people are going to war to perpetuate slavery, and the first gun fired in the war will be the knell of slavery.
> — 1861, prediction

651 I have been buffeted by the waves, as I have been borne along time's ocean, until shattered and worn, I approach the narrow isthmus, which divides it from the sea of eternity beyond.
> — 18 March 1863, speech in Houston, Texas

652 Once I dreamed of an empire for an united People...the dream is over.
> — 18 March 1863, speech in Houston, Texas

MRS. L.C. HOWARD

Mrs. Howard was a civilian in Mason, Illinois.

653 Lincoln you have committed the one great error of your life.
> — 17 September 1861, letter to President Lincoln after he had revoked Frémont's emancipation proclamation in Missouri

JULIA WARD HOWE

Born 27 May 1819 in New York City. Her original name was Julia Ward; she married the educator-reformer Samuel Gridley Howe. She was an author, lecturer, and reformer (active in such fields as woman's suffrage, abolition of slavery, and prison reform). Died 17 October 1910 in Rhode Island.

654   Mine eyes have seen the glory of the coming of the Lord;
He is trampling out the vintage where the grapes of wrath are stored;
He hath loosed the fateful lightning of His terrible swift sword:
His truth is marching on.
  Glory, glory, hallelujah,
  Glory, glory, hallelujah,
  Glory, glory, hallelujah,
His truth is marching on.
> — 19 November 1861, "Battle Hymn of the Republic," poem first published in *The Atlantic Monthly* (February 1862), later a song to the tune of "John Brown's Body"

FRANCES HUNT

Frances Hunt was a 14-year-old Richmond girl when she made the following entry in her diary.

655   The Yankees are behaving very well, considering it is them.
> — April 1865, diary

JOHN HUNTER

Hunter was the mayor of Natchez, Mississippi.

656 Coming as a conqueror, you need not the interposition of the city authorities to possess this place. An unfortified city, an entirely defenseless people, have no alternative but to yield to an irresistible force, or uselessly to imperil innocent blood. Formalities are absurd in the face of such realities.
> — 13 May 1862, written reply to James S. Palmer, commander of the U.S.S. *Iroquois*, who had sent a formal demand for the surrender of Natchez

ROBERT MERCER TALIAFERRO HUNTER

Born 21 April 1809 in Essex County, Virginia. Before the Civil War, he was a lawyer and politician. During the war, he served as a Confederate congressman (1861), secretary of state (1861-62), and senator (1862-65). After the war, he was the treasurer of Virginia and a port collector. Died 18 July 1887 near Lloyds, Virginia.

657 If we are right in passing this measure, we were wrong in denying to the old government the right to interfere with the institution of slavery and to emancipate slaves.

> — 7 March 1865, speech to the Confederate Senate, against a bill to turn slaves into soldiers

RUFUS INGALLS

Born 23 August 1818 in Denmark, Maine. West Point class of 1843. A captain when the Civil War started, he rose to Union major (12 January 1862), brigadier general of volunteers (23 May 1863), brevet brigadier general of Regulars (6 July 1864), and brevet major general of volunteers and Regulars (13 March 1865). From 16 June 1864 to 9 May 1865, he was chief quartermaster of the Armies of the Potomac and the James. He retired from the army in 1883 as quartermaster general. Died 15 January 1893 in New York City.

658 Operations so extensive and important as the rapid and successful embarkation of such an army, with all its vast equipments, its transfer to the Peninsula, and its supply while there, under its many vicissitudes, had scarcely any parallel in history, certainly no precedent in our country.

> — 17 February 1863, report to R.B. Marcy on the Peninsula campaign

659 It must be borne in mind that war on a scale inaugurated by this rebellion was decidedly new to us, if not to the civilized world.

> — 28 September 1863, annual report, addressed to M.C. Meigs

CLAIBORNE FOX JACKSON

Born 4 April 1806 in Fleming County, Kentucky. He was a proslavery Democrat elected governor of Missouri in 1860. His pro-Confederate activity led to Unionist military intervention and his flight from the state capital in May 1861. Died of illness 2 December 1862 in Little Rock, Arkansas.

660 Not one man will the State of Missouri furnish to carry on any such unholy crusade.

> — 17 April 1861, letter to Simon Cameron, Federal secretary of war, refusing President Lincoln's call for troops

THOMAS JONATHAN JACKSON

Born 21 January 1824 in Clarksburg, Virginia. West Point class of 1846. In 1851 he resigned from the army to teach at the Virginia Military Institute. During the Civil War, he became a Confederate brigadier general (17 June 1861), major general (7 October 1861), and lieutenant general (10 October 1862). Nicknamed Stonewall (for the origin of this nickname, see the Barnard Elliott Bee entry). Accidentally wounded by his own men at Chancellorsville (2 May 1863), he died at nearby Guiney's Station, Virginia, on 10 May.

661 I am in favor of making a thorough trial for peace, and if we fail in this, and the state is invaded, to defend it with terrific resistance.
  — 26 January 1861, letter to his nephew

662 People who are anxious to bring on war don't know what they are bargaining for; they don't see all the horrors that must accompany such an event.
  — 26 January 1861, letter to his nephew

663 The time may be near when the state needs your services. If that time comes, then draw your swords and throw away the scabbard. (Alternate version: The time for war has not yet come, but it will come, and that soon; and when it does come, my advice is to draw the sword and throw away the scabbard.)
  — 13 April 1861, speech to the cadets at Virginia Millitary Institute

664 It is painful enough to discover with what unconcern they speak of war and threaten it. I have seen enough of it to make me look upon it as the sum of all evils.
  — April 1861, letter

665 Don't you know that it is unmilitary and unlike an officer to write news respecting one's post? You wouldn't wish your husband to do an unofficerlike thing, would you?
  — 4 June 1861, letter to his wife

666 This place should be defended with the spirit which actuated the defenders of Thermopylae, and if left to myself such is my determination.
  — June 1861, letter to Robert E. Lee, concerning Maryland Heights

667 Sir, we'll give them the bayonet!
  — 21 July 1861, reply to Barnard Bee after the latter had said that they were being beaten back at 1st Bull Run

668 Charge, men, and yell like furies! (Alternate version: Reserve your fire till they come within fifty yards, then fire and give them the bayonet; and when you charge, yell like furies!)

— 21 July 1861, order to his troops at 1st Bull Run

669 Whilst great credit is due to other parts of our gallant army, God made my brigade more instrumental than any other in repulsing the main attack. This is for your information only—say nothing about it. Let others speak praise, not myself.

— 22 July 1861, letter to his wife, after 1st Bull Run

670 So you think the papers ought to say more about your husband! My brigade is not a brigade of newspaper correspondents.

— 5 August 1861, letter to his wife

671 As my officers and soldiers are not permitted to go and see their wives and families, I ought not to see my *esposita*, as it might make the troops feel that they were badly treated, and that I consult my own pleasure and comfort regardless of theirs.

— August 1861, letter to his wife

672 Man, man, do you love your wife more than your country?

— August 1861, attributed comment to an officer who had requested leave to see his dying wife

673 What is life without honor? Degradation is worse than death.

— August 1861, written reply to an officer who had requested leave to visit a dying family member

674 Throughout the broad extent of country over which you have marched, by your respect for the rights and property of citizens, you have shown that you were soldiers not only to defend, but able and willing both to defend and protect.

— 4 November 1861, farewell speech to his men

675 In the army of the Shenandoah you were the First Brigade; in the army of the Potomac you were the First Brigade; in the second corps of this army you are the First Brigade; you are the First Brigade in the affections of your General; and I hope by your future deeds and bearing you will be handed down to posterity as the First Brigade in our second War of Independence. Farewell!

— 4 November 1861, farewell speech to his men

676 The sweetest music I have ever heard.

— 4 November 1861, remark to his staff, referring to the Rebel yell given by his men after his farewell speech

677 If officers desire to have control over their commands, they must remain habitually with them, industriously attend to their instruction and comfort, and in battle lead them well.

> — November 1861, letter to commanding officers at Winchester, Virginia

678 All I am and all I have is at the service of my country.

> — 1861, letter

679 The Service cannot afford to keep a man who does not succeed.

> — 1861, letter

680 The treadmill of the garrison.

> — 1861, letter

681 I never found anything impossible with this brigade.

> — 3 January 1862, comment to Richard B. Garnett, after the latter had said that it was impossible for the men to march without eating first

682 Your order requiring me to direct General Loring to return with his command to Winchester immediately has been received and promptly complied with. With such interference with my command I cannot expect to be of much service in the field.

> — 31 January 1862, letter to Judah P. Benjamin

683 If the Secretary persists in the ruinous policy complained of, I feel that no officer can serve his country better than by making his strongest possible protest against it...rather than be a willful instrument in prosecuting the war upon a ruinous principle.

> — 6 February 1862, letter to Governor John Letcher of Virginia, concerning Judah P. Benjamin's interference with Jackson's command

684 If this Valley is lost, Virginia is lost.

> — 3 March 1862, letter to Alexander R. Boteler, concerning the Shenandoah Valley

685 Merit should be the only basis of promotion.

> — 5 [15?] March 1862, letter to William P. Miles, complaining about political generals

686 Whilst I highly prize Military education, yet something more is required to make a general.

> — 5 [15] March 1862, letter to William P. Miles

687 If we cannot be successful in defeating the enemy should he advance, a kind Providence may enable us to inflict a terrible wound and effect a safe retreat in the event of having to fall back.

> — 8 March 1862, letter from Winchester to Joseph E. Johnston

688 Say nothing about it. We are in for it.

> — 23 March 1862, reply to Alexander Pendleton, who had said that they were trapped at Kernstown

689 Our gallant little army is increasing in numbers, and my prayer is that it may be an army of the living God as well as of its country.

> — 7 April 1862, letter to his wife

690 You appear much concerned at my attacking *on Sunday*. I was greatly concerned, too; but I felt it my duty to do it, in consideration of the ruinous effects that might result from postponing the battle until the morning.

> — 11 April 1862, letter to his wife

691 Arms is a profession that, if its principles are adhered to for success, requires an officer do what he fears may be wrong, and yet, according to military experience, must be done, if success is to be attained.

> — 11 April 1862, letter to his wife

692 Now, Major, we'll have war in earnest. Old Virginia has waken up!

> — April 1862, comment to John A. Harman, concerning the Confederate conscription act of 16 April 1862

693 Why does Colonel Grigsby refer to me to know what to do with a mutiny? He should shoot them where they stand.

> — 16 May 1862, comment on receiving a report of the refusal of duty by short-term volunteers whose enlistment had expired

694 Surely they need not have run, at least until they were hurt!

> — 24 May 1862, comment to a staff officer, referring to his fleeing cavalry near Winchester

695 I yield to no man in sympathy for the gallant men under my command; but I am obliged to sweat them tonight, that I may save their blood tomorrow.

> — 25 May 1862, comment to Colonel Sam Fulkerson, who had said that the men needed rest from their all-night marching, near Winchester

696 I am afraid you are a wicked fellow.

> — 25 May 1862, comment to Richard Taylor, who had cursed

697 Never was there such a chance for cavalry! Oh, that my cavalry were in place!

> — 25 May 1862, remark at Winchester

698 With God's blessing, let us make thorough work of it.
— May 1862, statement early in the Valley campaign

699 Shoot the brave officers, and the cowards will run away and take the men with them.
— June 1862, remark to Richard S. Ewell, after Cross Keys and Port Republic (8-9 June 1862)

700 Never take counsel of your fears.
— 18 June 1862, advice to Jedediah Hotchkiss

701 Tell them that this affair must hang in suspense no longer; sweep the field with the bayonet.
— 27 June 1862, order to division commanders during the Seven Days in Virginia

702 It is cheaper to feed them than to fight them.
— early July 1862, comment to an officer after Seven Days, concerning Federal prisoners

703 So great is my confidence in General Lee that I am willing to follow him blindfolded.
— July 1862, remark to Alexander R. Boteler

704 Who could not conquer, with such troops as these?
— 25 August 1862, remark to his staff

705 My men have sometimes failed to *take* a position, but to *defend* one, never!
— 13 December 1862, comment to Heros von Borcke, Fredericksburg

706 God has fixed the time of my death. I do not concern myself about that, but to be always ready, no matter when it may overtake me.—That is the way all men should live, and then all would be equally brave.
— 1862, letter

707 I do not want to make an appointment on my staff except of such as are early risers.
— 1862, letter to his wife

708 If I can deceive my own friends, I can make certain of deceiving the enemy.
— 1862, maxim

709 I had rather lose one man in marching than five in fighting.
— c. 1862, maxim

710 My opinion is that there ought not to be much firing at all. My idea is that the best mode of fighting is to reserve your fire till the enemy get—or

you get them—to close quarters. Then deliver one deadly, deliberate volley— and charge!

> — 1863, maxim

711 To move swiftly, strike vigorously, and secure all the fruits of victory, is the secret of successful war.

> — 1863, letter

712 After being fired upon by our artillery, they presented the aspect of a mass of disordered fugitives.

> — 10 April 1863, report on the Valley campaign

713 We must make this campaign an exceedingly active one. Only thus can a weaker country cope with a stronger; it must make up in activity what it lacks in strength.

> — April 1863, letter

714 I trust God will grant us a great victory. Keep closed on Chancellorsville.

> — 1 May 1863, order to J.E.B. Stuart

715 The Institute will be heard from today.

> — 2 May 1863, comment to Thomas T. Munford, who had noted the large number of Virginia Military Institute graduates and former professors at Chancellorsville

716 I have always been kind to their wounded, and I am sure they will be kind to me.

> — 3 May 1863, comment to Dr. Hunter McGuire the day after Jackson was wounded

717 My men sometimes fail to drive the enemy from a position, but they always fail to drive us away.

> — 4 May 1863, comment to the men in the ambulance taking him to safety

718 I prefer it.

> — 10 May 1863, reply to his wife when she asked him if he was ready to die

719 I will be an infinite gainer to be translated.

> — 10 May 1863, comment to his wife, on his imminent death

720 It is the Lord's Day. My wish is fulfilled. I have always desired to die on Sunday.

> — 10 May 1863, statement to Alexander S. Pendleton

721 It will only delay my departure, and do no good. I want to preserve my mind, if possible, to the last.
> — 10 May 1863, reply to Dr. Hunter McGuire, who had offered Jackson a drink of brandy

722 Order A.P. Hill to prepare for action! Pass the infantry to the front!
> — 10 May 1863, attributed semiconscious statement while dying

723 Duty is ours; consequences are God's.
> — 10 May 1863, attributed semiconscious statement while dying

724 Let us cross over the river and rest under the shade of the trees.
> — 10 May 1863, last words

725 My duty is to obey orders.
> — a favorite aphorism

726 Always mystify, mislead, and surprise the enemy. (Alternate version: Mystery, mystery is the secret of success.)
> — attributed maxim

MICAH JENKINS

Born 1 December 1835 on Edisto Island, South Carolina. South Carolina Military Academy class of 1855. Before the war, he helped establish other military schools. He became a colonel in the Confederate service, led the famed Palmetto Sharpshooters, and rose to brigadier general (22 July 1862). Died 6 May 1864 at the Wilderness, Virginia, after being mistakenly shot by Confederate troops.

727 Come on, Georgia; I want you!
> — 31 May 1862, invitation to the adjutant of Lieutenant Colonel C.T. Zachry, of the 27th Georgia, who had offered support to Jenkins's South Carolina troops

728 The wounded gave no groans of anguish as the fatal blow was received, and instead of asking to be carried from the field encouraged their comrades to press on. The dying fell with their faces to the foe, all seeming actuated by a spirit like that of the noble Captain Carpenter, who advanced by my colors until his gallant little band of 28 dwindled to 12 and ever in their front, when the fatal ball pierced his heart turned to his company and, in words fit to be the last of a dying hero and patriot, said, "Boys, I am killed, but you press on!" then yielded up his spirit to the cause.
> — [June ?] 1862, report on Fair Oaks (31 May and 1 June 1862)

CIVIL WAR QUOTATIONS

R.P. JENNINGS

Jennings was a captain with the 23rd Virginia.

729 I may as well be killed running as lying still.
> — 17 September 1862, comment to another Rebel when Jennings, with a wounded hip, decided to head for the rear at Antietam

ANDREW JOHNSON

Born 29 December 1808 in Raleigh, North Carolina. Tailor and politician. During the Civil War, he served as the Union military governor of Tennessee (4 March 1862 to 3 March 1865, with the rank of brigadier general), vice president (4 March to 15 April 1865), and president (15 April 1865 to 4 March 1869). Died 31 July 1875 in Carter's Station, Tennessee.

730 For myself, I care not whether treason be committed North or South; he that is guilty of treason is entitled to a traitor's fate!
> — February 1861, speech in United States Senate

731 It seems to me that if I could not unsheath my sword in vindication of the flag of my country...I would return the sword to its scabbard. I would never sheathe it in the bosom of my mother!
> — February 1861, speech in United States Senate

732 I return to you with no hostile purpose....I come with the olive branch in one hand and the Constitution in the other, to render you whatever aid may be in my power, in re-erecting...the Star Spangled Banner.
> — 13 March 1862, speech in Nashville as the new military governor of Tennessee

733 What will the aristocrats do, with a railsplitter for President, and a tailor for Vice President.
> — November 1864, attributed comment

734 It is not promulging anything that I have not heretofore said to say that traitors must be made odious, that treason must be made odious, that traitors must be punished and impoverished.
> — 21 April 1865, speech in Washington, D.C.

HERSCHEL VESPASIAN JOHNSON

Born 18 September 1812 in Burke County, Georgia. Lawyer and politician, serving as Stephen A. Douglas's running mate in the 1860 presidential election. From November 1862 on, he was a member of the Confederate Congress. After the war, he was a politician and judge. Died 16 August 1880 near Louisville, Kentucky.

735 One revolution at a time is enough.
> — 29 November 1863, letter to Alexander H. Stephens, concerning the movement to revolt against Jefferson Davis

ALBERT SIDNEY JOHNSTON

Born 2 February 1803 in Washington, Kentucky. West Point class of 1826. On 10 April 1861, he resigned from the United States Army as a brevet brigadier general. Joining the Confederacy, he was named a full general (30 August 1861, to rank from 30 May). At Shiloh, Tennessee, he was shot in the right leg and bled to death on 6 April 1862.

736 I have put you in motion to offer battle to the invaders of your country. With the resolution and disciplined valor becoming men fighting, as you are, for all worth living or dying for, you can but march to a decisive victory over the agrarian mercenaries sent to subjugate and despoil you of your liberties, property, and honor. Remember the precious stake involved; remember the dependence of your mothers, your wives, your sisters, and your children on the result; remember the fair, broad, abounding land, the happy homes, and the ties that would be desolated by your defeat.
> — 3 April 1862, notice to the soldiers of the Army of the Mississippi

737 I would fight them if they were a million.
> — 5 April 1862, boast at a war council before Shiloh

738 Tonight we will water our horses in the Tennessee River.
> — 6 April 1862, boast to his staff just before Shiloh (some authorities give the date as 5 April and the first word as *Tomorrow*)

739 These men were our enemies a moment ago. They are our prisoners now. Take care of them.
> — 6 April 1862, attributed remark shortly before his death at Shiloh

JOSEPH EGGLESTON JOHNSTON

Born 3 February 1807 in Farmville, Virginia. West Point class of 1829. In 1837 he resigned from the army to work as a civil engineer. Later he returned to the army and rose to the rank of brigadier general (28 June 1860). During the Civil War, he left the United States Army (22 April 1861), became a Confederate brigadier general (14 May 1861), and was promoted to full general (31 August 1861, to rank from 4 July). He surrendered the Army of Tennessee on 26 April

1865. After the war, he worked in the insurance business and served in the United States Congress. Died 21 March 1891 in the District of Columbia.

740 The only way in which this force can be made useful, I think, is by rendering it movable, and employing it to prevent or retard the enemy's passage of the Potomac, and, should he effect the crossing, in opposing his advance into the country.
> — 26 May 1861, memorandum on Harpers Ferry

741 The battle is there. I am going.
> — 21 July 1861, comment to Beauregard at 1st Bull Run

742 Go to where the fire is hottest.
> — 21 July 1861, comment to Edmund Kirby Smith at 1st Bull Run

743 I am confident from observation that the Northern troops, like other raw soldiers, fear artillery unreasonably, and that we shall gain far more by an addition of these guns than by one of a thousand men.
> — 10 August 1861, letter to Jefferson Davis

744 I now and here declare my claims, that notwithstanding these nominations by the President and their confirmation by Congress I still rightfully hold the rank of first general in the Armies of the Southern Confederacy.
> — September 1861, letter to Jefferson Davis, protesting Johnston's fourth-place ranking among Confederate generals

745 If that miserable little Jew is retained in his place our country will never be able to defend itself.
> — 13 February 1862, letter to his wife, concerning Judah P. Benjamin, Confederate secretary of war at the time

746 No one but McClellan could have hesitated to attack.
> — 22 April 1862, letter to Robert E. Lee, concerning McClellan's siege of Yorktown

747 We are engaged in a species of warfare at which we can never win.

It is plain that General McClellan will...depend for success upon artillery and engineering. We can compete with him in neither.

We must therefore change our course, take the offensive, collect all the troops we have in the East and cross the Potomac with them.
> — 30 April 1862, letter to Robert E. Lee

748 You must be astonished to find how fond all Americans are of titles, though they are republicans; and as they can't get any other sort, they all take military ones.
> — 21 May 1863, comment to British visitor Arthur Fremantle

749   I would rather anything but this.
> — 14 June 1864, comment on the death of Leonidas Polk

750   Confident language by a military commander is not usually regarded as evidence of competency.
> — 18 July 1864, letter to Samuel Cooper

751   Sherman's course cannot be hindered by the small force I have. I can do no more than annoy him.
> — March 1865, message to Robert E. Lee

752   Our people are tired of war, feel themselves whipped, and will not fight. Our country is overrun, its military reserves greatly diminished, while the enemy's military power and resources were never greater, and may be increased to any extent desired.
> — April 1865, comment to Jefferson Davis

753   My small force is melting away like snow before the sun, and I am hopeless of recruiting it.
> — April 1865, comment to Jefferson Davis

JOHN BEAUCHAMP JONES

Born 6 March 1810 in Baltimore, Maryland. Writer and editor who served as a Confederate war clerk in Richmond during the Civil War. He wrote an important diary of the period. Died 4 February 1866 in Burlington, New Jersey.

754   Fighting is a sport our men always have an appetite for.
> — 10 July 1861, diary

755   Our generals will resolve never to survive a defeat.
> — 17 July 1861, diary

756   *Our* generals *never* modify their reports of victories.
> — 1 September 1862, diary

757   What a blunder France and England made in hesitating to espouse our cause!
> — 26 November 1862, diary

758   Let them come! They will be annihlated.
> — 4 February 1863, diary

759   Numbers have now no terror for the Southern people. They are willing to wage the war against quadruple their number.
> — 9 May 1863, diary

760   I am told the very *name* of Richmond is a terror to the foe.
> — 12 September 1863, dairy

761   Sherman's army is *doomed.*
        — 2 August 1864, diary

762   Many of the privates in our armies are fast becoming what is termed machine soldiers, and will ere long cease to fight well—having nothing to fight for.
        — September 1864, diary

763   Yesterday Gen. Lee surrendered the "Army of Northern Virginia."...If Mr. Davis had been present, he never would have consented to it; and I doubt if he will ever forgive Gen. Lee.
        — 10 April 1865, diary

J.H. JORDAN

Jordan was a civilian from Cincinnati, Ohio

764   The most fatal infatuation that ever did or can possess a statesman is the idea of a *Peace Policy* in the present emergency! It only encourages and strengthens the enemy, while it disheartens the friends of the Union in the seceded States, as well as the *real* friends of the Union every where!
        — 4 April 1861, letter to President Lincoln

PHILIP KEARNY

Born 1 June 1815 in New York City. In the Mexican War, he lost his left arm and earned a brevet to major. In 1851 he resigned from the army as a captain. A wealthy man, he then traveled. In 1859 he fought for France in a war against Austria. During the Civil War, he became a Union brigadier general (to rank from 17 May 1861) and major general (to rank from 4 July 1862). Killed in action 1 September 1862 at Chantilly (Ox Hill), Virginia.

765   With one arm gone, I am a better soldier than those who treat me so cavalierly!
        — spring 1861, comment when the War Department rejected him for military service

766   You understand that with one arm lost in Mexico I might easily have kept out of the war, without anyone charging a want of zeal against me. But as a gentleman I felt called on to act and not be idle. Besides, I firmly believe in the Union.
        — c. early August 1861, comment to his wife

767   We are superior to them and I do not see why we should not fight as well, and if we are beaten, then the oftener we are beaten the sooner we will learn to fight.
      — early 1862, letter to John W. De Peyster

768   I now proclaim distinctly...that unless a chief of proven military prestige—success under fire with troops—is put in command of the Army of the Potomac, leaving to McClellan the staff duties of General in Chief, we will come in for some awful disaster.
      — 4 March 1862

769   Don't flinch, boys! They're shooting at me, not at you!
      — early May 1862, attributed remark to his men at Williamsburg, Virginia

770   Go in anywhere, Colonel! You'll find lovely fighting all along the line.
      — 31 May 1862, comment to the colonel of a reinforcing regiment at Seven Pines

771   I respectfully submit that it is to the disadvantage of a constituted command to take men from their habitual leaders, and not to be anticipated that a brave though weak division can accomplish the same results with its regiments thus allotted out to those whom they neither know nor have fought under.
      — 2 June 1862, report on Fair Oaks

772   War is horrible because it strangles youth.
      — early June 1862

773   Here we are at deadlock again. Manassas over again—both parties entrenched up to the eyes; both waiting for something to occur.
      — 22 June 1862, letter to his wife

774   It only requires McClellan to put forth...his military might and Richmond would have been ours. But no; delay upon delay.
      — 22 June 1862, letter to his wife

775   A soldier can fight in soiled underwear but not without bullets.
      — 30 June 1862, quip at White Oak Swamp, where he ordered personal items to be left behind while knapsacks and pockets were stuffed with cartridges

776   Good-bye, Rebels! I'll see you all in Hell!
      — 30 June 1862, taunt orally hurled at Confederate troops as he rode away at Glendale

777   I, Philip Kearny, an old soldier, protest this order for retreat. We ought, instead of retreating, to follow up the enemy and take Richmond. And in

full view of all the responsibility of such a declaration I say to you all, such an order can only be prompted by cowardice or treason.
> — early July 1862, angry comment when McClellan ordered a retreat after the Union victory at Malvern Hill

778 It is fortunate in my Nature to feel that with my regiments, particularly whilst I am at the front, all enemies must yield before us.
> — July 1862, letter to his wife

779 Had the South kept to the Constitution and not resorted to revolution, I know the Northerners to be so contemptible that I would nearly have joined them.
> — July 1862, letter to his wife

780 The Virginia Creeper.
> — 1862, epithet for McClellan, during the Peninsula campaign

781 The Rebel bullet that can kill me has not yet been molded.
> — 1 September 1862, boast to David Birney, shortly before Kearny was shot dead

782 Dulce et decorum est pro patria mori.
> — his motto, Latin for "It is sweet and fitting to die for one's country"

J.H. KENDIG

Kendig was a Union soldier from Pennsylvania.

783 It bloud up a storm and knocked us about and made some of the boys very sick and ye gods what a time some was praying and some was swaring and others wanted to be throd overboard.
> — December 1861, letter to his brother, describing a troop movement by ship to South Carolina

EDWARD HALLOCK KETCHAM

Ketcham, though a Quaker, fought with the 120th New York as a second lieutenant. Killed in action 2 July 1863 at Gettysburg.

784 *It does men good to suffer for a good cause.* It somehow identifies them with it; and, as one good cause is linked with everything else that is good and noble, a man in fighting for liberty somehow fights his way to goodness. The general effect on the men here will be humanizing, and with peace—an honorable one, as we mean to win—will come national virtue.
> — 12 May 1863, letter to his mother

JOHN JAMES KEY

Key was a major in the Union army. Lincoln dismissed him from the service shortly after verifying that Key had made the statement quoted below.

785 The object is that neither army shall get much advantage of the other; that both shall be kept in the field till they are exhausted, when we will make a compromise and save slavery.

> — fall 1862, reply to Major Levi C. Turner when the latter asked, "Why was not the rebel army bagged immediately after the battle near Sharpsburg?"

HORATIO KING

Born 21 June 1811 in Paris, Maine. Postal clerk who rose to postmaster general under President Buchanan. President Lincoln appointed King to a commission that determined the compensation for slaves emancipated within the District of Columbia before the general Emancipation Proclamation. Later he worked at law. Died 20 May 1897 in Washington, D.C.

786 The celebrated Woman Order, I at first regarded as rather unfortunately worded, but I have the authority of a most intelligent lady, who resided in the South when the rebellion broke out, and remained there,...for saying that it was exactly what was required, and that it produced the desired effect. It brought ladies to their senses, and taught them to see what they should never have overlooked, that to insult an officer or soldier in the manner so many of them had done was a pretty sure sign that they had no claim to the title of lady.

> — 25 February 1863, letter to Professor J.W. Marshall

WALTER KITTREDGE

Born 8 October 1834 in Merrimac, New Hampshire. Songwriter. He continued to live in New Hampshire in his later years. Died 1905.

787   Many are the hearts that are weary tonight,
Wishing for the war to cease;
Many are the hearts looking for the right
To see the dawn of peace.
  Tenting tonight, tenting tonight,
  Tenting on the old camp ground.

> — 1864, "Tenting on the Old Camp Ground," song

KNOXVILLE WHIG AND REBEL VENTILATOR

The Knoxville Whig and Rebel Ventilator *was a pro-Union periodical in Knoxville, Tennessee.*

788 The *mediation* we shall advocate, is that of the *cannon* and the *sword*, and our motto is—no armistice on sea or land, until *all*, ALL the rebels, both front and rear, in arms, and in ambush, are subjugated or exterminated!
— 11 November 1863

PRINCE LAMBKIN

Lambkin was a Union corporal with the 1st South Carolina Volunteers, a regiment of former slaves.

789 Our mas'rs dey hab lib under de flag, de got dere wealth under it, and ebryting beautiful for dere chilen. Under it dey hab grind us up, and put us in dere pocket for money. But de fus' minute dey tink dat ole flag mean freedom for we colored people, dey pull it right down, and run up de rag ob dere own. But we'll neber desert de ole flag, boys, neber; we hab lib under it for *eighteen hundred sixty-two years*, and we'll die for it now.
— 5 December 1862, speech to the regiment

JAMES H. LANGHORNE

Langhorne was a lieutenant with the 4th Virginia, of the Stonewall Brigade, when he wrote the following quotation.

790 If a man had told me 12 months ago that men could stand such hardship I would have called him a fool.
— January 1862, letter to his mother, during the march to Romney

M.P. LARRY

Larry was a Union soldier from Maine.

791 Death is the common lot of all and the difference between dyeing to day and to morrow is not much but we all prefer to morrow.
— 26 February 1864, letter to his sister

HENRIETTA E. LEE

Mrs. Lee was the wife of Edmund J. Lee, a prominent Virginian and a relative of Robert E. Lee.

792 Hyena-like, you have torn my heart to pieces! For all hallowed memory clustered around that homestead; and demonlike, you have done it without even the pretext of revenge, for I never saw or harmed you. Your office is not to lead, like a brave man and soldier, your men to fight in the ranks of war, but your work has been to separate yourself from all danger, and with your incendiary band steal unaware upon helpless women and children, to insult and destroy...Were it possible for human lips to raise your name heavenward, angels would thrust the foul thing back again, and demons claim their own.
>   — 20 July 1864, letter to Union Major General David Hunter, who had burned her home

ROBERT EDWARD LEE

Born 19 January 1807 in Westmoreland County, Virginia. West Point class of 1829. He distinguished himself in the Mexican War, served as superintendent of West Point (1852-55), led marines in the capture of John Brown at Harpers Ferry (1859), and rose to colonel (spring 1861). In April 1861 he was offered field command of the Federal army. However, he rejected that offer, resigned, and became a major general in the Virginia forces (23 April 1861). Soon he joined the Confederate army as a brigadier general (14 May 1861) and won a promotion to full general (confirmed 31 August 1861, to rank as of 14 June). From 1 June 1862 to 9 April 1865, he commanded the Army of Northern Virginia. After the war, he was president of Washington College (later called Washington and Lee University), Lexington, Virginia. Died 12 October 1870 in Lexington.

793 Secession is nothing but revolution....Still, a Union that can only be maintained by swords and bayonets, and in which strife and civil war are to take the place of brotherly love and kindness, has no charm for me. If the Union is dissolved, the government disrupted, I shall return to my native state and share the miseries of my people. Save in her defense, I will draw my sword no more.
>   — 23 January 1861, letter to his son

794 I must say that I am one of those dull creatures that cannot see the good of secession.
>   — 19 April 1861, comment to a druggist in Alexandria, Virginia

795 Since my interview with you on the 18th inst. I have felt that I ought not longer to retain my commission in the army. I therefore tender my

resignation, which I request you will recommend for acceptance. It would have been presented at once, but for the struggle it has cost me to separate myself from a service to which I have devoted the best years of my life and all the ability I possessed...Save in defence of my native State, I never desire again to draw my sword.

— 20 April 1861, letter to Winfield Scott

796 Now we are in a state of war which will yield to nothing. The whole South is in a state of revolution, into which Virginia, after a long struggle, has been drawn; and, though I recognize no necessity for this state of things, and would have forborne and pleaded to the end for redress of grievances, real or supposed, yet in my own person I had to meet the question whether I should take part against my native State. With all my devotion to the Union, and the feeling of loyalty and duty of an American citizen, I have not been able to make up my mind to raise my hand against my relatives, my children, my home. I have therefore resigned my commission in the army, and, save in defence of my native State, with the sincere hope that my poor services may never be needed, I hope I may never be called on to draw my sword.

— 20 April 1861, letter to his sister

797 Whatever may be the result of the contest, I foresee that the country will have to pass through a terrible ordeal, a necessary expiation, perhaps, of our national sins.

— 5 May 1861, letter to "My dear Little H—-," a Northern girl

798 I agree with you in thinking that the inflammatory articles in the papers do us much harm. I object particularly to those in the Southern papers, as I wish them to take a firm, dignified course, free from bravado and boasting.

— 13 May 1861, letter to his wife

799 I prefer annihilation to submission. They may destroy but I trust never conquer us.

— 27 July 1861, letter to a relative

800 Our enemy is so strong at all points that we can only hope to give him an effective blow by a concentration of our forces, and, that this may be done surely and rapidly, their movements and actions must be controlled by one head.

— 8 August 1861, letter to Henry A. Wise

801 Our poor sick I know suffer much. They bring it on themselves by not doing what they are told. They are worse than children, for the latter can be forced.

— 17 September 1861, letter to his wife

802 I beg therefore, if not too late, that the troops be united, and that we conquer or die together.

— 21 September 1861, letter to Henry A. Wise

803 I begin to fear the enemy will not attack us. We shall therefore have to attack him.

— 30 September 1861, letter to John B. Floyd

804 For the bad behavior of a few it would not appear just to punish the whole.

— 25 April 1862, letter to Theophilus H. Holmes, concerning the suggestion that whole companies should be punished for the misconduct of some of their men

805 We cannot afford to be idle, and though weaker than our opponents in men and military equipments, must endeavor to harass if we cannot destroy them.

— 3 September 1862, letter to Jefferson Davis

806 Stragglers are usually those who desert their comrades in peril.

— 4 September 1862, General Order No. 102

807 Here is my old war horse at last! (Alternate version: Here comes my old war horse from the field he has done so much to save!)

— 17 September 1862, greeting to James Longstreet at Antietam

808 The army is resting to-day....Its present efficiency is greatly paralyzed by the loss to its ranks of the numerous stragglers. I have taken every means in my power from the beginning to correct this evil, which has increased instead of diminished.

— 21 September 1862, letter to Jefferson Davis

809 We may be annihilated, but we cannot be conquered.

— 3 November 1862, letter to his brother Charles

810 We can only act upon probabilities and endeavor to avoid greater evils.

— 12 November 1862, letter to Stonewall Jackson

811 It is well that war is so terrible—we should grow too fond of it.

— 13 December 1862, comment to James Longstreet and other officers at Fredericksburg

812 But what a cruel thing is war. To separate & destroy families & friends & mar the purest joys & happiness God has granted us in this world. To fill our hearts with hatred instead of love for our neighbours & to devastate the fair face of this beautiful world.

— 25 December 1862, letter to his wife

813 More than once have most promising opportunities been lost for want of men to take advantage of them, and victory itself has been made to put on the appearance of defeat, because our diminished and exhausted troops have been unable to renew a successful struggle against fresh numbers of the enemy. The lives of our soldiers are too precious to be sacrificed in the attainment of successes that inflict no loss upon the enemy beyond the actual loss in battle.

> — 10 January 1863, letter to James A. Seddon, secretary of war, asking for more men

814 The greatest difficulty I find is in causing orders and regulations to be obeyed. This arises not from a spirit of disobedience but from ignorance. We therefore have a need of a corps of officers to teach others their duty, see to the observance of orders, and to the regularity and precision of all movements.

> — 21 March 1863, letter to Davis

815 There is no better way of defending a long line than by moving into the enemy's territory.

> — 21 March 1863, letter to John R. Jones

816 Could I have directed events, I should have chosen for the good of the country to have been disabled in your stead.

> — 3 May 1863, letter to Stonewall Jackson after learning of the latter's being wounded

817 Give him my affectionate regards, and tell him to make haste and get well, and come back to me as soon as he can. He has lost his left arm, but I have lost my right arm.

> — 6 May 1863, oral message given to Rev. Beverly T. Lacy to pass along to the wounded Stonewall Jackson

818 Such an executive officer the sun never shone on. I have but to show him my design, and I know that if it can be done, it will be done. No need for me to send or watch him. Straight as the needle to the pole he advanced to the execution of my purpose.

> — c. 6 May 1863, statement to a visitor about Stonewall Jackson

819 I agree with you in believing that our army would be invincible if it could be properly organized and officered. There never were such men in an army before. They will go anywhere and do anything if properly led. But there is the difficulty—proper commanders. Where can they be obtained.

> — 21 May 1863, letter to John B. Hood

820 There is always hazard in military movements, but we must decide between the positive loss of inactivity and the risk of action.

> — 8 June 1863, letter to James A. Seddon

821 We should neglect no honorable means of dividing and weakening our enemies, that they may experience some of the difficulties experienced by ourselves. It seems to me that the most effectual mode of accomplishing this object, now within our reach, is to give all the encouragement we can, consistently with truth, to the rising peace party of the North.

Nor do I think we should, in this connection, make nice distinction between those who declare for peace unconditionally and those who advocate it as a means of restoring the Union, however much we may prefer the former.
    — 10 June 1863, letter to Jefferson Davis

822 General Meade will commit no blunder in my front, and if I make one he will make haste to take advantage of it.
    — late June or early July 1863

823 If the enemy is there, we must attack him.
    — 1 July 1863, comment to James Longstreet at Gettysburg

824 The enemy is here, and if we do not whip him, he will whip us.
    — 2 July 1863, comment to John B. Hood at Gettysburg

825 What *can* detain Longstreet?
    — 2 July 1863, question to Armistead L. Long at Gettysburg

826 I have not heard a word from you for days, and you the eyes and ears of my army.
    — 2 July 1863, remark to Jeb Stuart, at Gettysburg

827 The enemy is there, and I am going to strike him.
    — 3 July 1863, remark to James Longstreet at Gettysburg

828 Never mind, general; all this has been my fault. It is I who have lost this fight, and you must help me out of it in the best way you can. (Alternate version: Your men have done all that men could do; the fault is entirely my own.)
    — 3 July 1863, comment to George E. Pickett after the disastrous Pickett's Charge at Gettysburg

829 I am very sorry—the task was too great for you. But we musn't despond. Another time we shall succeed.
    — 3 July 1863, remark to Captain Randolph A. Shotwell at Gettysburg

830 All this has been my fault.
    — 3 July 1863, comment to Cadmus M. Wilcox at Gettysburg

831 It's all my fault. I thought my men were invincible.
    — 4 July 1863, comment to James Longstreet after Gettysburg

832 They have but little courage.
> — 13 July 1863, comment about the Yankees digging in instead of attacking after Gettysburg

833 I...request Your Excellency to take measures to supply my place....I cannot even accomplish what I myself desire. How can I fulfil the expectations of others? In addition I sensibly feel the growing failure of my bodily strength.... Everything, therefore, points to the advantages to be derived from a new commander, and I the more anxiously urge the matter upon Your Excellency from my belief that a younger and abler man than myself can readily be attained.
> — 8 August 1863, letter to Jefferson Davis after the Confederate retreat from Gettysburg

834 To prolong a state of affairs in every way desirable, and not to permit the season for active operations to pass without endeavoring to inflict further injury upon the enemy, the best course appeared to be the transfer of the army into Maryland.
> — 19 August 1863, report to Samuel Cooper on the capture of Harpers Ferry

835 Men seem to prefer sowing discord to inculcating harmony.
> — 9 September 1863, letter to James A. Seddon, concerning newspaper correspondents

836 Well, well, General, bury these poor men and let us say no more about it.
> — 15 October 1863, comment to Ambrose P. Hill after Hill's error at Bristoe Station

837 I fear that pardons, unless for the best of reasons, will not only make all the blood that has been shed for the maintenance of discipline useless, but will result in the painful necessity of shedding a great deal more.
> — 30 October 1863, letter to James A. Seddon

838 I have never witnessed on any previous occasion such entire disregard of the usages of civilized warfare and the dictates of humanity.
> — 27 April 1864, report on the November 1863 operations against Meade in Virginia, concerning Federal destruction of private property

839 If victorious, we have everything to live for. If defeated, there will be nothing left to live for.
> — 3 May 1864, prediction before the Wilderness

840 I think General Grant has managed his affairs remarkably well up to the present time.
> — 11 May 1864, remark to his officers who had criticized Grant

841 This army cannot stand a siege. We must end this business on the battlefield, not in a fortified place.
> — 11 May 1864, statement to his officers at Spotsylvania

842 He never brought me a piece of false information.
> — 12 May 1864, comment about Jeb Stuart while the latter was dying

843 I can scarcely think of him without weeping!
> — 12 May 1864, comment about Jeb Stuart after the latter had died

844 These men are not an army; they are citizens defending their country.
> — 15 May 1864, comment to A.P. Hill

845 The soldiers know their duties better than the general officers do, and they have fought magnificently.
> — 15 May 1864, comment to A.P. Hill

846 When a man makes a mistake, I call him to my tent, talk to him, and use the authority of my position to make him do the right thing the next time.
> — 15 May 1864, comment to A.P. Hill

847 It seems to me that we must choose between employing negroes ourselves and having them employed against us.
> — 2 September 1864, letter to Davis

848 I think...we must decide whether slavery shall be extinguished by our enemies and the slaves be used against us, or use them ourselves at the risk of the effects which may be produced upon our social institutions. My own opinion is that we should employ them without delay. I believe that with proper regulations they can be made efficient soldiers.
> — 11 January 1865, letter to Andrew Hunter

849 The surest foundation upon which the fidelity of an army can rest, especially in a service which imposes peculiar hardships and privations, is the personal interest of the soldier in the issue of the contest. Such an interest we can give our negroes by giving immediate freedom to all who enlist, and freedom at the end of the war to the families of those who discharge their duties faithfully.
> — 11 January 1865, letter to Andrew Hunter

850 We should not expect slaves to fight for prospective freedom when they can secure it at once by going to the enemy, in whose service they incur no greater risk than in ours....The best means of securing the efficiency and

fidelity of this auxiliary force would be to accompany the measure with a well-digested plan of gradual and general emancipation. As that will be the result of the continuance of the war, and will certainly occur if the enemy succeed, it seems to me most advisable to adopt it at once, and thereby obtain all the benefits that will accrue to our cause.
— 11 January 1865, letter to Andrew Hunter

851   Every citizen who prevents a carbine or pistol from remaining unused will render a service to his country. Those who think to retain arms for their own defence should remember that if the army cannot protect them, the arms will be of little use.
— 25 January 1865, circular

852   They cannot barter manhood for peace nor the right of self-government for life or property.
— 14 February 1865, General Order No. 2

853   The advantages of the enemy will have but little value if we do not permit them to impair our resolution. Let us then oppose constancy to adversity, fortitude to suffering, and courage to danger, with the firm assurance that He who gave freedom to our fathers will bless the efforts of their children to preserve it.
— 14 February 1865, General Order No. 2

854   I shall...endeavor to do my duty and fight to the last.
— 22 February 1865, letter to his wife

855   They should be made to understand that discipline contributes no less to their safety than to their efficiency. Disastrous surprises and those sudden panics which lead to defeat and the greatest loss of life are of rare occurrence among disciplined troops.... Let officers and men be made to feel that they will most effectually secure their safety by remaining steadily at their posts, preserving order, and fighting with coolness and vigor.
— 22 February 1865, circular

856   He is at rest now, and we who are left are the ones to suffer.
— 2 April 1865, comment to Sergeant G.W. Tucker on the death of A.P. Hill

857   My God! Has the army dissolved?
— 6 April 1865, comment to William Mahone on the Confederate defeat at Sayler's Creek

858   I have recd your note of this date. Though not entertaining the opinion you express of the hopelessness of further resistance on the part of the Army of N. Virginia—I reciprocate your desire to avoid useless effusion of blood,

and therefore before considering your proposition ask the terms you will offer on condition of its surrender.

> — 7 April 1865, note to Ulysses S. Grant

859   I have probably to be General Grant's prisoner and thought I must make my best appearance.

> — 9 April 1865, comment to William N. Pendleton, explaining Lee's fancy attire

860   There is nothing left me to do but to go and see General Grant, and I would rather die a thousand deaths.

> — 9 April 1865, comment to his staff before meeting Grant to surrender at Appomattox

861   The question is, Is it right to surrender this army? If it is right, then I will take all the responsibility.

> — 9 April 1865, reply when asked what history would say of his surrender

862   If I took your advice, the men would be without rations and under no control of officers. They would be compelled to rob and steal in order to live. They would become mere bands of marauders, and the enemy's cavalry would pursue them and overrun many wide sections they may never have occasion to visit. We would bring on a state of affairs it would take the country years to recover from.

> — 9 April 1865, reply to E. Porter Alexander's suggestion that Lee's soldiers should slip away and continue the fight

863   I suppose, General Grant, that the object of our present meeting is fully understood. I asked to see you to ascertain upon what terms you would receive the surrender of my army.

> — 9 April 1865, remark to Grant at Appomattox

864   This will have the best possible effect upon the men. It will be very gratifying and will do much toward conciliating our people.

> — 9 April 1865, comment to Grant at Appomattox, after Grant had offered to let Lee's men keep their own animals

865   Men, we have fought the war together, and I have done the best I could for you. You will all be paroled and go to your homes until exchanged.

> — 9 April 1865, brief address while riding back to his lines from the Appomattox surrender

866   Go home, all you boys who fought with me, and help to build up the shattered fortunes of our old state.

> — 9 April 1865, attributed remark to his men

867 After four years of arduous service marked by unsurpassed courage and fortitude, the Army of Northern Virginia has been compelled to yield to overwhelming numbers and resources....With an unceasing admiration of your constancy and devotion to your Country, and a grateful remembrance of your kind and generous consideration for myself, I bid you an affectionate farewell.

> — 10 April 1865, formal farewell address to his army; written by Colonel Charles Marshall and modified by Lee (many different people made copies of the speech at the time, creating slightly different versions)

868 Go home now, and if you make as good citizens as you have soldiers, you will do well, and I shall always be proud of you.

> — 12 April 1865, comment to some Confederate soldiers (also attributed to 9 April)

869 It is with pain that I announce to Your Excellency the surrender of the Army of Northern Virginia.

> — 12 April 1865, report to Davis

870 Upon arriving at Amelia Court-house on the morning of the 4th with the advance of the army,...and not finding the supplies ordered to be placed there, nearly twenty-four hours were lost in endeavoring to collect in the country subsistence for men and horses. This delay was fatal, and could not be retrieved.

> — 12 April 1865, report to Davis

871 Go home and take up any work that offers. Accept conditions as you find them. Consider only the present and the future. Do not cherish bitterness.

> — mid-April 1865, repeated comment to Southerners he met while going home after his surrender

872 It is always well to expect the enemy to do what he should do.

> — a favorite maxim

873 Private and public life are subject to the same rules; and truth and manliness are two qualities that will carry you through this world much better than *policy*, or *tact*, or *expediency*, or any other word that was ever devised to conceal or mystify a deviation from a straight line.

> — a favorite maxim

874 We must strike them a blow.

> — a frequent saying

STEVEN DILL LEE

Born 22 September 1833 in Charleston, South Carolina. West Point class of 1854. He resigned as a first lieutenant from the United States Army (20 February 1861) and became a Confederate captain (1861), major (1861), lieutenant colonel (June 1862), colonel (c. July 1862), brigadier general (6 November 1862), major general (3 August 1863), and lieutenant general (23 June 1864). After the war, he was a planter, legislator, and college president. Died 28 May 1908 in Vicksburg, Mississippi.

875 Sharpsburg was artillery hell.
— November 1862, comment to Edward P. Alexander

JOSEPH LESTER

Lester was a Union volunteer.

876 It is Gods inexorable Law that wrong "doing" must receive Punishment, whether it is Nations or Individuals, and our Sin has found us out, and the Penalty is being meted out to us.
— 1 November 1862, letter to his father and sisters

CYRUS H. LEWIS

Lewis served the Union with the 1st Missouri Engineers.

877 I have read and studied the Chicago Platform, and I pronounce it treason of the darkest hue....It is like a thief feigning to be a clergyman or a wolf in lamb's clothing.
— 3 November 1864, letter to his parents

ABRAHAM LINCOLN

Born 12 February 1809 near Hodgenville, Hardin County, Kentucky. He became a lawyer in 1836 and, as a Whig, served several terms in the Illinois state legislature and one term (1847-49) in the United States House of Representatives. In 1858 he ran as the Republican nominee against the Democrat Stephen A. Douglas for a seat in the United States Senate. Lincoln lost that election but in 1860 won a race against the same opponent for the office of president of the United States, which he held from 4 March 1861 till his death. Shot by John

Wilkes Booth on 14 April 1865 in Washington, D.C., Lincoln died the following day.

878   I am for those means which will give the greatest good to the greatest number.

> — 12 February 1861, speech in Cincinnati; a paraphrase of Jeremy Bentham's "The greatest happiness of the greatest number is the foundation of morals and legislation," itself from Francis Hutcheson's "That action is best which procures the greatest happiness for the greatest numbers"

879   If all do not join now to save the good old ship of the Union this voyage nobody will have a chance to pilot her on another voyage. (Alternate version: If we do not make common cause to save the good old ship of the Union on this voyage, nobody will have a chance to pilot her on another voyage.)

> — 15 February 1861, speech in Cleveland

880   But if this country cannot be saved without giving up that principle—I was about to say I would rather be assassinated on this spot than to surrender it.

> — 22 February 1861, speech in Philadelphia; the "principle" was the idea of liberty for all in the Declaration of Independence

881   I take the official oath to-day, with no mental reservations, and with no purpose to construe the Constitution or laws, by any hypercritical rules.

> — 4 March 1861, 1st Inaugural Address

882   It is safe to assert that no government proper, ever had a provision in its organic law for its own termination.

> — 4 March 1861, 1st Inaugural Address

883   If, by the mere force of numbers, a majority should deprive a minority of any clearly written constitutional right, it might, in a moral point of view, justify revolution—certainly would, if such right were a vital one. But such is not our case. All the vital rights of minorities, and of individuals, are so plainly assured to them, by affirmations and negations, guarranties and prohibitions, in the Constitution, that controversies never arise concerning them.

> — 4 March 1861, 1st Inaugural Address

884   Suppose you go to war, you cannot fight always; and when, after much loss on both sides, and no gain on either, you cease fighting, the identical old questions, as to terms of intercourse, are again upon you.

> — 4 March 1861, 1st Inaugural Address

885 This country, with its institutions, belongs to the people who inhabit it. Whenever they shall grow weary of the existing government, they can exercise their *constitutional* right of amending it, or their *revolutionary* right to dismember, or overthrow it.
— 4 March 1861, 1st Inaugural Address

886 Why should there not be a patient confidence in the ultimate justice of the people? Is there any better, or equal hope, in the world?
— 4 March 1861, 1st Inaugural Address

887 While the people retain their virtue, and vigilance, no administration, by any extreme of wickedness or folly, can very seriously injure the government, in the short space of four years.
— 4 March 1861, 1st Inaugural Address

888 In *your* hands, my dissatisfied fellow countrymen, and not in *mine*, is the momentous issue of civil war. The government will not assail *you*. You can have no conflict, without being yourselves the aggressors.
— 4 March 1861, 1st Inaugural Address

889 I am loth to close. We are not enemies, but friends. We must not be enemies. Though passion may have strained, it must not break our bonds of affection. The mystic chords of memory, stretching from every battle-field, and patriot grave, to every living heart and hearthstone, all over this broad land, will yet swell the chorus of the Union, when again touched, as surely they will be, by the better angels of our nature.
— 4 March 1861, 1st Inaugural Address

890 I think the necessity of being *ready* increases. Look to it.
— 8 April 1861, letter to Andrew G. Curtin, governor of Pennsylvania

891 Our men are not moles, and can't dig under the earth; they are not birds, and can't fly through the air. There is no way but to march across, and that they must do. But in doing this there is no need of collision. Keep your rowdies in Baltimore, and there will be no bloodshed. Go home and tell your people that if they will not attack us, we will not attack them; but if they do attack us, we will return it, and that severely.
— 22 April 1861, reply to a Baltimore committee advocating peace at any price

892 You are green, it is true, but they are green also; you are all green alike.
— 29 June 1861, comment to Irvin McDowell, who wanted to delay an offensive till he could train more men

893 If, at any point, on or in the vicinity of any military line which is now, or which shall be used, between the City of New York and the City of

Washington, you find resistance which renders it necessary to suspend the writ of Habeas Corpus for the Public Safety, you, personally, or through the Officer in command, at the point where resistance occurs, are authorized to suspend that writ.

— 2 July 1861, letter to Winfield Scott (in future letters, Lincoln extended the suspension to other areas)

894 It presents to the whole family of man, the question, whether a constitutional republic, or a democracy—a government of the people, by the same people—can, or cannot, maintain its territorial integrity, against its own domestic foes....It forces us to ask:..."Must a government, of necessity, be too *strong* for the liberties of its own people, or too *weak* to maintain its own existence?"

— 4 July 1861, message to Congress; the "it" referred to here was the Confederate attack on Fort Sumter

895 This is essentially a People's contest. On the side of the Union, it is a struggle for maintaining in the world, that form, and substance of government, whose leading object is, to elevate the condition of men—to lift artificial weights from all shoulders—to clear the paths of laudable pursuit for all—to afford all, an unfettered start, and a fair chance, in the race of life.

— 4 July 1861, message to Congress

896 All I have to say is what the girl said when she stuck her foot into the stocking. It strikes me there's something in it.

— 13 September 1861, comment on being shown an ironclad model

897 I think to lose Kentucky is nearly the same as to lose the whole game. Kentucky gone, we cannot hold Missouri, nor, I think, Maryland. These all against us, and the job on our hands is too large for us. We would as well consent to separation at once, including the surrender of this capital.

— September 1861, remark at a cabinet meeting

898 I will hold McClellan's horse if he will only bring us success.

— 13 November 1861, comment to John Hay after McClellan had snubbed Lincoln

899 Labor is prior to, and independent of, capital. Capital is only the fruit of labor, and could never have existed if labor had not first existed. Labor is the superior of capital, and deserves much the higher consideration.

— 3 December 1861, message to Congress

900 One war at a time.

— December 1861, comment to William H. Seward, concerning the *Trent* affair, which many believed could start a war with England

901 He who does *something* at the head of one Regiment, will eclipse him who does *nothing* at the head of a hundred.

> — 31 December 1861, letter to David Hunter

902 The Doll Jack is pardoned by order of the President.

> — 1861, written pardon for his sons' soldier doll, who was forever getting into trouble for serious offenses, such as desertion and sleeping on duty

903 General, what shall I do? The people are impatient; Chase has no money and tells me he can raise no more; the General of the Army has typhoid fever. The bottom is out of the tub.

> — 10 January 1862, comment to Quartermaster General Montgomery C. Meigs

904 If General McClellan does not want to use the army, I would like to borrow it, provided I could see how it could be made to do something.

> — 10 January 1862, comment during a White House war council, recorded in paraphrase by Irvin McDowell

905 I state my general idea of this war to be that we have the *greater* numbers, and the enemy has the *greater* facility of concentrating forces upon points of collision; that we must fail, unless we can find some way of making *our* advantage an over-match for *his*; and that this can only be done by menacing him with superior forces at *different* points, at the *same* time; so that we can safely attack, one, or both, if he makes no change; and if he *weakens* one to strengthen the other, forbear to attack the strengthened one, but seize, and hold the weakened one, gaining so much.

> — 13 January 1862, letter to Don C. Buell

906 Why in the Nation, General Marcy, couldn't the General have known whether a boat would go through that lock before spending a million dollars getting them there? I am no engineer, but it seems to me that if I wished to know whether a boat would go through a hole or a lock, common sense would teach me to go and measure it.

> — 27 February 1862, comment to Randolph B. Marcy, concerning George B. McClellan's failure to get his boats through the lock between the Chesapeake and Ohio Canal and the Potomac River

907 In my judgment, gradual, and not sudden emancipation, is better for all.

> — 6 March 1862, message to Congress, recommending compensated emancipation

908 Stanton's navy is as useless as the paps of a man to a sucking child. There may be some show to amuse the child, but they are good for nothing for service.

> — spring 1862, remark concerning the boats that the Federals intended to fill with stones and sink in the Potomac, blocking the C.S.S. *Virginia*; the operation was never carried out

909 The country will not fail to note—is noting—that the present hesitation to move upon an intrenched enemy, is but the story of Manassas repeated.

I beg to assure you that I have never written you, or spoken to you, in greater kindness of feeling than now, nor with a fuller purpose to sustain you....*But you must act.*

> — 9 April 1862, letter to McClellan

910 I can't spare this man; he fights.

> — April 1862, comment to Alexander K. McClure, referring to Grant

911 I expect to maintain this contest until successful, or till I die, or am conquered, or my term expires, or Congress or the country forsakes me.

> — 28 June 1862, letter to William H. Seward

912 The severest justice may not always be the best policy.

> — 17 July 1862, message to Congress

913 If there be those who would not save the Union, unless they could at the same time *save* slavery, I do not agree with them. If there be those who would not save the Union unless they could at the same time *destroy* slavery, I do not agree with them. My paramount object in this struggle *is* to save the Union, and is *not* either to save or to destroy slavery. If I could save the Union without freeing *any* slave I would do it, and if I could save it by freeing *all* the slaves I would do it; and if I could save it by freeing some and leaving others alone I would also do that....

I have here stated my purpose according to my view of *official* duty; and I intend no modification of my oft-expressed *personal* wish that all men every where could be free.

> — 22 August 1862, letter to Horace Greeley, in response to Greeley's "The Prayer of Twenty Millions"

914 I shall try to correct errors when shown to be errors; and I shall adopt new views so fast as they shall appear to be true views.

> — 22 August 1862, letter to Greeley

915 Broken eggs can never be mended, and the longer the breaking proceeds the more will be broken.

> — 22 August 1862, deleted sentence from his letter to Greeley

916   Well, John, we are whipped again.

> — 1 September 1862, comment to John Hay after the Union defeat at 2nd Bull Run

917   On the first day of January in the year of our Lord, one thousand eight hundred and sixty-three, all persons held as slaves within any state, or designated part of a state, the people whereof shall then be in rebellion against the United States shall be then, thenceforward, and forever free.

> — 22 September 1862, preliminary Emancipation Proclamation (the passage was repeated, with slight changes in punctuation and capitalization, in the final proclamation, issued on 1 January 1863)

918   The Writ of Habeas Corpus is suspended in respect to all persons arrested, or who are now, or hereafter during the rebellion shall be, imprisoned...by any military authority or by the sentence of any Court Martial or Military Commission.

> — 24 September 1862, proclamation

919   So it is called, but that is a mistake; it is only McClellan's bodyguard.

> — 2 October 1862, remark to Ozias M. Hatch, concerning the Army of the Potomac

920   Are you not over-cautious when you assume that you can not do what the enemy is constantly doing?

> — 13 October 1862, letter to McClellan

921   I have just read your despatch about sore tongued and fatigued horses. Will you pardon me for asking what the horses of your army have done since the battle of Antietam that fatigue anything?

> — 24 October 1862, telegram to McClellan

922   If I had had my way, this war would never have been commenced; if I had been allowed my way, this war would have been ended before this.

> — 26 October 1862, reply to Eliza P. Gurney

923   Somewhat like the boy in Kentucky who stubbed his toe while running to see his sweetheart. The boy said he was too big to cry, and far too badly hurt to laugh.

> — November 1862, reply when asked how he felt about the New York elections, published in *Frank Leslie's Illustrated Weekly* (22 November 1862)

924   I certainly know that if the war fails, the administration fails, and that I *will* be blamed for it, whether I deserve it or not. And I ought to be blamed, if I could do better. You think I could do better; therefore you blame me already. I think I could not do better; therefore I blame you for blaming me.

— 24 November 1862, letter to Carl Schurz

925 So you're the little woman who wrote the book that made this great war.

— November 1862, attributed remark when meeting Harriet Beecher Stowe, author of *Uncle Tom's Cabin*

926 Whichever way it ends, I have the impression that I shan't last long after it's over.

— November 1862, attributed remark to Harriet Beecher Stowe

927 A nation may be said to consist of its territory, its people, and its laws. The territory is the only part which is of certain durability.

— 1 December 1862, message to Congress

928 If there ever could be a proper time for mere catch arguments, that time surely is not now. In times like the present, men should utter nothing for which they would not willingly be responsible through time and in eternity.

— 1 December 1862, message to Congress

929 The dogmas of the quiet past, are inadequate to the stormy present. The occasion is piled high with difficulty, and we must rise with the occasion. As our case is new, so we must think anew, and act anew.

— 1 December 1862, message to Congress

930 Fellow-citizens, *we* cannot escape history. We of this Congress and this administration, will be remembered in spite of ourselves. No personal significance, or insignificance, can spare one or another of us. The fiery trial through which we pass, will light us down, in honor or dishonor, to the latest generation....We—even *we here*—hold the power, and bear the responsibility. In *giving* freedom to the *slave*, we *assure* freedom to the *free*—honorable alike in what we give, and what we preserve. We shall nobly save, or meanly lose, the last best, hope of earth.

— 1 December 1862, message to Congress

931 If there is a worse place than hell, I am in it.

— December 1862, comment to Andrew Curtin, concerning recent military and political setbacks

932 McClellan's got the slows.

— 1862, frequent observation

933 We are a good deal like whalers who have been long on a chase. At last we have got our harpoon fairly into the monster; but we must now look how we steer, or with one flop of his tail, he will yet send us all into eternity!
> — early 1863, comment to Edwin D. Morgan, concerning the Emancipation Proclamation

934 I am a slow walker, but I never walk back.
> — early 1863, expression of his refusal to alter or revoke his Emancipation Proclamation

935 To use a coarse, but an expressive figure, broken eggs can not be mended. I have issued the emancipation proclamation, and I can not retract it.
> — 8 January 1863, letter to John A. McClernand

936 I believe you to be a brave and skilful soldier, which, of course, I like. I also believe you do not mix politics with your profession, in which you are right. You have confidence in yourself, which is a valuable, if not an indispensable quality. You are ambitious, which, within reasonable bounds, does good rather than harm. But I think that during Gen. Burnside's command of the Army, you have taken counsel of your ambition, and thwarted him as much as you could, in which you did a great wrong to the country, and to a most meritorious and honorable brother officer.
> — 26 January 1863, letter to Joseph Hooker, new head of the Army of the Potomac

937 I have heard, in such a way as to believe it, of your recently saying that both the Army and the Government needed a Dictator. Of course it was not *for* this, but in spite of it, that I have given you the command. Only those generals who gain successes, can set up dictators. What I now ask of you is military success, and I will risk the dictatorship.
> — 26 January 1863, letter to Hooker

938 Beware of rashness, but with energy, and sleepless vigilance, go forward, and give us victories.
> — 26 January 1863, letter to Hooker,

939 The bare sight of fifty thousand armed, and drilled black soldiers on the banks of the Mississippi, would end the rebellion at once.
> — 26 March 1863, letter to Andrew Johnson

940 The hen is the wisest of all the animal creation because she never cackles until after the egg is laid.
> — spring 1863, comment on Hooker's boasting

941 My God! My God! What will the country say! What will the country say?

> — 6 May 1863, comment to White House visitors, including Noah Brooks, after the Union defeat at Chancellorsville

942 Must I shoot a simple-minded soldier boy who deserts, while I must not touch a hair of a wiley agitator who induces him to desert?

> — 12 June 1863, letter to Erastus Corning and others

943 If the head of Lee's army is at Martinsburg and the tail of it on the Plank road between Fredericksburg and Chancellorsville, the animal must be very slim somewhere. Could you not break him?

> — 14 June 1863, message to Hooker

944 I long ago made up my mind that if anybody wants to kill me, he will do it. If I wore a shirt of mail, and kept myself surrounded by a body-guard, it would be all the same. There are a thousand ways of getting at a man if it is desired that he should be killed.

> — early summer 1863, comment to Noah Brooks

945 Drive the invader from our soil? My God! Is that all?

> — early July 1863, comment on George G. Meade's stated objective after Gettysburg; Lincoln wanted to destroy Lee's army

946 Halleck knows better than I what to do. He is a military man, has had a military education. I brought him here to give me military advice. His views and mine are widely different. It is better that I, who am not a military man, should defer to him, rather than he to me.

> — 14 July 1863, comment recorded by Gideon Welles

947 We had them within our grasp. We had only to stretch forth our hands & they were ours. And nothing I could say or do could make the Army move.

> — 14 July 1863, lament after the Union forces under Meade failed to pursue and crush the Confederate army under Lee after Gettysburg, even when Lee was trapped at the swollen Potomac River

948 Our Army held the war in the hollow of their hand and they would not close it.

> — 19 July 1863, comment on Meade's failure to attack Lee after Gettysburg

949 I was deeply mortified by the escape of Lee across the Potomac, because the substantial destruction of his army would have ended the war, and because I believed, such destruction was perfectly easy—believed that Gen. Meade

and his noble army had expended all the skill, and toil, and blood, up to the ripe harvest, and then let the crop go to waste.

— 21 July 1863, letter to Oliver O. Howard

950   When differences of opinion arise between officers of the Government, the ranking officer must be obeyed.

— 31 July 1863, letter to Samuel W. Moulton

951   Negroes, like other people, act upon motives. Why should they do anything for us, if we will do nothing for them? If they stake their lives for us, they must be prompted by the strongest motive—even the promise of freedom. And the promise being made, must be kept.

— 26 August 1863, letter to James C. Conkling

952   The Father of Waters again goes unvexed to the sea.

— 26 August 1863, letter to James C. Conkling, concerning the Mississippi River

953   Nor must Uncle Sam's Web-feet be forgotten. At all the watery margins they have been present. Not only on the deep sea, the broad bay, and the rapid river, but also up the narrow muddy bayou, and wherever the ground was a little damp, they have been, and made their tracks.

— 26 August 1863, letter to James C. Conkling; "web-feet" were navy personnel (in other contexts, infantrymen)

954   Peace does not appear so distant as it did. I hope it will come soon, and come to stay; and so come as to be worth the keeping in all future time. It will then have been proved that, among free men, there can be no successful appeal from the ballot to the bullet.

— 26 August 1863, letter to James C. Conkling

955   Are we degenerate? Has the manhood of our race run out?

— [14 September?] 1863, excerpt from a paper aimed at critics of the draft

956   I desire to so conduct the affairs of this administration that if, at the end, when I come to lay down the reins of power, I have lost every other friend on earth, I shall at least have one friend left, and that friend shall be down inside of me.

— 30 September 1863, comment to a joint committee from Missouri and Kansas

957   [Rosecrans is] confused and stunned like a duck hit on the head.

— 24 October 1863, remark recorded by John Hay, a Lincoln secretary and later a journalist, historian, and diplomat

958 I have endured a great deal of ridicule without much malice; and have received a great deal of kindness, not quite free from ridicule. I am used to it.

> — 2 November 1863, letter to James H. Hackett

959 Four score and seven years ago our fathers brought forth on this continent, a new nation, conceived in Liberty, and dedicated to the proposition that all men are created equal.

Now we are engaged in a great civil war, testing whether that nation, or any nation so conceived and so dedicated, can long endure. We are met on a great battle-field of that war. We have come to dedicate a portion of that field, as a final resting place for those who here gave their lives that that nation might live. It is altogether fitting and proper that we should do this.

But, in a larger sense, we can not dedicate—we can not consecrate—we can not hallow—this ground. The brave men, living and dead, who struggled here, have consecrated it, far above our poor power to add or detract. The world will little note, nor long remember what we say here, but it can never forget what they did here. It is for us the living, rather, to be dedicated here to the unfinished work which they who fought here have thus far so nobly advanced. It is rather for us to be here dedicated to the great task remaining before us—that from these honored dead we take increased devotion to that cause for which they gave the last full measure of devotion—that we here highly resolve that these dead shall not have died in vain—that this nation, under God, shall have a new birth of freedom—and that government of the people, by the people, for the people, shall not perish from the earth.

> — 19 November 1863, Gettysburg Address

960 That speech won't scour. It is a flat failure.

> — 19 November 1863, comment to Ward Hill Lamon, immediately after the Gettysburg Address; "scour," of agricultural origin, means succeed, do well

961 In our respective parts yesterday, you could not have been excused to make a short address, nor I a long one. I am pleased to know that, in your judgment, the little I did say was not entirely a failure.

> — 20 November 1863, letter to Edward Everett

962 I hope to "stand firm" enough to not go backward, and yet not go forward fast enough to wreck the country's course.

> — 20 November 1863, letter to Zachariah Chandler

963 I would be very happy to oblige you, if my passes were respected. But the fact is, sir, I have, within the last two years, given passes to two hundred and fifty thousand men to go to Richmond, and not one has got there yet.

> — 1863, reply to a man who had asked for "safe conduct" to Richmond, Virginia

964 This war is eating my life out. I have a strong impression that I shall not live to see the end.

> — early 1864, comment to Owen Lovejoy

965 If slavery is not wrong, nothing is wrong.

> — 4 April 1864, letter to Albert G. Hodges

966 By general law life and limb must be protected; yet often a limb must be amputated to save a life; but a life is never wisely given to save a limb.

> — 4 April 1864, letter to Albert G. Hodges, concerning Lincoln's use of extreme measures to save the Union

967 I claim not to have controlled events, but confess plainly that events have controlled me.

> — 4 April 1864, letter to Albert G. Hodges

968 The shepherd drives the wolf from the sheep's throat, for which the sheep thanks the shepherd as a *liberator*, while the wolf denounces him for the same act as the destroyer of liberty, especially as the sheep was a black one.

> — 18 April 1864, speech in Baltimore

969 The particulars of your plans I neither know, or seek to know. You are vigilant and self-reliant; and, pleased with this, I wish not to obtrude any constraints or restraints upon you....If there is anything wanting which is within my power to give, do not fail to let me know it.

> — 30 April 1864, letter to Ulysses S. Grant

970 Those not skinning can hold a leg.

> — 30 April 1864, remark after approving Grant's strategy of moving the Union armies against all Confederate fronts simultaneously

971 Grant has gone into the Wilderness, crawled in, drawn up the ladder, and pulled in the hole after him.

> — 6 May 1864, comment during the battle of the Wilderness

972 I have not permitted myself, gentlemen, to conclude that I am the best man in the country; but I am reminded, in this connection, of a story of an old Dutch farmer, who remarked to a companion once that "it was not best to swap horses when crossing streams."

> — 9 June 1864, reply to a delegation from the National Union League, which had just endorsed his renomination

973 Oh, he is intrenching.

> — mid-June 1864, reply to the Rev. J.P. Thompson when the latter asked why McClellan had not responded to a letter from the Chicago Convention

974 When Grant once gets possession of a place, he holds on to it as if he had inherited it.

> — 22 June 1864, remark to Benjamin F. Butler

975 Truth is generally the best vindication against slander.

> — 14 July 1864, letter to Stanton, concerning Halleck's complaint against Postmaster General Blair's criticism of the army

976 This morning, as for some days past, it seems exceedingly probable that this Administration will not be re-elected. Then it will be my duty to so co-operate with the President elect, as to save the Union between the election and the inauguration; as he will have secured his election on such ground that he can not possibly save it afterwards.

> — 23 August 1864, memorandum to his cabinet

977 Your people—the Friends—have had, and are having, a very great trial. On principle, and faith, opposed to both war and oppression, they can only practically oppose oppression by war. In this hard dilemma, some have chosen one horn and some the other.

> — 4 September 1864, letter to Mrs. Eliza P. Gurney, wife of a prominent English Quaker

978 I began to fear he was playing false—that he did not want to hurt the enemy.

> — 25 September 1864, comment concerning McClellan's failure to advance after Antietam in 1862

979 It has long been a grave question whether any government, not *too* strong for the liberties of its people, can be strong *enough* to maintain its own existence, in great emergencies.

> — 10 November 1864, response to a serenade

980 I have been shown in the files of the War Department a statement of the Adjutant General of Massachusetts, that you are the mother of five sons who have died gloriously on the field of battle.

I feel how weak and fruitless must be any words of mine which should atempt to beguile you from the grief of a loss so overwhelming. But I cannot refrain from tendering to you the consolation that may be found in the thanks of the Republic they died to save.

I pray that our Heavenly Father may assuage the anguish of your breavement, and leave you only the cherished memory of the loved and lost, and the solemn pride that must be yours, to have laid so costly a sacrifice upon the altar of Freedom.

> — 21 November 1864, letter to Mrs. Lydia Bixby of Massachusetts; Lincoln had been misinformed about her sons, only two of whom had been killed in action, while one had deserted, another had either deserted or died in a Confederate prison, and one would be honorably discharged in December 1864

981 We all know where he went in at, but I can't tell where he will come out at.

> — 6 December 1864, brief speech in response to a serenade, a reference to Sherman's March to the Sea; during this period, Lincoln told Senator John Sherman, General Sherman's brother, "I know what hole he went in at, but I can't tell what hole he will come out of"

982 I never knew a man who wished himself to be a slave. Consider if you know any *good* thing that no man desires for himself.

> — 1864, inscription in an album at a Sanitary fair

983 If the people over the river had behaved themselves, I could not have done what I have.

> — early 1865, comment on the passage of the 13th Amendment

984 While the inaugural address was being delivered from this place, devoted altogether to *saving* the Union without war, insurgent agents were in the city seeking to *destroy* it without war.

> — 4 March 1865, 2nd Inaugural Address

985 Both parties deprecated war; but one of them would *make* war rather than let the nation survive; and the other would *accept* war rather than let it perish. And the war came.

> — 4 March 1865, 2nd Inaugural Address

986 Both read the same Bible, and pray to the same God; and each invokes His aid against the other. It may seem strange that any men should dare to ask a just God's assistance in wringing their bread from the sweat of other men's faces; but let us judge not that we be not judged.

> — 4 March 1865, 2nd Inaugural Address

987 Fondly do we hope—fervently do we pray—that this mighty scourge of war may speedily pass away. Yet, if God wills that it continue, until all the

wealth piled by the bond-man's two hundred and fifty years of unrequited toil shall be sunk, and until every drop of blood drawn with the lash, shall be paid with another drawn with the sword, as was said three thousand years ago, so still it must be said "the judgments of the Lord, are true and righteous altogether."

— 4 March 1865, 2nd Inaugural Address

988 With malice toward none; with charity for all; with firmness in the right, as God gives us to see the right, let us strive on to finish the work we are in; to bind up the nation's wounds; to care for him who shall have borne the battle, and for his widow, and his orphan—to do all which may achieve and cherish a just, and a lasting peace, among ourselves, and with all nations.

— 4 March 1865, 2nd Inaugural Address

989 Whenever [I] hear any one, arguing for slavery I feel a strong impulse to see it tried on him personally.

— 17 March 1865, speech to 140th Indiana

990 I want no one punished. Treat them liberally all around. We want those people to return to their allegiance to the Union and submit to the laws.

— 28 March 1865, remark to Grant, Sherman, and David D. Porter

991 Grant has the bear by the hind leg while Sherman takes off the hide.

— early spring 1865, comment to a White House visitor

992 Don't kneel to me. You must kneel to God only and thank him for your freedom.

— 4 April 1865, comment to freedmen at Richmond, Virginia

993 They will never shoulder a musket in anger again. And if Grant is wise he will leave them their guns to shoot crows with, and their horses to plow with. It would do no harm.

— 5 April 1865, comment to David D. Porter, concerning Confederate prisoners at Richmond

994 Gen. Sheridan says "If the thing is pressed I think that Lee will surrender." Let the *thing* be pressed.

— 7 April 1865, telegram to Grant

995 I have always thought "Dixie" one of the best tunes I have ever heard. Our adversaries over the way attempted to appropriate it, but I insisted yesterday that we fairly captured it....I now request the band to favor me with its performance.

— 10 April 1865, response to a serenade

996 Concede that the new government of Louisiana is only to what it should be as the egg is to the fowl, we shall sooner have the fowl by hatching the egg than by smashing it?

> — 11 April 1865, last public address

997 Important principles may, and must, be inflexible.

> — 11 April 1865, last public address

998 I soon began to dream. There seemed to be a deathlike stillness about me. Then I heard subdued sobs, as if a number of people were weeping. I thought I left my bed and wandered downstairs. There the silence was broken by the same pitiful sobbing, but the mourners were invisible. I went from room to room; no living person was in sight, but the same mournful sounds of distress met me as I passed along. It was light in all the rooms; every object was familiar to me; but where were all the people who were grieving as if their hearts would break? I was puzzled and alarmed. What could be the meaning of all this? Determined to find the cause of a state of things so mysterious and shocking, I kept on until I arrived at the East Room, which I entered. There I met with a sickening surprise. Before me was a catafalque, on which rested a corpse wrapped in funeral vestments. Around it were stationed soldiers who were acting as guards; and there was a throng of people, some gazing mournfully upon the corpse, whose face was covered, others weeping pitifully. "Who is dead in the White House?" I demanded of one of the soldiers. "The President," was his answer; "he was killed by an assassin!" Then came a loud burst of grief from the crowd.

> — 2nd week of April 1865, description of a dream to his wife and others

999 When you have got an elephant by the hind leg, and he's trying to run away, it's best to let him run.

> — 14 April 1865, comment to Charles A. Dana when the latter asked if he should arrest Jacob Thompson, a fleeing Rebel official

1000 I had this strange dream again last night, and we shall, judging from the past, have great news very soon.

> — 14 April 1865, comment to members of his cabinet; in the dream, which had preceeded many important events of the war, Lincoln was in a strange vessel moving quickly toward an indefinite shore

1001 If I were to try to read, much less answer, all the attacks made on me, this shop might as well be closed for any other business. I do the very best I know how—the very best I can; and I mean to keep doing so until the end. If the end brings me out all right, what is said against me won't amount to

anything. If the end brings me out wrong, ten angels swearing I was right would make no difference.
> — comment to an officer who wanted Lincoln to respond to criticism from the Committee on the Conduct of the War

1002 If they kill me, the next man will be just as bad for them.
> — a common remark to friends who feared for his safety

THOMAS LINCOLN

Born 4 April 1853 in Springfield, Illinois. Nicknamed Tad. Son of President Lincoln. Died 15 July 1871 in Chicago.

1003 Oh, Mr. Welles, who killed my father?
> — 15 April 1865, query to Gideon Welles

WILLIAM WALLACE LINCOLN

Born 21 December 1850 in Springfield, Illinois. Known as Willie. Son of President Lincoln. Died 20 February 1862 in Washington, D.C.

1004 There was no patriot like Baker,
So noble and so true;
He fell as a soldier on the field,
His face to the sky of blue.
> — 1861, poem (published in the *Washington National Republican*, 4 November 1861) on the death of Lincoln family friend Edward Dickinson Baker at Ball's Bluff

JOHN ALEXANDER LOGAN

Born 9 February 1826 in Jackson County, Illinois. Before the Civil War, he was a lawyer and politician. During the war, he became a Union colonel (18 September 1861), brigadier general (21 March 1862), and major general (29 November 1862). After the war, he was a United States congressman and senator. Died 26 December 1886 in the District of Columbia.

1005 Damn it, that's the place to kill them—where they are thick!
> — 16 May 1863, reply to the adjutant of the 34th Indiana who had said that "the Rebels are awful thick up there"

1006 My God! They are killing my bravest men in that hole!
> — 25 June 1863, exclamation at a crater near Vicksburg

1007 McPherson and revenge, boys, McPherson and revenge.
> — 22 July 1864, exhortation to his men at Atlanta, where McPherson had been killed earlier that day

HENRY WADSWORTH LONGFELLOW

Born 27 February 1807 in Portland, Maine. Poet. His books of poems include The Song of Hiawatha *(1855) and* Tales of a Wayside Inn *(in three parts: 1863, 1872, and 1874). Died 24 March 1882 in Cambridge, Massachusetts.*

1008 Weary days with wars and rumors of wars, and marching of troops, and flags waving, and people talking.
> — 23 April 1861, journal

1009 The civil war grumbles and growls and gathers; but the storm-clouds do not yet break....It is indeed a heavy atmosphere to breathe—the impending doom of a nation!
> — 2 May 1861, journal

1010 Of the civil war I say only this. It is not a revolution, but a Catalinian conspiracy. It is Slavery against Freedom; the north wind against the southern pestilence. I saw lately, at a jeweller's, a slave's collar of iron, with an iron tongue as large as a spoon, to go into the mouth. Every drop of blood in me quivered! The world forgets what Slavery really is!
> — 8 May 1862, letter to "Miss F —"

1011 Every shell from the cannon's mouth bursts not only on the battle-field, but in far-away homes, North or South, carrying dismay and death. What an infernal thing war is!
> — 1 September 1862, journal

1012 Listen, my children, and you shall hear
Of the midnight ride of Paul Revere,

....

Through all our history, to the last,
In the hour of darkness and peril and need,
The people will waken and listen to hear
The hurrying hoof-beats of that steed,
And the midnight message of Paul Revere.
> — 1863, "Paul Revere's Ride," poem

JAMES LONGSTREET

Born 8 January 1821 in Edgefield District, South Carolina. West Point class of 1842. He stayed in the army and rose to major before resigning on 1 June 1861. Joining the Confederate forces, he became a brigadier general (17 June 1861), major general (7 October 1861), and lieutenant general (9 October 1862). After the war, he worked in the insurance business, joined the Republican party, and held political appointments, such as minister resident to Turkey. Died 2 January 1904 in Gainesville, Georgia.

1013   Retreat! Hell, the Federal army has broken to pieces!
— 21 July 1861, response when ordered to withdraw at 1st Bull Run

1014   This is a hard fight and we had better all die than lose it.
— 17 September 1862, note to Roger Pryor at Antietam

1015   The General is a little nervous this morning; he wishes me to attack; I do not wish to do so without Pickett. I never like to go into battle with one boot off.
— 2 July 1863, comment to John B. Hood at Gettysburg; the "General" was Robert E. Lee

1016   I don't want to make this charge. I don't believe it can succeed. I would stop Pickett now, but that General Lee has ordered it and expects it.
— 3 July 1863, comment to E. Porter Alexander

1017   We must make up our minds to get into line of battle and to stay there; for that man will fight us every day and every hour till the end of this war. In order to whip him we must outmanoeuver him, and husband our strength as best we can.
— spring 1864, warning to a Confederate officer who had expressed contempt for Grant

1018   If General Lee doesn't know when to surrender until I tell him, he will never know.
— 8 April 1865, comment to William N. Pendleton, who wanted Longstreet to ask Lee to surrender

1019   General, unless he offers us honorable terms, come back and let us fight it out!
— 9 April 1865, comment to Lee as the latter rode off to meet Grant at Appomattox

WILLIAM WING LORING

Born 4 December 1818 in Wilmington, North Carolina. He lost his left arm in the Mexican War and rose to colonel before resigning from the United States Army on 13 May 1861. Joining the Confederate forces, he became a brigadier general (20 May 1861) and major general (17 February 1862). From 1869 to 1879, he was in the military service of the khedive of Egypt. Died 30 December 1886 in New York City.

1020   Give them blizzards, boys! Give them blizzards!
> — March 1863, attributed comment to his men at Fort Pemberton, outside Vicksburg

OWEN LOVEJOY

Born 6 January 1811 in Albion, Maine. Christian minister who served as a Republican in the Illinois state legislature and in the United States House of Representatives (1857-64). Died 25 March 1864 in Brooklyn, New York.

1021   I hate the British government. I now here publicly avow and record my inextinguishable hatred....I mean to cherish it while I live, and to bequeath it as a legacy to my children when I die. And if I am alive when war with England comes, as sooner or later it must, for we shall never forget this humiliation, and if I can carry a musket in that war, I will carry it.
> — January 1862, speech in the House of Representatives, after the United States capitulated to British pressure and released two Confederate diplomats seized aboard the British vessel *Trent*

JAMES RUSSELL LOWELL

Born 22 February 1819 in Cambridge, Massachusetts. Poet, essayist, and editor. He was the first editor of the Atlantic Monthly *(1857-61) and then served as joint editor of the* North American Review *(1863-72). Died 12 August 1891 in Cambridge.*

1022   The fault of the free states in the eyes of the South is not one that can be atoned for by any yielding of special points here and there. Their offence is that they are free, and that their habits and prepossessions are those of freedom. Their crime is the census of 1860. Their increases in numbers, wealth and power is a standing aggression. It would not be enough to please the Southern states that we should stop asking them to abolish slavery: what

they demand is nothing less than we should abolish the spirit of the age. Our very thoughts are a menace.
— February 1861, essay in the *Atlantic Monthly*

1023 "Tears may be ours, but proud, for those who win
Death's royal purple in the foeman's lines;
Peace, too, brings tears; and mid the battle-din,
The wiser ear some text of God divines,
For the sheathed blade may rust with darker sin.
— October 1861, "The Washers of the Shroud," poem

1024 It is curious, that, as gunpowder made armour useless on shore, so armour is having its revenge by baffling its old enemy at sea; and that, while gunpowder robbed land warfare of nearly all its picturesqueness to give even greater stateliness and sublimity to a sea-fight, armour bids fair to degrade the latter into a squabble between two iron-shelled turtles.
— 10 March 1862, observation on ironclads

1025 Right in the van,
On the red rampart's slippery swell,
With the heart that beat a charge, he fell
Foeward, as fits a man.
— August 1863, "Memoriae Positum," in memory of Robert Gould Shaw

THEODORE LYMAN

Born 23 August 1833 in Waltham, Massachusetts. Union lieutenant colonel (2 September 1863). After the war, he was a zoologist, overseer of Harvard University (1868-80), and United States congressman (1883-85). Died 9 September 1897 in Nahant, Massachusetts.

1026 General Custer...is one of the funniest-looking beings you ever saw, and looks like a circus rider gone mad!
— 17 September 1863, letter to his wife

1027 He habitually wears an expression as if he had determined to drive his head through a brick wall, and was about to do it.
— 12 April 1864, letter to his wife, a description of Grant

1028 Lee is not retreating. He is a brave and skillful soldier and will fight while he has a division or a day's rations left.
— 18 May 1864, letter to his wife

1029 Their great characteristic is their stoical manliness. They never beg or whimper or complain, but look you straight in the face with as little animosity as if they had never heard a gun fired.

> — 18 May 1864, letter to his wife, on Confederate soldiers

1030 Ben F. Butler...*is* the strangest sight on a horse you ever saw: it is hard to keep your eyes off him. With his head set immediately on a stout shapeless body, his very squinting eyes, and a set of legs and arms that look as if made for somebody else, and hastily glued to him by mistake.

> — 20 July 1864, letter to his wife

1031 Sherman...is a very remarkable-looking man, such as could not be grown out of America—the concentrated quintessence of Yankeedom.

> — 29 March 1865, letter to his wife

WILLIAM HAINES LYTLE

Born 2 November 1826 in Cincinnati, Ohio. Lawyer, politician, and poet. He joined the Ohio militia (1857) and during the Civil War became a Union colonel (3 May 1861) and brigadier general (29 November 1862). Killed in action 20 September 1863 at Chickamauga.

1032 If I must die, I will die as a gentleman.

> — 20 September 1863, statement at Chickamauga

1033 All right, men, we can die but once. This is the time and place. Let us charge.

> — 20 September 1863, command just before his death

HARRY MACARTHY

Born 1834 in England. He came to the United States in 1849 and became an entertainer known as the Arkansas Comedian. Died 1888 in Oakland, California.

1034 Hurrah! hurrah! for Southern rights! hurrah! / Hurrah! for the bonnie blue flag that bears a single star.

> — 1861, "The Bonnie Blue Flag," song (in 1862, Mrs. Annie Chambers-Ketchum, of Memphis, wrote new lyrics to the song, initiating a confusion over the authorship of the song's text; however, the above quotation, from the chorus, was published in the original, 1861, version)

GEORGE BRINTON MCCLELLAN

Born 3 December 1826 in Philadelphia, Pennsylvania. West Point class of 1846. In 1857 he resigned as a captain from the United States Army to enter the railroad business. During the Civil War, he was appointed a major general of Ohio volunteers (April 1861) and then a major general in the Regular Army (May 1861). In late July 1861 he was called to Washington, D.C. to take command of what later became the Army of the Potomac, which he headed till November 1862. From November 1861 to March 1862, he also served as the Union general in chief. In 1864 he was the Democratic nominee for president. After the war, he turned to business and served a term as governor of New Jersey. Died 29 October 1885 in Orange, New Jersey.

1035 Your enemies have violated every moral law—neither God nor man can sustain them. They have without cause rebelled against a mild and paternal government.
> — 25 June 1861, message to his troops

1036 Soldiers! I have heard that there was danger here. I fear now but one thing—that you will not find foemen worthy of your steel.
> — 25 June 1861, message to his troops

1037 Assure the General that no prospect of a brilliant victory shall induce me to depart from my intention of gaining success by maneuvering rather than by fighting....Say to the General, too, that I am trying to follow a lesson long ago learned from him; *i.e.*, not to move until I know that everything is ready, and then to move with the utmost rapidity and energy.
> — 5 July 1861, letter to E.D. Townsend, assistant to Winfield Scott

1038 All private property whether of secessionists or others must be strictly respected, and no one is to be molested merely because of political opinions.
> — 14 July 1861, letter to Jacob Beyers, a mustering agent for the militia of the Unionist government of western Virginia

1039 I find myself in a new & strange position here—Presdt, Cabinet, Genl Scott & all deferring to me—by some strange operation of magic I seem to have become *the* power of the land. I almost think that were I to win some small success now I could become Dictator or anything else that might please me—but nothing of that kind would please me—*therefore* I *won't* be Dictator. Admirable self denial!
> — 27 July 1861, letter to his wife

1040 Who would have thought when we were married, that I should so soon be called upon to save my country?
> — 30 July 1861, letter to his wife

1041 "The Young General" has no bed of roses on which to recline.
— 6 August 1861, letter to his mother

1042 How does he [Seward] think I can save this country when stopped by Genl Scott—I do not know whether he is a *dotard* or a *traitor*! I can't tell which. Every day strengthens me—I am leaving nothing undone to increase our force—but that confounded old Genl always comes in the way—he is a perfect imbecile. He understands nothing, appreciates nothing & is ever in my way.
— 8 August 1861, letter to his wife

1043 I am here in a terrible place—the enemy have from 3 to 4 times my force—the Presdt is an idiot, the old General [Scott] in his dotage—they cannot or will not see the true state of affairs.
— 16 August 1861, letter to his wife

1044 I can't tell you how disgusted I am becoming with these wretched politicians—they are a most dispicable set of men & I think Seward is the meanest of them all—a meddling, officious, incompetent little puppy....The Presdt is nothing more than a well meaning baboon.
— c. 11 October 1861, letter to his wife

1045 It is terrible to stand by & see the cowardice of the Presdt, the vileness of Seward, & the rascality of Cameron—Welles is an old woman—Bates an old fool. The only man of courage & sense in the Cabinet is Blair, & I do not altogether fancy him!
— 31 October 1861, letter to his wife

1046 For a long time I have kept you inactive, but not without a purpose: you were to be disciplined, armed and instructed....I shall demand of you great, heroic exertions, rapid and long marches, desperate combats, privations, perhaps. We will share all these together; and when this sad war is over we will all return to our homes, and feel that we can ask no higher honor than the proud consciousness that we belonged to the Army of the Potomac.
—14 Mar, 1862, message to his troops

1047 I prefer Lee to Johnston—the former is too cautious & weak under grave responsibility—personally brave & energetic to a fault, he yet is wanting in moral firmness when pressed by heavy responsibility & is likely to be timid & irresolute in action.
— 20 April 1862, letter to President Lincoln

1048 I am tired of the sickening sight of the battlefield, with its mangled corpses & poor suffering wounded! Victory has no charms for me when purchased at such cost.
— 2 June 1862, letter to his wife

1049 If I save this Army now I tell you plainly that I owe no thanks to you or any other persons in Washington—you have done your best to sacrifice this Army.

> — 28 June 1862, telegram to Edwin M. Stanton; before the message was delivered to Stanton, this sentence was deleted by Edward S. Sanford, head of the War Department's telegraphic office

1050 Never did such a change of base, involving a retrograde movement, and under incessant attacks from a most determined and vastly more numerous foe, partake so little of disorder.

> — 4 July 1862, telegram to President Lincoln, describing McClellan's retreat during the Peninsula campaign

1051 It should not be, at all, a War upon a population; but against armed forces and political organizations. Neither confiscation of property, political executions of persons, territorial organization of States or forcible abolition of slavery should be contemplated for a moment.

> — 7 July 1862, letter to President Lincoln

1052 I am willing to serve you in such position as you may assign me and I will do so as faithfully as ever subordinate served superior.

> — 7 July 1862, letter to President Lincoln

1053 I have not come here to wage war upon the defenseless, upon non-combatants, upon private property, nor upon the domestic institutions of the land.

> — 11 July 1862, letter to Hill Carter, a Virginia landowner

1054 I think that he is the most unmitigated scoundrel I ever knew, heard or read of; I think that (& I do not wish to be irreverent) had he lived in the time of the Saviour, Judas Iscariot would have remained a respected member of the fraternity of the Apostles, & that the magnificent treachery & rascality of E.M. Stanton would have caused Judas to have raised his arms in holy horror & unaffected wonder—he would certainly have claimed & exercised the right to have been the Betrayer of his Lord & Master.

> — 13 July 1862, letter to his wife

1055 I see it reported in this evening's papers that Halleck is to be the new Genl in Chief. Now let them take the next step & relieve me & I shall once more be a free man.

> — 20 July 1862, letter to his wife

1056 Again I have been called upon to save the country.

> — 5 September 1862, letter to his wife

1057 Here is a paper with which if I cannot whip Bobbie Lee, I will be willing to go home.

> — 13 September 1862, comment to John Gibbon on finding Lee's Lost Order

WILLIAM WHANN MACKALL

Born 18 January 1817 in Cecil County, Maryland. West Point class of 1837. He resigned from the United States Army on 3 July 1861 and soon joined the Confederate forces as a lieutenant colonel (July 1861). Later he became a brigadier general (6 March 1862, to rank from 27 February) and served as chief of staff for the Army of Tennessee (April-fall 1863 and January-July 1864). After the war, he was a farmer. Died 12 August 1891 in Fairfax County, Virginia.

1058 We have to keep close up to the enemy, watch carefully every movement, and then try and take advantage of every mistake he makes; by so doing, we have thus far succeeded in making him pay three or four for one of ours out of a state of service by death or wounds; if we can keep this up, we win.

> — 29 May 1864, letter to his family

JOHN HANSON MCNEILL

Born 12 June 1815 in Moorefield, Virginia. Nicknamed Hanse. Farmer and cattle breeder who operated as a Confederate partisan ranger during the Civil War. Wounded 3 October 1864 at Mount Jackson, Virginia, and died 9 November 1864 in Moorefield, Virginia.

1059 Good-bye, boys. Go on and leave me. I've done all I can for my country.

> — 3 October 1864, remark to his men after being mortally wounded at Mount Jackson

MACON TELEGRAPH

The Macon Telegraph *was a newspaper in Macon, Georgia.*

1060 It would seem as if in him all the attributes of man were merged in the enormities of the demon, as if Heaven intended in him to manifest depths of depravity yet untouched by a fallen race.

> — 5 December 1864, article on Sherman

1061 Unsated still in his demoniac vengeance he sweeps over the country like a simoom of destruction.
— 5 December 1864, article on Sherman

JOHN NEWLAND MAFFITT

Born 22 February 1819 at sea. At thirteen, he became a midshipman in the United States Navy and eventually rose to the rank of lieutenant before resigning (2 May 1861). He then joined the Confederate navy as a lieutenant (8 May 1861) and later rose to commander (29 April 1863). Maffitt served on both combat vessels and merchant ships, and he won renown for capturing Northern ships and for running the blockade. After the war, he briefly commanded foreign ships and then turned to writing. Died 16 May 1886 in Wilmington, North Carolina.

1062 I regret that it is necessary to burn your vessel. The consequences of this unnatural war often fall most heavily upon those who disapprove of it. I trust your vessel is owned by abolitionists.
— 19 January 1863, comment to John Brown, master of the New York brig *Estelle*, when it was captured by Maffitt

JOHN BANKHEAD MAGRUDER

Born 1 May 1807 in Port Royal, Virginia. West Point class of 1830. At the beginning of the Civil War, he resigned from the United States Army. He became a Confederate colonel (June 1861), brigadier general (17 June 1861), and major general (7 October 1861). After the war, he fought under Maximilian in Mexico. Died 18 February 1871 in Houston, Texas.

1063 Give me 5000 men and if I don't take Washington, you may take not only my sword but my life!
— April 1861, boast to the Virginia Governor's Advisory Council

1064 We part as friends, but on the field of battle we meet as enemies.
— 10 June 1861, attributed comment to a Federal lieutenant at Big Bethel

STEPHEN RUSSELL MALLORY

Born 1813 in Trinidad. He grew up in Florida. Before the Civil War, he was a lawyer, judge, and politician. During the war, he served as the Confederate secretary of the navy. After the war, he returned to the law. Died 9 November 1873 in Pensacola, Florida.

1065 I regard the possession of an iron-armored ship as a matter of the first necessity. Such a vessel at this time could traverse the entire coast of the United States, prevent all blockades, and encounter, with fair prospect of success, their entire Navy.
— May 1861, letter to Charles M. Conrad

1066 Not only does economy but naval success dictate the wisdom and expediency of fighting with iron against wood, without regard to first cost.
— May 1861, letter to Charles M. Conrad

1067 Naval engagements between wooden frigates, as they are now built and armed, will prove to be the forlorn hopes of the sea, simply contests in which the question, not of victory, but of who shall go to the bottom first, is to be solved.
— May 1861, letter to Charles M. Conrad

1068 Naval education and training lie at the foundation of naval success; and the power that neglects this essential element of strength will, when the battle is fought, find that its ships, however formidable, are but built for a more thoroughly trained and educated enemy.
— 1864, annual report

THOMAS MANDEVILLE

Mandeville was a Confederate soldier.

1069 Stand firmly by your cannon,
Let ball and grape-shot fly,
And trust in God and Davis
But keep your powder dry.
— 31 August 1861, letter to Ellwyn Mandeville

AMBROSE DUDLEY MANN AND WILLIAM LOWNDES YANCEY

Mann, born 26 April 1801 in Hanover Court House, Virginia, was a lawyer and diplomat. Yancey, born 10 August 1814 in Ogeechee Shoals, Warren County, Georgia, was a lawyer and journalist. In 1861 both were sent to England to try to gain official recognition for the Confederate States of America. Later in the war, Mann was the Confederate representative to the Vatican (1863-64) and Yancey held a seat in the Confederate Senate (1862-63). Mann died in November

1889 in or near Paris, France. Yancey died in July 1863 near Montgomery, Alabama.

1070 The public mind here is entirely opposed to the Government of the Confederate States of America on the question of slavery....The sincerity and universality of this feeling embarass the Government in dealing with the question of our recognition.
— 21 May 1861, letter from England to Robert A. Toombs

EMMERY MATLOCK

Matlock was a member of the 15th Indiana Battery.

1071 He isn't much for looks, but if we'd had him we wouldn't have been caught in this trap.
— 15 September 1862, comment to his fellow prisoners at Harpers Ferry, referring to Stonewall Jackson

GEORGE GORDON MEADE

Born 31 December 1815 in Cádiz, Spain, of American parents. West Point class of 1835. Before the Civil War, he served in the United States Army. During the war, he became a brigadier general of volunteers (31 August 1861), major general of volunteers (29 November 1862), commander of the Army of the Potomac (28 June 1863), brigadier general in the Regular Army (3 July 1863), and major general in the Regular Army (18 August 1864). After the war, he stayed in the army and helped with Reconstruction. Died 6 November 1872 in Philadelphia, Pennsylvania.

1072 The men are good material, and with good officers might readily be moulded into soldiers; but the officers, as a rule, with but very few exceptions, are ignorant, inefficient and worthless....We have been weeding out some of the worst, but owing to the vicious system of electing successors which prevails, those who take their places are no better.
— 24 November 1861, letter to his wife

1073 War is a game of chance, and besides the chances of service, the accidents and luck of the field, in our army, an officer has to run the chances of having his political friends in power, or able to work for him.
— 10 May 1862, letter to his wife

1074 I hear the reaction in favor of McClellan since he has had some men killed is very great, and that even Greeley has begun to praise him. Poor Mac, if he is in this strait, he is in a pretty bad way! Greeley's enmity he might stand, but his friendship will kill him.

— 14 May 1862, letter to his wife

1075 I go into the action to-day as the commander of an army corps. If I survive, my *two* stars are secure, and if I fall, you will have my reputation to live on.

— September 1862, letter to his wife just before Antietam

1076 I am tired of this playing war without risks. We must encounter risks if we fight, and we cannot carry on war without fighting.

— 2 January 1863, letter to his wife

1077 Hurrah for old Joe! We're on Lee's flank, and he doesn't know it!

— 30 April 1863, exclamation to Henry W. Slocum, praising Joseph Hooker at Chancellorsville

1078 If we can't hold the top of a hill, we certainly can't hold the bottom of it.

— 1 May 1863, complaint when ordered to retreat at Chancellorsville

1079 We have got another Gettysburg in front of us.

— 28 November 1863, comment to Sedgwick and others while viewing Confederate works at Mine Run

1080 Soldiers! the eyes of the whole country are looking with anxious hope to the blow you are about to strike in the most sacred cause that ever called men to arms.

— 4 May 1864, address to the Army of the Potomac, before launching the six bloodiest weeks of the war

1081 Be not over-elated by reported successes, nor over-depressed by exaggerated rumors of failures.

— 6 June 1864, letter to his wife

1082 I believe these two armies would fraternize and make peace in an hour, if the matter rested with them; not on terms to suit politicians on either side, but such as the world at large would acknowledge as honorable, and which would be satisfactory to the mass of people on both sides.

— 24 June 1864, letter to his wife

1083 Grant says the Confederates, in their endeavors to get men, have robbed the cradle and the grave; if that *is* the case, I must say their ghosts and babies fight very well!

— 12 December 1864, comment to his staff

1084 The war is over, and we are going home!

— 9 April 1865, news shouted as he rode through the Union troops

1085 *You* are responsible for my gray hairs.

> — April 1865, comment to Lee soon after the latter's surrender (so recorded in Lee's *Memoirs*; according to Theodore Lyman, Lee asked, "But what are you doing with all that gray in your beard?" to which Meade responded, "You have to answer for most of it")

1086 My God, what misery this dreadful war has produced, and how it comes home to the doors of almost every one!

> — 13 April 1865, letter to his wife, after learning of the death of his wife's brother

JOSEPH MEHARRY MEDILL

Born 6 April 1823 near St. John, New Brunswick, Canada. At the age of nine, he moved with his parents to the United States. He was a lawyer and journalist (best known for his association with the Chicago Tribune*) who helped to form, and may have named, the Republican party. Died 16 March 1899 in San Antonio, Texas.*

1087 Don't be in too much hurry for Peace. Don't *coax* the rebel chiefs, but pound them a little more.

> — 15 January 1865, letter to President Lincoln

JOHN STUART MILL

Born 20 May 1806 in London, England. English economist, philosopher, and radical reformer. Died 8 May 1873 in Avignon, France.

1088 A man who has nothing which he is willing to fight for, nothing which he cares more about than he does about his personal safety, is a miserable creature who has no chance of being free, unless made and kept so by the exertions of better men than himself.

> — February 1862, "The Contest in America," published in *Fraser's Magazine*

LINDLEY MILLER

Miller was a captain in the 7th New York before being given command of the 1st Arkansas, a black regiment.

1089   Oh! we're de bully soldiers of de "First of Arkansas";
We are fightin' for de Union, we are fightin' for de law;
We can hit a Rebel furder dan a white man eber saw;
As we go marching on.
> — 1863, "Marching Song of the First Arkansas," sung to the tune of "John Brown's Body"

IRA MILTIMORE

Miltimore (or Miltmore) was a captain with the 33rd Wisconsin from October 1862 to August 1863, when he resigned.

1090   The backbone of the Rebellion is this day broken. The Confederacy is divided—Pemberton is a prisoner. Vicksburg is ours. The Mississippi River is opened, and Gen. Grant is to be our next President.
> — 4 July 1863, letter to his wife

W.J. MIMS

Mims was a Confederate major when he wrote the following letter.

1091   I will state as a matter of history that female virtue if it ever existed in this Country seems now almost a perfect wreck. Prostitutes are thickly crowded through mountain & valley, in hamlet & city.
> — 6 June 1863, letter to his wife written from eastern Tennessee

ANDREW J. MOON

Moon was a private with the 104th Ohio.

1092   I went over in front of the works to see what we had done. Well, for 400 yards in front, I could hardly step without stepping on dead and wounded men. The ground was in a perfect slop and mud with blood and, oh, such cries that would come up from the wounded was awful. Oh, how they suffered that night was terrible, they had to lay just as they were shot down all night without anything done for them.
> — 4 December 1864, letter to his sister, after the battle of Franklin, Tennessee

BENJAMIN MORAN

Born 1 August 1820 in West Marlboro Township, Pennsylvania. Diplomat and author. He was assistant secretary (1857-64) and secretary (1864-74) of the American legation in England. Died 20 June 1886 in Braintree, Essex County, England.

1093   That pink of modesty and refinement, *The Times*, is filled with such slatternly abuse of us and ours, that it is fair to conclude that all the Fishwifes of Billingsgate have been transferred to Printing House Square to fill the ears of the writers there with their choicest phraseology.
— December 1861, diary entry concerning the *Trent* affair

SARAH IDA FOWLER MORGAN

Born 28 February 1842 in Baton Rouge, Louisiana. An important Southern diarist during the Civil War and a writer after the war. Died 5 May 1909 in Paris, France.

1094   "Why wasn't I born old and ugly?" Suppose I should unconsciously entrap some magnificent Yankee? What an awful thing it would be!!
— 3 June 1862, diary

GEORGE POPE MORRIS

Born 10 October 1802 in Philadelphia, Pennsylvania. Poet and journalist. Known for his poem "Woodman, Spare That Tree!" (1830). Founder and editor of Morris's National Press *(renamed* Home Journal; *1846-64). Died 6 July 1864 in New York City.*

1095   The Union of lakes—the union of lands,
The union of States none can sever,
The union of hearts, the union of hands,
And the flag of our Union forever.
— 1862, "The Flag of Our Union," poem

HAYWARD MORTON

Morton was a private with the 7th Massachusetts.

1096   We took several prisoners. It was quite interesting to talk with them. Someone asked one of them how far it was to Richmond. He said we should

have to go over two Hills, then get over a Stonewall, go through a Longstreet and by that time we should end up on a Lee shore. Pretty good, that.
— 19 December 1862, letter to his sister

FRANK MOSS

Frank Moss was a Confederate soldier from Texas. Brother of W.M. Moss.

1097 [Our] poor Buck and Grind Stone bread would kill the Devil.
— 7 December 1864, letter to one of his sisters

W.M. MOSS

W.M. Moss was a Confederate soldier from Texas. Brother of Frank Moss.

1098 I am so sick of war that I dont want to heare it any more till old Abes time is out and then let a man say war to me and I will choke him.
— 28 December 1863, letter to his sisters

CHARLES R. MUDGE

Mudge was a Union lieutenant colonel when he was killed in action on 3 July 1863 at Gettysburg.

1099 Well, it is murder, but it's the order. Up, men, over the works.
— 3 July 1863, comment on hearing the order to charge the Confederates at Spangler's Spring, Gettysburg

JAMES ADELBERT MULLIGAN

Born 25 June 1830 in Utica, New York. His parents were Irish immigrants. Before the Civil War, he was a lawyer and Irish politician in Chicago. He helped form the 23rd Illinois, known as the Irish Brigade, and became its colonel (18 June 1861). Mortally wounded at Winchester, Virginia, during 2nd Kernstown on 23 July 1864, he died three days later (26 July 1864). He was posthumously breveted a brigadier general.

1100 Lay me down and save the flag!
— 23 July 1864, last commmand to his men; before they could return to him, he was captured by the Confederates, in whose hands he died

JOHNNY C. MURRAY

Murray was a Confederate soldier from Louisiana.

1101 If any person offers me cornbread after this war comes to a close, I shall probably tell him to—go to hell!
— 28 March 1865, letter to "Sig"

EDWARD DUFFIELD NEILL

Born 9 August 1823 in Philadelphia, Pennsylvania. Clergyman, educator, and historian. From February 1864 on, he was an assistant secretary to President Lincoln. Died 26 September 1893 in St. Paul, Minnesota.

1102 Keep the champagne, but return the negro.
— February 1865, remark to the Confederate commissioners at the Hampton Roads Peace Conference, when a bottle was sent to them through a black servant

WILLIAM NELSON

Born 27 September 1824 in Maysville, Kentucky. Before the Civil War, he was in the United States Navy and rose to the rank of lieutenant. During the war, he was commissioned a Union brigadier general of army volunteers (16 September 1861) and was later promoted to major general (July 1862). On 29 September 1862, in Louisville, Kentucky, he was mortally shot by the Union's Brigadier General Jefferson C. Davis, after an argument. Nelson lingered for an hour before dying.

1103 Damn your souls, if you won't fight get out of the way of men who will!
— 6 April 1862, command to fleeing Federal soldiers

1104 Send for a clergyman; I wish to be baptized. I have been basely murdered.
— 29 September 1862, statement after being shot

NEW ORLEANS CRESCENT

The New Orleans Crescent *was a newspaper in New Orleans, Louisiana.*

1105 Such men as these will make quick work of the Yankee racers when they get a chance.
— 1861, statement quoted in the *Richmond Examiner* (3 September 1861)

NEW YORK EVENING DAY-BOOK

The New York Evening Day-Book *was a periodical in New York, New York.*

1106 Mr. Lincoln is evidently a believer in the savageries of old Europe, and thinks that the only way to "save the Union" is to resort to the bayonet....But he is behind the times, behind 1776, when the great and immortal truth that *governments must rest on the consent of the governed, was instituted for the benefit of all coming generations of men.*
— 18 April 1861

NEW YORK HERALD

The New York Herald *was a newspaper in New York, New York.*

1107 There is no longer any apprehension of disturbance at the capital; but the little cloud "the size of a man's hand" which appeared in the Southern horizon on the morning after the 6th of November has grown and spread and become darker and darker, till now the whole Southern heavens are overcast, and tempest seems almost inevitable.
— 4 March 1861

1108 All our women are Florence Nightingales.
— 5 April 1864

1109 The world has seen its iron age, its silver age, its golden age and its bronze age. This is the age of shoddy.
— editorial comment on poorly manufactured goods sold to the Union army

NEW YORK TIMES

The New York Times *was a newspaper in New York, New York.*

1110 In a great crisis like this, there is no policy so fatal as that of having no policy at all.
— 3 April 1861

NEW YORK TRIBUNE

The New York Tribune *was a newspaper in New York, New York.*

1111 Forward to Richmond!
— June 1861, slogan printed daily on the editorial page

1112 The first era of the supremacy of the rights of man in this country dates from the Declaration of Independence; the second began on the 6th of March, 1862, with the Emancipation Message of President Lincoln.

> — 8 March 1862, comment on Lincoln's call for compensated emancipation

1113 Every gun fired in this struggle, no matter on which side, no matter what else it hits or misses, lodges a ball in the carcase of the writhing monster. Man may hesitate or vacillate, but the judgment of God is sure, and under that judgment Slavery reels to its certain downfall.

> — 20 May 1862

1114 There is no jeering or tormenting from our men....We have even refrained from cheering, and nothing—absolutely nothing—has been done to add humiliation to the cup of sorrows which the Rebels have been compelled to drink.

> — 15 July 1863, dispatch dated 4 July

NEW YORK WORLD

The New York World *was a newspaper in New York, New York.*

1115 Mrs. Willow and a free colored woman named Hannah Courtena, were arrested yesterday for selling poisoned pies to the soldiers at Camp Benton.

> — 12 September 1861, news item from St. Louis, concerning Southern women and Federal soldiers

OLIVER WILLCOX NORTON

Born 17 December 1839 in Allegany County, New York. Early in the Civil War, he volunteered as a private with the 83rd Pennsylvania. Later he was commissioned a first lieutenant with a black regiment (5 November 1863). After the war, he was a manufacturer. Died 1 October 1920 in Chicago.

1116 The first thing in the morning is drill, then drill, then drill again. Then drill, drill, a little more drill. Then drill, and lastly drill. Between drills, we drill and sometimes stop to eat a little and have a roll-call.

> — 1861, letter

1117 We've been fooling about this thing long enough, and now we want a change....We must take the offensive and destroy their army and take their capital. When this is done, the clouds will begin to break.

> — 13 July 1862, letter to his brother and sister

1118 Shoddycracy is pretty large in New York,...the hideous offspring of the monster war.

— 1863, letter

WILLIAM L. NUGENT

Nugent was a captain with the 28th Mississippi Cavalry.

1119 I feel that I would like to shoot a Yankee, and yet I know that this would not be in harmony with the spirit of Christianity.

— early in the war

1120 The idea of being continually employed in the destruction of human life is revolting in the extreme. Necessity, imperious and exacting, forces us along and we hurry through the dreadful task apparently unconscious of its demoralizing influences and destructive effects both upon the nation and individuals.

— 7 September 1863, letter to his wife

OHIO STATESMAN

The Ohio Statesman *was a newspaper.*

1121 The slaves who run away from their masters in Virginia, are set to work at once by Gen. Butler, and made to keep at it, much to their annoyance. One of them having been put to it rather strong, said, "Golly, Massa Butler, dis nigger never had to work so hard before; guess dis chile will secede once moah."

— 2 August 1861

DENNIS O'KANE

O'Kane was a colonel with the 69th Pennsylvania when he was mortally wounded on 3 July 1863 at Gettysburg; he died the next day.

1122 Let your work this day be for victory or death!

— 3 July 1863, command to his men at Gettysburg

JOHN GIBSON PARKHURST

Born 17 April 1824 in Oneida Castle, New York. Lawyer who became a Union lieutenant colonel (10 September 1861), colonel (February 1863), and brevet brigadier general (22 May 1865). After the war, he returned to the law and entered politics. Died 1906 in Coldwater, Michigan.

1123 In relation to guerrillas, General Forrest remarked that he was as anxious to rid the country of them as was any officer in the U.S. Army, and that he would esteem it a favor if General Thomas would hang every one he caught.

> — 1 March 1865, letter to William D. Whipple

1124 No man who runs away ranks me.

> — 20 September 1863, attributed remark at Chickamauga, to a fleeing officer who had said, "Get out of my way! I rank you"

E.D. PATTERSON

Patterson was a Confederate private.

1125 When a fellow's time comes, down he goes. Every bullet has its billet.
> — 4 April 1862, diary

HENRY PEARSON

Pearson was a captain with the 6th New Hampshire. when he wrote the letter below. Later he rose to lieutenant colonel before he was killed in action on 26 May 1864 at North Anna River, Virginia.

1126 The Northern people get not the faintest idea from the newspapers of the true state of affairs at the seat of operations. The lying reports of our general and reporters beat anything that ever existed among the rebels.

> — 5 September 1862, letter to a "Friend" regarding 2nd Bull Run; his general was John Pope

WILLIAM DORSEY PENDER

Born 6 February 1834 in Edgecomb County, North Carolina. West Point class of 1854. He resigned from the United States Army in March 1861 to become a Confederate colonel. Later he rose to brigadier general (3 June 1862) and major general (27 May 1863). Wounded 2 July 1863 at Gettysburg, he died 8 July in Staunton, Virginia.

1127 The whole of our time is taken up by two things, marching and fighting. Some of the Army have a fight nearly every day, and the more we fight, the less we like it.

> — 22 September 1862, letter to his wife

1128 Our Army has shown itself incapable of invasion and we had best stick to the defensive.

— 22 September 1862, letter to his wife

1129 I think if it were hinted around in Yankee land that we would be satisfied with the Potomac as the line that the people would soon bring the government to it.

— 22 September 1862, letter to his wife

1130 I am tired of invasion for altho they have made us suffer all that people can suffer, I cannot get my resentment to that point to make me indifferent to what goes on here.

— 28 June 1863, letter from Pennsylvania to his wife

WILLIAM NELSON PENDLETON

Born 26 December 1809 in Richmond, Virginia. West Point class of 1830. After three years in the army, he resigned to become an educator and Episcopal minister. During the Civil War, he was commissioned a Confederate captain (1 May 1861) and won promotions to colonel (13 July 1861) and brigadier general (26 March 1862). After the war, he returned to the ministry. Died 15 January 1883 in Lexington, Virginia.

1131 Fire, boys! and may God have mercy on their guilty souls!

— 21 July 1861, statement at 1st Bull Run

THOMAS G. PENN

Penn was a Confederate soldier.

1132 The smell of blood is sickening.

— 27 June 1862, letter to his mother

ABNER MONROE PERRIN

Born 2 February 1827 in Edgefield District, South Carolina. After fighting in the Mexican War as a lieutenant in the United States Army, he became a lawyer. During the Civil War, he was commissioned a Confederate captain (summer 1861) and won promotions to colonel (20 February 1863) and brigadier general (10 September 1863). Killed in action 12 May 1864 at Spotsylvania.

1133 I shall come out of this fight a live major general or a dead brigadier.

— May 1864, comment before the engagement in which he was killed at Spotsylvania

SETH LEDYARD PHELPS

Born 13 January 1824 in Parkman, Ohio. He became a United States Navy midshipman in 1841 and later rose to lieutenant (1855) and lieutenant commander (1862). After the war, he was vice president of a steamship company. In 1883 he was named minister to Peru, where he died c. 1885.

1134 Every day we heard great things threatened only to realize fizzles. I fear that both S.P. Lee and Palmer had too much influence with Commander Farragut in the matter of the attacks on the *Arkansas*, but that does not excuse his "great talk and little action." I tell you, my old commander, I would rather have your little finger at the head than he who led the attack at New Orleans.
— 29 July 1862, letter to Flag Officer Andrew H. Foote

GEORGE EDWARD PICKETT

Born 25 January 1825 in Richmond, Virginia. West Point class of 1846. On 25 June 1861, he resigned from the United States Army as a captain. Joining the Confederate forces, he became a colonel (summer 1861), brigadier general (13 February 1862, to rank from 14 January), and major general (10 October 1862). After the war, he entered the insurance business. Died 30 July 1875 in Norfolk, Virginia.

1135 The war was never really contemplated in earnest. I believe if either the North or the South had expected that their differences would result in this obstinate struggle, the cold-blooded Puritan and the cock-hatted Huguenot and Cavalier would have made a compromise.
— 27 June 1862, letter to his fiancée

1136 When your official report of the battle was published there was a universal feeling of mortification and sense of injustice felt in my command, both by the officers and the men. We were barely mentioned as having been in the original line of battle, but no notice was made of their gallant unsupported charge made through an open field for 150 or 200 yards under a galling fire against a concealed foe, and of their holding the enemy in check for so long a space of time considerably in advance of the rest of our line.
— 10 July 1862, letter to Leonidas Polk, concerning an engagement at Belmont

1137 If General Lee had Grant's resources he would soon end the war; but Old Jack can do it without resources.
— 11 October 1862, letter to his fiancée; "Jack" was Stonewall Jackson

1138 Up, men, and to your posts! Don't forget today that you are from Old Virginia. (Alternate version: Charge the enemy and remember Old Virginia.)
> — 3 July 1863, command to his men just before Pickett's Charge at Gettysburg

1139 General Lee, I have no division now.
> — 3 July 1863, reply to Lee's order to prepare his division to repel a possible Union counterattack

1140 It is all over now. Many of us are prisoners, many are dead, many wounded, bleeding and dying. Your soldier lives and mourns and but for you, my darling, he would rather be back there with his dead, to sleep for all time in an unknown grave.
> — 4 July 1863, letter to his fiancée, after Gettysburg

1141 War and its horrors, and yet I sing and whistle.
> — May 1864, letter to his wife

1142 It is finished! Oh, my beloved division! Thousands of them have gone to their eternal home, having given up their lives for the cause they knew to be just. The others, alas, heartbroken, crushed in spirit, are left to mourn its loss.
> — "Midnight—the night of the 8th and the dawn of the 9th" April 1865, letter to his wife

JAMES PLEASANTS

Pleasants was a young Confederate captain when he wrote the following letter.

1143 The campaign is a failure and the worst failure that the South has ever made. Gettysburg sets off Fredericksburg. Lee seems to have become as weak as Burnside. And no blow since the fall of New Orleans has been so telling against us.
> — 17 July 1863, letter to Mrs. D.H. Gordon

LEONIDAS POLK

Born 10 April 1806 in Raleigh, North Carolina. West Point class of 1827. He soon resigned from the army to become an Episcopal minister. During the Civil War, he was commissioned a Confederate major general (25 June 1861) and was promoted to lieutenant general (10 October 1862). Killed in action 14 June 1864 at Pine Mountain, Georgia.

1144 I cannot describe the field. It was one of great carnage, and as it was the second battle I have been in—the other being a bloody one also—I felt somewhat more accustomed to it. This one was on a large scale, and a magnificent affair.

— 10 April 1862, letter to his wife after Shiloh

1145   How can you subdue such a nation as this?

— 29 May 1863, comment to Arthur Fremantle after relating the story of a Southern woman who, after losing three sons in battle, was willing to give her fourth and last son to the cause

JOHN POPE

Born 16 March 1822 in Louisville, Kentucky. West Point class of 1842. When the Civil War began, he was a captain in the Regular Army. During the war, he became a Union brigadier general of volunteers (14 June 1861, to rank from 17 May), major general of volunteers (21 March 1862), and brigadier general in the Regular Army (14 July 1862). From 26 June to 2 September 1862, he commanded the Army of Virginia. After the war, he remained in the army and rose to major general. Died 23 September 1892 in Sandusky, Ohio.

1146   I have come to you from the West, where we have always seen the backs of our enemies—from an army whose business it has been to seek the adversary, and to beat him when found, whose policy has been attack and not defence....Let us look before us and not behind. Success and glory are in the advance; disaster and shame lurk in the rear.

— 14 July 1862, address to the Army of Virginia

1147   My headquarters will be in the saddle.

— July 1862, press statement when he took command of the Army of Virginia

DAVID DIXON PORTER

Born 8 June 1813 in Chester, Pennsylvania. Foster brother of David G. Farragut and cousin of Fitz-John Porter. David D. Porter entered the navy in 1829. During the Civil War, he became a Union commander (22 April 1861) and rear admiral (acting, September 1862; permanent, July 1863). After the war, he served as superintendent of the Naval Academy (1865-69) and became a full admiral (1870). Died 13 February 1891 in Washington, D.C.

1148   Mobile is so ripe now that it would fall to us like a mellow pear.

— 3 June 1862, report to David G. Farragut

1149 A greater pack of knaves never went unhung.
> — 29 October 1863, letter to William T. Sherman, regarding Treasury aides who were supposed to regulate trade with the South

1150 I have seen death in so many shapes within the last year, that I consider the change from life to eternity very philosophically, it is our doom.
> — 29 December 1863, letter to his mother

1151 A ship without Marines is like a garment without buttons.
> — 1863, letter to John Harris

1152 There is but one chance for wooden vessels in attacking an ironclad. You will, in case she comes out, make a dash at her with every vessel you have, and "lay her on board," using canister to fire into her ports, while the ram strikes her steering apparatus and disables her.
> — 22 October 1864, letter to William H. Macomb

1153 The chances are death, capture, glory, and promotion.
> — 5 November 1864, order requesting volunteers for hazardous duty

1154 This war is not being conducted for the benefit of officers or to enrich them by the capture of prizes, and every commander is deficient in the high moral character which has always been inherent in the Navy who for a moment consults his private interests in preference to the public good, hesitates to destroy what is the property of the enemy, or attempts to benefit himself at the expense of others.
> — 9 November 1864, General Order No. 41

1155 Honor and glory should be the watchword of the Navy, and not profit.
> — 9 November 1864, General Order No. 41

1156 I have seen so many ill effects from leaving guns (those that we have captured) on shore, that I am convinced it is best always to ship them.
> — 28 November 1864, order to William H. Macomb

1157 The picket boats must always be kept in readiness at night, with their torpedoes ready for instant service, and if an ironclad should come down they must destroy her even if they are all sunk. For this purpose you must select men of nerve to command them, who will undertake anything, no matter how desperate.
> — 2 December 1864, order to the James River Division of the North Atlantic Squadron

1158 While in action an officer will be kept by the compass to see that the vessel heads the course she anchored on, for, if she should swing in the smoke, broadsides might be fired in the wrong direction.
> — 19 December 1864, Special Order No. 2

1159 The object is to lodge the shell in the parapets, and tear away the traverses under which the bombproofs are located. A shell now and then exploding over a gun en barbette may have good effect, but there is nothing like lodging the shell before it explodes.

> — 2 January 1865, General Order No. 78 for the bombardment of Fort Fisher

1160 We regret our companions in arms and shed a tear over their remains, but if these rebels should succeed we would have nothing left us and our lives would be spent in terror and sorrow.

> — 17 January 1865, report to Gideon Welles

FITZ-JOHN PORTER

Born 31 August 1822 in Portsmouth, New Hampshire. Cousin of David D. Porter. West Point class of 1845. A career army man, he was a brevet captain when the Civil War began. During the war, he became a colonel (14 May 1861), brigadier general of volunteers (August 1861, to rank from 17 May), brevet brigadier general in the Regular Army (27 June 1862), and major general of volunteers (4 July 1862). Court-martialed for misconduct, he was cashiered on 21 Jan 1863. In 1878 he was exonerated, and in 1886 he was reinstated as a colonel. Died 21 May 1901 in Morristown, New Jersey.

1161 This army moves as a disciplined body—not an armed mob—compelled to respect private rights and to win the respect of the people we will mingle with.

> — 21 May 1862, comment to Manton Marble, a newspaper editor

ROGER ATKINSON PRYOR

Born 19 July 1828 near Petersburg, Dinwiddie County, Virginia. Before the Civil War, he was a lawyer, writer, publisher, and politician. In April 1861, he roamed Charleston, South Carolina, and urged the Confederate authorities to open fire on Fort Sumter. On 12 April 1861 he accompanied the party of Confederate officers who delivered Beauregard's ultimatum to the Union garrison at the fort. Early in the war, Pryor was a member of the Confederate Congress. Joining the army, he became a colonel (1861) and brigadier general (16 April 1862) before resigning in 1863. He then served as a scout and courier for the cavalry till he was captured (27 November 1864). In 1865 he was exchanged.

After the war, Pryor was a journalist, lawyer, and judge. Died 14 March 1919 in New York City.

1162 I will tell you, gentlemen, what will put her [Virginia] in the Southern Confederacy in less than an hour by Shrewsbury clock—strike a blow! The very moment that blood is shed, old Virginia will make common cause with her sisters of the South.
> — 10 April 1861, speech in Charleston, South Carolina

1163 I could not fire the first gun of the war.
> — 12 April 1861, reply to Captain George S. James, who had offered to let Pryor fire the first shot at Fort Sumter

S.G. PRYOR

S.G. Pryor was a Confederate lieutenant from Georgia.

1164 To think of it among civilized people killing one another like beasts one would think that the supreme ruler would put a stop to it but wee sinned as a nation and must suffer in the fleash as well as spiritually those things wee cant account for.
> — 18 May 1862, letter to his wife

ISAAC C. PUGH

Born c. 1822. Illinois lawyer who, during the Civil War, became a Union captain (25 April 1861), colonel (5 August 1861), and brevet brigadier general (10 March 1865). Died 1874.

1165 Fill your canteens, boys! Some of you will be in hell before night and you'll need water!
> — April 1862, order to his men at Shiloh

WILLIAM CLARKE QUANTRILL

Born 31 July 1837 in Canal Dover, Ohio. Before the Civil War, he was a gambler and thief. During the war, he performed guerrilla operations for the Confederacy and was given the ranks of captain (August 1862) and colonel (November 1862). On 10 May 1865 he was fatally wounded while raiding in Kentucky. He died 6 June as a prisoner in Louisville.

1166 Kill! Kill! Lawrence must be cleansed, and the only way to cleanse it is to kill! Kill!
> — 21 August 1863, command to his men at Lawrence, Kansas

CIVIL WAR QUOTATIONS

V.S. RABB

Rabb was a Confederate soldier from Texas.

1167   These Arkansaw hoosiers ask from 25 to 30 cents a pound for there pork, but the Boys generally get it a little *cheaper than that* I reckon you understand how they get it.
— 4 January 1863, letter to his brother

JAMES RYDER RANDALL

Born 1 January 1839 in Baltimore, Maryland. Poet and journalist. After some moves to other areas, he returned to Baltimore for the rest of his life. Died 14 January 1908.

1168   The despot's heel is on thy shore,
  Maryland!
His torch is at thy temple door,
  Maryland!
Avenge the patriotic gore
That flecked the streets of Baltimore,
And be the battle queen of yore,
  Maryland! My Maryland!
— 1861, "Maryland! My Maryland!" poem published in the *New Orleans Delta* (26 April 1861); later slightly altered by others into a song fitting the tune of "O Tannenbaum"

JOHN L. RANSOM

Ransom was a 1st sergeant with the 9th Michigan Cavalry. His Andersonville diary, published in 1881, chronicles his experiences as a military prisoner in Georgia.

1169   The prison is a success as regards safety; no escape except by death, and very many take advantage of that way.
—8 July 1864, diary

1170   It's "bite dog, bite bear" with most of us prisoners; we don't care which licks, what we want is to get out of this pen. Of course, we all care and want our side to win, but it's tough on patriotism.
— 14 July 1864, diary

1171   Four out of five prefer to stay inside and die with their friends rather than go to the hospital. Hard stories reach us of the treatment of the sick out there, and I am sorry to say the cruelty emanates from our own men who act as nurses. These deadbeats and bummer nurses are the same bounty jumpers the U.S. authorities have had so much trouble with.

— 18 July 1864, diary

1172   There is no such thing as delicacy here. Nine out of ten would as soon eat with a corpse for a table as any other way. In the middle of last night I was awakened by being kicked by a dying man. He was soon dead. In his struggles he had floundered clear into our bed. Got up and moved the body off a few feet, and again went to sleep to dream of the hideous sights.

— 19 July 1864, diary

1173   Lay in the sun for some hours to be examined, and finally my turn came, and I tried to stand up, but was so excited I fainted away. When I came to myself I lay along with the row of dead on the outside. Raised up and asked a Rebel for a drink of water, and he said: "Here, you Yank, if you ain't dead, get inside there!

— 25 July 1864, diary

1174   Ain't dead yet.

— 26 July 1864, dairy

1175   Rebels say we go during the night when transportation comes. Battese grinned when this news come and can't get his face straightened out again.

— 7 September 1864, diary

JESSE LEE RENO

Born 20 June 1823 in Wheeling, western Virginia. West Point class of 1846. A career officer, he rose to captain before the Civil War. During the war, he became a brigadier general (12 November 1861) and major general (18 July 1862). Killed in action 14 September 1862 at South Mountain, Maryland.

1176   Hallo, Sam. I'm dead!

— 14 September 1862, comment to Samuel D. Sturgis, shortly after Reno was fatally wounded

ALEXANDER C. RHIND

Born 31 October 1821 in New York City. He entered the United States Navy as a midshipman (1838) and rose to lieutenant (1854), lieutenant commander

(1862), commander (1863), and rear admiral (1883). Died 8 November 1897 in New York City.

1177   There's a fizzle.

> — 24 December 1864, comment after a powder boat explosion failed to do any damage to Fort Fisher

ELISHA HUNT RHODES

Born 21 March 1842 in Pawtuxet village, Cranston, Rhode Island. Before the Civil War, he was a clerk. He enlisted as a private with the 2nd Rhode Island (1861), rose to lieutenant colonel (6 February 1865), and saw action in every campaign of the Army of the Potomac, from 1st Bull Run to Appomattox. He wrote one of the Civil War's most famous diaries. After the war, he was a businessman, public official, and brigadier general in the Rhode Island militia. Died 14 January 1917 in Rhode Island.

1178   Mud, mud. I am thinking of starting a steamboat line to run on Penn. Avenue....If I was owner of this town I would sell it very cheap. Will the mud never dry up so that the Army can move?...I want to see service and have the war over so that I can go home.

> — 31 January 1862, diary, Washington, D.C.

1179   Sleeping on the ground is fun, and a bed of pine boughs better than one of feathers.

> — 21 March 1862, diary

1180   We have to detail a good many men to protect the gardens, or the people would starve. I do not see what they can do for food next winter, but they are reaping the fruits of their folly.

> — 15 June 1862, diary, near Mechanicsville, Virginia

1181   Soldiering is not fun, but duty keeps us in the ranks.

> — 4 July 1862, diary

1182   O, why did we not attack them and drive them into the river? I do not understand these things. But then I am only a boy.

> — 23 September 1862, diary, after Antietam

1183   How I would like to have some of those "On to Richmond" fellows out here with us in the snow.

> — 8 November 1862, diary, White Plains, Virginia

1184   Was ever the Nation's Birthday celebrated in such a way before[?] This morning the 2nd Rhode Island was sent out to the front and found that during the night General Lee and his Rebel Army had fallen back....At 12

M. a National Salute with shotted guns was fired from several of our Batteries, and the shells passed over our heads toward the Rebel lines.
— 4 July 1863, diary, after Gettysburg

1185 I wonder what the South thinks of us Yankees now. I think Gettysburg will cure the Rebels of any desire to invade the North again.
— 9 July 1863, diary

1186 If we were under any other General except Grant I should expect a retreat, but Grant is not that kind of a soldier, and we feel that we can trust him.
— 7 May 1864, diary, the Wilderness

1187 Early should have attacked early in the morning. "Early was Late."
— 12 July 1864, diary, near Washington D.C.

1188 Well I have seen the end of the Rebellion. I was in the first battle fought by the dear old Army of the Potomac, and I was in the last. I thank God for all his blessings to me and that my life has been spared to see this glorious day. Hurrah, Hurrah, Hurrah!
— 9 April 1865, diary

RICHMOND DISPATCH

The Richmond Dispatch *was a newspaper in Richmond, Virginia.*

1189 McClellan consistently thinks no more of attacking the Confederate Army...than of attacking the man in the moon.
— 23 September 1861

1190 Nor is it very important whether the President is a high-minded statesman or a vulgar demagogue. If he is the first, the people will desert him, and if he is the last, he will desert the people. A gentleman in the Presidency would give mortal offense to the magnificent vulgar.
— 8 January 1862

1191 Posterity will scarcely believe that the wonderful campaign which has just ended with its terrible marches and desperate battles, was made by men, one-fourth of whom were entirely barefooted, and one-half of whom were as ragged as scarecrows....We cease to wonder at the number of stragglers, when we hear how many among them were shoeless, with stone bruises on their feet.
— 9 October 1862, article concerning Lee's army during the Antietam campaign

1192 We are by no means sure that the removal of McClellan from command is calculated to do the Yankee cause any great harm. It is said that he is the best General they have, and we think it probable he is. Yet they could have fallen upon no man who could have made a more signal failure than he did in his campaign against Richmond. If he be the best, they must all be exceedingly bad.
— 17 November 1862

RICHMOND ENQUIRER

The Richmond Enquirer *was a newspaper in Richmond, Virginia.*

1193 Never defeated, never surprised, always at the right place at the right time, he has earned and well merits the title of General.
— 18 June 1862, praise of Richard S. Ewell

RICHMOND EXAMINER

The Richmond Examiner *was a newspaper in Richmond, Virginia.*

1194 There are officers as well as privates among these absentees; drones in uniform, who smoke or guzzle about the hotels, and are made parlor pets by some of the social noodles of Richmond.
—21 July 1862

1195 There was the stuff of Cromwell in Jackson. Hannibal might have been proud of his campaign in the Valley, and the shades of the mightiest warriors should rise to welcome his stern ghost.
— 11 May 1863, article on the death of Stonewall Jackson

M.F. ROBERTS

Roberts was a Union soldier from Ohio.

1196 The surgeon insisted on Sending me to the hospital for treatment. I insisted on takeing the field and prevailed—thinking that I had better die by Rebel bullets than Union Quackery.
— 3 May 1864, diary

CIVIL WAR QUOTATIONS

FANNIE J. ROBERTSON

Robertson was a Confederate civilian.

1197 Independence has few charms to me when the anguish of my heart is stretched to the utmost.
> — 10 July 1862, letter to "Dear Afflicted Daniel," after her brother's death

G.L. ROBERTSON

Robertson was a Confederate soldier.

1198 I may run, but if I do I wish that some of our own men would shoot me down.
> — 19 January 1862, letter to his mother

JOHN S. ROCK

Born 1825, probably in Salem, New Jersey. Black physician, lawyer, and antislavery leader. Died 3 December 1866 in Boston, Massachusetts.

1199 Had it not been for slavery, we should have had no war! Through 240 years of indescribable tortures, slavery has wrung out of the blood, bones, and muscles of the Negro hundreds of millions of dollars and helped much to make this nation rich. At the same time, it has developed a volcano which has burst forth, and, in a less number of days than years, has dissipated this wealth and rendered the government bankrupt! And, strange as it may appear, you still cling to this monstrous iniquity, notwithstanding it is daily sinking the country lower and lower! Some of our ablest and best men have been sacrificed to appease the wrath of this American god.
> — 23 January 1862, speech to the Massachusetts Anti-Slavery Society

1200 Many of those who advocate emancipation as a military necessity seem puzzled to know what is best to be done with the slave if he is set at liberty. Colonization in Africa, Haiti, Florida, and South America are favorite theories with many well-informed persons. This is really interesting! No wonder Europe does not sympathize with you. You are the only people, claiming to be civilized, who take away the rights of those people whose color differs from your own. If you find that you cannot rob the Negro of his labor and of himself, you will banish him! What a sublime idea! You are certainly a great people!... When the orange is squeezed, we throw it aside. The black man is a good fellow while he is a slave and toils for nothing; but the moment he claims his own flesh and blood and bones, he is a most obnoxious creature, and there is a propostion to get rid of him!...This country and climate are perfectly adapted to Negro slavery, it is the free black that the air is not good for! What an idea! A country good for slavery and not good for freedom!

— 23 January 1862, speech to the Massachusetts Anti-Slavery Society

1201   It is true the government is but little more antislavery now than it was at the commencement of the war; but while fighting for its own existence, it has been obliged to take slavery by the throat and sooner or later, *must* choke her to death.

— 23 January 1862, speech to the Massachusetts Anti-Slavery Society

GEORGE FREDERICK ROOT

Born 30 August 1820 in Sheffield, Massachusetts. Composer and music educator. Died 6 August 1895 in Bailey Island, Maine.

1202   The Union forever,
Hurrah, boys, hurrah!
Down with the Traitor,
Up with the Star;
While we rally round the flag, boys,
Rally once again,
Shouting the battle-cry of Freedom.

— 1861 (published 1862), "The Battle-cry of Freedom," aka "Rally round the Flag, Boys," song

1203   Tramp! Tramp! Tramp! the boys are marching,
Cheer up comrades they will come,
And beneath the starry flag,
We shall breathe the air again,
Of the freeland in our own beloved home.

— 1864, "Tramp! Tramp! Tramp!" song

WILLIAM STARKE ROSECRANS

Born 6 September 1819 in Kingston, Ohio. West Point class of 1842. In 1854 he resigned from the army as a 1st lieutenant and entered business. During the Civil War, he became a colonel of engineers and aide-de-camp with the Ohio volunteers (23 April 1861), colonel of the 23rd Ohio (12 June 1861), brigadier general in the Regular Army (17 June 1861, to rank from 16 May), and major general of volunteers (17 September 1862; reappointed 25 October 1862, to rank from 21 March). After the war, he was minister to Mexico (1868-69), a civil engineer, a United States congressman (1881-85) and register of the United States Treasury (1885-93). Died 11 March 1898 in Redondo Beach, California.

1204 Citizens of Western Virginia, your fate is mainly in your own hands.

If you allow yourselves to be trampled under foot by hordes of disturbers, plunderers, and murderers, your land will become a desolation. If you stand firm for law and order and maintain your rights, you may dwell together peacefully and happily as in former days.

> — 20 August 1861, proclamation to the people of West Virginia

1205 Watch your language. Remember, the first bullet may send you to eternity.

> — 31 December 1862, warning to Philip H. Sheridan at Stones River

1206 Men, do you know how to be safe? Shoot low! But to be safest of all, give them a blizzard, and then charge with cold steel!

> — 31 December 1862, admonition to his men at Stones River

1207 Some of us must die. Cross yourselves and march forward.

> — 31 December 1862, attributed admonition to his men at Stones River

1208 Brave men die in battle.

> — 31 December 1862, comment when informed of the death of Julius P. Garesché

DANIEL RUGGLES

Born 31 January 1810 in Barre, Massachusetts. West Point class of 1833. He resigned from the United States Army as a captain (7 May 1861), having already joined the Virginia volunteers as a brigadier general (Ap 1861). On 9 August 1861 he became a brigadier general in the Confederate army. After the war, he was a farmer and real-estate manager. Died 1 June 1897 in Fredericksburg, Virginia.

1209 It is to be observed that the first great law of nature, the right of self-defense, is inherent in communities as well as individuals. No law condemns the individual who slays the robber or assassin, and no just law can condemn a community for using all its power to resist the Invader and drive him from their soil.

> — 15 July 1862, letter to Benjamin F. Butler

ABRAM JOSEPH RYAN

Born 5 February 1838 in Hagerstown, Maryland. Catholic priest and poet. On 1 September 1862, he entered Confederate service as a free-lance chaplain. His collected poems are in Father Ryan's Poems *(1879). Died 22 April 1886 in Louisville, Kentucky.*

1210   Furl that banner! for 'tis weary;
Round its staff 'tis drooping, dreary;
Furl it, fold it, it is best;

....

Furl it, hide it, let it rest.
    — April 1865, "The Conquered Banner," poem written after Lee's surrender

HORACE BINNEY SARGENT

Born 1821 in Massachusetts. A Union lieutenant colonel (19 November 1861), colonel (1 November 1862), and brevet brigadier general (21 March 1864).

1211   A policy of extermination alone can achieve the end expected. Every man and horse must be sent within the lines, every house destroyed, every tree girdled and set on fire, before we can approach security against the secret combination of a sudden force within musket range of our outposts. Attila, King of the Huns, adopted the only method that can exterminate these citizen soldiers.
    — 2 September 1863, report on cavalry operations in Virginia

1212   I can clean this country with fire and sword, and no mortal can do it in any other way.
    — 2 September 1863, report on cavalry operations in Virginia

N. SARGENT

Sargent was a Washington, D.C., civilian.

1213   This is the season when you and I are apt to be afflicted with disordered bowels; & as my black berry cordial, like the rebellion, is pretty well "played out," or "used up," I send you for trial, an article which is *highly* reputed, but which I have not had occasion to try since its appearance in the shops. I hope you will find it beneficial.
    — 12 September 1863, letter to President Lincoln

CHARLES C. SAWYER

Born 1833 in Mystic, Connecticut. Songwriter. Died after 1890.

1214   Weeping, sad and lonely,
      Hopes and fears, how vain,
    Yet praying, when this cruel war is over,
      Praying, that we meet again!
           — 1863, "Weeping, Sad and Lonely; or, When This Cruel War Is Over," song

MARY L. SCALES

Scales was a Southern civilian.

1215   I know my country needs all her children and I had thought I could submit to her requisitions. I have given her cause my prayers, my time, my means and my children but now the last lamb of the fold is to be taken, the mother and helpless woman triumph over the patriot.
           — 8 September 1862, letter to the Confederate secretary of war

SCIENTIFIC AMERICAN

The Scientific American *was a periodical.*

1216   It may well surprise ourselves and all other nations that, during a year of the greatest civil war on record, our country has been wonderfully prosperous.
           — 17 January 1863

WINFIELD SCOTT

Born 13 June 1786 near Petersburg, Virginia. The hero of the War of 1812 and the Mexican War, he was general in chief of the army from 1841 to 1861. He was known as Old Fuss and Feathers because of his strict military protocol (fuss) and his vanity about his appearance (feathers). He proposed the Anaconda Plan of avoiding outright war by blockading Confederate ports, occupying positions along the Mississippi River, and "squeezing" the South till the crisis had passed. He resigned on 1 November 1861. Died 29 May 1866 at West Point, New York.

1217   I am amazed that any man of judgment should hope for the success of any cause in which Jefferson Davis is a leader. There is contamination in his touch. If secession was "the holiest cause that tongue or sword of mortal ever lost or gained," he would ruin it! He will bear a great amount of

watching....He is not a cheap Judas. I do not think he would have sold the Saviour for thirty shillings; but for the successorship to Pontius Pilate he would have betrayed Christ and the apostles and the whole Christian Church.
> — February 1861, outburst to a group of listeners after Davis was elected to the Confederate presidency

1218 Say to the seceded States, Wayward Sisters, depart in peace!
> — 3 March 1861, letter to William H. Seward, one of four alternate courses of action offered to President Lincoln

1219 It will require the exercise of the full powers of the Federal Government to restrain the fury of the noncombatants.
> — April 1861, statement after the attack on Fort Sumter (12-14 April)

1220 Lee, you have made the greatest mistake of your life; but I feared it would be so.
> — 18 April 1861, comment to Robert E. Lee when the latter declined the command of the Federal army

1221 We rely greatly on the sure operation of a complete blockade of the Atlantic and Gulf ports soon to commence. In connection with such blockade we propose a powerful movement down the Mississippi to the ocean, with a cordon of posts at proper points, and the capture of Forts Jackson and Saint Philip; the object being to clear out and keep open this great line of communication in connection with the strict blockade of the sea-board, so as to envelop the insurgent States and bring them to terms with less bloodshed than by any other plan....Finally, it will be necessary that New Orleans should be strongly occupied and securely held until the present difficulties are composed.

A word now as to the greatest obstacle in the way of this plan—the great danger now pressing upon us—the impatience of our patriotic and loyal Union friends. They will urge instant and vigorous action, regardless, I fear, of consequences.
> — 3 May 1861, letter to George B. McClellan

1222 Boldness in execution is nearly always necessary, but in planning and fitting out expeditions or detachments great circumspection is a virtue.
> — 18 May 1861, letter to Benjamin F. Butler

JAMES M. SCOVEL

Scovel was a civilian from Philadelphia.

1223 George Washington made the Republic. Abraham Lincoln will save it.
— 9 November 1864, letter to President Lincoln

JOHN SEATON

Seaton was a captain with the 22nd Illinois when he uttered the following remark. He resigned on 13 June 1862.

1224 Many of us have seen the sun rise for the last time. I do not know what the crucial test may cause, but—if I should show the white feather, shoot me dead in my tracks and my family will feel that I died for my country.
— 7 November 1861, request of his men at Belmont

JOHN SEDGWICK

Born 13 September 1813 in Cornwall Hollow, Connecticut. West Point class of 1837. A career officer, he was a major at the start of the Civil War. During the war, he became a Union lieutenant colonel (16 March 1861), colonel (25 March 1861), brigadier general (31 August 1861), and major general (4 July 1862). Killed in action 9 May 1864 at Spotsylvania Court House, Virginia.

1225 We have done an incredible amount of labour, if we have accomplished but little.
— 26 July 1863, letter after Lee escaped following Gettysburg

1226 They couldn't hit an elephant at this distance.
— 9 May 1864, comment just before being shot dead

PAUL JONES SEMMES

Born 6 June 1815 in Wilkes County, Georgia. Banker and planter who, during the Civil War, became a Confederate colonel (1861) and brigadier general (to rank from 11 March 1862). Wounded 2 July 1863 at Gettysburg, he died 10 July in Martinsburg, Virginia.

1227 I consider it a privilege to die for my country.
— July 1863, comment after being wounded

WILLIAM HENRY SEWARD

Born 16 May 1801 in Florida, New York. Before the Civil War, he was a lawyer and politician. He served as the United States secretary of state from 1861 to 1869. In 1867 he arranged for the purchase of Alaska from Russia. Died 10 October 1872 in Auburn, New York.

1228 I close. We are not we must not be aliens or enemies but fellow countrymen and brethren. Although passion has strained our bonds of affection too hardly they must not, I am sure they will not be broken. The mystic chords which proceeding from so many battle fields and so many patriot graves pass through all the hearts and all the hearths in this broad continent of ours will yet again harmonize in their ancient music when breathed upon by the guardian angel of the nation.
> — February 1861, a suggested closing paragraph for President-elect Lincoln's 1st Inaugural Address

1229 We are at the end of a month's administration and yet without a policy, either domestic or foreign.
> — 1 April 1861, memorandum to President Lincoln

1230 We must change the question before the public from one upon slavery, or about slavery, for a question upon union or disunion: In other words, from what would be regarded as a party question, to one of partiotism or union.
> — 1 April 1861, memorandum to President Lincoln

1231 I would demand explanations from Spain and France, categorically, at once.
I would seek explanations from Great Britain and Russia, and send agents into Canada, Mexico, and Central America to rouse a vigorous continental spirit of independence on this continent against European intervention.
And, if satisfactory explanations are not received from Spain and France, Would convene Congress and declare war against them.
> — 1 April 1861, memorandum to President Lincoln

1232 I can touch a bell on my right hand and order the imprisonment of a citizen of Ohio; I can touch a bell again and order the imprisonment of a citizen of New York; and no power on earth, except that of the President, can release them. Can the Queen of England do so much?
> — 1861, attributed remark to Lord Lyons, the British ambassador; the story was widely circulated in August

1233 Assassination is not an American practice or habit, and one so vicious and so desperate cannot be engrafted into our political system.
— 15 July 1862, letter to John Bigelow

1234 It is a truism, that in times of peace there are always instigators of war. So soon as a war begins there are citizens who impatiently demand negotiations for peace. The advocates of war...generally gain their fearful end, though the war declared is not unfrequently unnecessary and unwise. So peace agitators in time of war ultimately bring about an abandonment of the conflict, sometimes without securing the advantages which were originally expected from the conflict.
— 7 February 1865, letter to Charles Francis Adams

ROBERT GOULD SHAW

Born 10 October 1837 in Boston, Massachusetts. Before the Civil War, he was a student at Harvard, a mercantile businessman, and a member of the 7th New York National Guard. In May 1861 the 7th was disbanded and he joined the 2nd Massachusetts as a second lieutenant. He rose to first lieutenant (July 1861) and captain (August 1862) before being promoted to colonel (early 1863) and taking command of the 54th Massachusetts, the first regiment of black troops from the Northern states. Killed in action 18 July 1863 on Morris Island, South Carolina.

1235 We have a very pleasant feeling towards Rebel soldiers now, because our prisoners were treated so well by them, and because we have had very pleasant interviews with many of their officers and men, but the *citizens* of the towns we have passed through seem to hate us much more bitterly, as a general thing.
— 25 June 1862, letter to his mother, written in Virginia

1236 If we only went in for sink or swim, we should finish the thing up; Stanton wants to be economical. It was for that he stopped recruiting at one time, without which an army in the field must dwindle to half its size in a short time. I don't mean that money should be wasted, but that there should be no economy which is sure to be waste in the end. Like buying bad boots, because they are cheap.
— 4 July 1862, letter to his mother

1237 At last, night came on, and, with the exception of an occasional shot from the outposts, all was quiet. The crickets chirped, and the frogs croaked, just as if nothing had happened all day long, and presently the stars came

out bright, and we lay down among the dead, and slept soundly until daylight. There were twenty dead bodies within a rod of me.
— 21 September 1862, letter to his father, after Antietam

1238 One of the most noticable things in a battle is the perfect calmness of the wounded men; they will lie in the most exposed positions under fire from both sides, without apparently noticing it, and some have told me that when once hit, they felt as if the thing were done, and they couldn't be touched again.
— 28 September 1862, letter to one of his sisters, Sue

1239 For myself, I have gone through the war so far without dishonor, and I do not like to degenerate into a plunderer and robber,—and the same applies to every officer in my regiment.
— 9 June 1863, letter to his wife, concerning his forced participation in the burning of Darien, Georgia, under orders from Colonel James M. Montgomery

PHILIP HENRY SHERIDAN

Born 6 March 1831 in Albany, New York. West Point class of 1853. A career soldier, he became a second lieutenant (1854), first lieutenant (1 March 1861), captain (14 May 1861), colonel (25 May 1862), brigadier general of volunteers (1 July 1862), major general of volunteers (31 December 1862), brigadier general in the Regular Army (20 September 1864), and major general in the Regular Army (8 November 1864). In 1883 he succeeded William T. Sherman as commander in chief, and in 1888 Sheridan rose to full general. Died 5 August 1888 in Nonquitt, Massachusetts.

1240 Unless I swear like hell the men won't take me seriously.
— 31 December 1862, reply to William S. Rosecrans, who had told Sheridan to watch his language

1241 Remember Chickamauga!
— November 1863, battle cry to his men before Missionary Ridge

1242 Run, boys, run! Don't wait to form! Don't let 'em stop! If you can't run, then holler!
— 25 November 1863, command to his men at Missionary Ridge

1243 I shall expect nothing short of success.
— 8 March 1864, order to his division commanders

1244 I do not advise rashness, but I do desire resolute and actual fighting, with necessary casualties.
— 23 September 1864, message to William W. Averell

1245 To-morrow I will continue the destruction of wheat, forage, etc., down to Fisher's Hill. When this is completed the Valley, from Winchester up to Staunton, ninety-two miles, will have but little in it for man or beast.
— 7 October 1864, report to Ulysses S. Grant

1246 God damn you! Don't cheer me. Fight!
— 19 October 1864, command to his troops when he rejoined them at Cedar Creek

1247 Retreat, hell! We'll be back in our camps tonight.
— 19 October 1864, comment to William H. Emory at Cedar Creek

1248 There, there, old fellow; don't capture me!
— 19 October 1864, remark to George Armstrong Custer when the latter picked up and whirled Sheridan in the victory celebration after Cedar Creek

1249 I long ago made up my mind that it was not a good plan to fight battles with paper orders—that is, for the commander to stand on a hill in the rear and send his aides-de-camp with written orders to the different commanders. My practice has always been to fight in the front rank.
— 24 October 1864, statement to Charles A. Dana

1250 A crow could not fly over it without carrying his rations with him.
— October 1864, boast after his destruction of the Shenandoah Valley

1251 I will soon commence on Loudoun County, and let them know there is a God in Israel.
— 26 November 1864, telegram to Henry W. Halleck

1252 Those who live at home, in peace and plenty, want the duello part of this war to go on; but when they have to bear their burden by loss of property and comforts they will cry for peace.
— 26 November 1864, telegram to Henry W. Halleck

1253 I tell you, I'm ready to strike out tomorrow and go to smashing things.
— 30 March 1865, boast to Grant's staff officers

1254 We'll get the twist on 'em, boys! There won't be a grease spot of 'em left!
— 1 April 1865, boast at Five Forks

1255 If the thing is pressed I think Lee will surrender.
— 6 April 1865, telegram to Grant

E.J. SHERLOCK

Sherlock was a Union soldier.

1256   Emancipation without deportation
Sequestration without Litigation
Condemnation without mitigation
Extermination without procrastination
Confiscation without Botheration
Damnation without reservation
And no hesitation until
there is a Speedy termination
to this Southern Confederation.
     — 25 August 1863, diary

WILLIAM TECUMSEH SHERMAN

Born 8 February 1820 in Lancaster, Ohio. West Point class of 1840. In 1853 he resigned as a captain to enter banking. Later he turned to law (1858) and served as superintendent of a Louisiana military academy (1859-61; later known as Louisiana State University). After Louisiana seceded, he left the state and briefly headed a St. Louis streetcar company. During the Civil War, he became a Union colonel (14 May 1861), brigadier general of volunteers (August 1861, to rank from 17 May), major general of volunteers (1 May 1862), brigadier general in the Regular Army (4 July 1863), and major general in the Regular Army (12 August 1864). After the war, he became a lieutenant general (1866), rose to full general (1869), and served as commander in chief (1869-83). Died 14 February 1891 in New York City.

1257   I have seen enough of war not to be caught by its first glittering bait, and when I engage in this it must be with a full consciousness of its real character.
     — 23 May 1861, letter to Thomas Ewing, Jr.

1258   A fatal mistake in war is to underrate the strength, feeling and resources of an enemy.
     — 23 May 1861, letter to Thomas Ewing, Jr.

1259   But as soon as real war begins, new men, heretofore unheard of, will emerge from obscurity, equal to any occasion. Only I think it is to be a long war,—very long,—much longer than any politician thinks.
     — 3 June 1861, letter to Thomas Ewing, Jr.

1260 You are a soldier, and must submit to orders till you are properly discharged. If you attempt to leave without orders, it will be mutiny, and I will shoot you like a dog!
> — late July 1861, warning to a captain who wanted to leave the army after his original three-month enlistment was up

1261 Then for the first time I saw the carnage of battle, men lying in every conceivable shape, and mangled in a horrible way; but this did not make a particle of impression on me, but horses running about riderless with blood streaming from their nostrils, lying on the ground hitched to guns, gnawing their sides in death.
> — 28 July 1861, letter to his wife, after 1st Bull Run

1262 Our men are not good soldiers. They brag, but do not perform, complain sadly if they don't get everything they want, and a march of a few miles uses them up.
> — 28 July 1861, letter to his wife

1263 'Tis said I am to be Brigadier General. If so, I know not it yet. I have closely minded my business, which is a bad sign for favor.
> — 3 August 1861, letter to his wife

1264 The bluer the times the more closely should one cling to his country.
> — 17 August 1861, letter to his wife

1265 Not till I see day light ahead do I want to lead, but when danger threatens and others slink away I am and will be at my post.
> — August 1861, unaddressed letter, probably to his wife

1266 The great difficulty is, and has been, that as volunteers offer we have not arms and clothing to give them. The arms sent us are, as you already know, European muskets of uncouth pattern, which the volunteers will not touch.
> — 22 October 1861, letter to Lorenzo Thomas

1267 She would not be comforted, saying that the camp was made up of the young men from the first and best families...and that they were proud, and would fight. I explained that young men of the best families did not like to be killed better than ordinary people.
> — 1861

1268 Well, Grant, we've had the devil's own day, haven't we?
> — 6 April 1862, question to Ulysses S. Grant at Shiloh, to which Grant replied, "Yes, lick 'em tomorrow, though"

1269 I will get even with the miserable class of corrupt editors yet. They are the chief cause of this unhappy war. They fan the flames of local hatred

and keep alive those prejudices which have forced friends into opposing hostile ranks.
— 6 June 1862, letter to his wife

1270 The very object of war is to produce results by death and slaughter, but the moment a battle occurs the newspapers make the leader responsible for the death and misery, whether of victory or defeat.
— 6 June 1862, letter to his wife

1271 Success is demanded, and yet the means to attain success are withheld.
— 25 August 1862, letter to Colonel W.H.H. Taylor, concerning the lack of support for military leaders among the Northern press and people

1272 I have no hesitation in saying that the possession of the Mississippi River by us is an advantage to our enemy, for by it and the commercial spirit of our people they (the enemy) get, directly or indirectly, all the means necessary to carry on the war.
— 25 August 1862, letter to Colonel W.H.H. Taylor

1273 They cannot be made to love us, but may be made to fear us.
— 4 October 1862, letter to Grant

1274 We cannot change the hearts of those people of the South, but we can make war so terrible that they will realize the fact that, however brave and gallant and devoted to their country, still they are mortal and should exhaust all peaceful remedies before they fly to war.
— 4 October 1862, letter to Grant

1275 If we allow the passions of our men to get full command then indeed will this war become a reproach to the names of liberty and civilization.
— 17 October 1862, letter to Confederate Major General Thomas C. Hindman

1276 We are willing to meet you anywhere and everywhere in manly fight, but to the assassin who fires from the river bank on an unarmed boat we will not accord the title, name, or consideration of an honorable soldier.
— 17 October 1862, letter to Confederate Major General Thomas C. Hindman

1277 If, as you threaten in your letter, you hang an officer, a prisoner in your hands, in retaliation of some act of ours, conjured up by false statements of interested parties, remember that we have hundreds of thousands of men bitter and yearning for revenge....You initiate the game, and my word for it your people will regret it long after you pass from earth.
— 17 October 1862, letter to Confederate Major General Thomas C. Hindman

1278 Thousands will perish by the bullet or sickness; but war must go on—it can't be stopped. The North must rule or submit to degradation and insult forevermore.

 — 24 November 1862, letter to his brother

1279 Complete military success can only be accomplished by an united action on some general plan embracing usually a large district of country.

 — 23 December 1862, letter to his division commmanders

1280 I will never again command an army in America if we must carry along paid spies. I will banish myself to some foreign country first.

 — 28 January 1863, letter to his wife; the "spies" were newspaper correspondents

1281 Who gave notice of McDowell's movement on Manassas, and enabled Johnston so to reinforce Beauregard that our army was defeated? The press. Who gave notice of the movement on Vicksburg? The press. Who has prevented all secret combinations and movements against our enemy? The press.... What has paralyzed the Army of the Potomac? Mutual jealousies kept alive by the press. What has enabled the enemy to combine so as to hold Tennessee after we have twice crossed it with victorious armies? What defeats and will continue to defeat our best plans here and elsewhere? The press....Tis folly to say the people must have news.

 — 18 February 1863, letter to his brother

1282 It is done of course by the cursed stragglers who won't fight, but hang behind and disgrace our cause and country....But this universal burning and wanton destruction of private property is not justified in war.

 — 6 May 1863, letter to his wife

1283 What I want is mules. If they will send me the mules, they can keep the brigadiers.

 — May 1863, comment when three brigadiers arrived at his headquarters

1284 Vox populi, vox humbug.

 — 2 June 1863, letter to his wife; Latin for "The voice of the people, the voice of humbug," his comment on the fickle opinions of the Union press and public

1285 I doubt if history affords a parallel to the deep and bitter enmity of the women of the South.

 — 27 June 1863, letter to his wife

1286 Vicksburg contains many of my old pupils and friends; should it fall into our hands I will treat them with kindness, but they have sowed the wind and must reap the whirlwind. Until they lay down their arms and submit to the rightful authority of the government they must not appeal to me for mercy or favors.

— 27 June 1863, letter to his wife

1287 A government resting immediately on the caprice of a people is too unstable to last....

Supposing the pilot of a ship should steer his vessel according to the opinion of every fellow who watched the clouds above or the currents below, where would his ship land? No, the pilot has before him a little needle; he watches that, and he never errs. So if we make that our simple code, the law of the land must and shall be executed; no matter what the consequences, we cannot err....

We have for years been drifting toward an unadulterated democracy or demagogism, and its signs were manifest in "mob" laws and vigilance committees all over our country.

The South that lived on slavery saw the United States yield to Abolition pressure at the North, to pro-slavery pressure at the South, to the miners of California, the rowdies of Baltimore, and to the people everywhere. They paved the way to this rebellion....

Our government should become a machine, self-regulating, independent of the man.

— 3 August 1863, letter to his brother

1288 War was not the remedy for grievances, or supposed grievances, for which our forefathers provided the Supreme Court of the United States to arbitrate and remove.

— 3 August 1863, letter to Jesse Reed and other Mississippians

1289 The young bloods of the South: sons of planters, lawyers about towns, good billiard-players and sportsmen, men who never did work and never will. War suits them, and the rascals are brave, fine riders, bold to rashness, and dangerous subjects in every sense....These men must all be killed or employed by us before we can hope for peace.

— 17 September 1863, letter to Henry W. Halleck; Sherman specifically mentioned Nathan B. Forrest and Stonewall Jackson as being among the "young bloods"

1290 War....should be "pure and simple" as applied to the belligerents. I would keep it so, till all traces of the war are effaced; till those who appealed to it are sick and tired of it, and come to the emblem of our nation, and sue for peace. I would not coax them, or even meet them half-way, but make them so sick of war that generations would pass away before they would again appeal to it.

— 17 September 1863, letter to Halleck

1291 I would make this war as severe as possible, and show no symptoms of tiring till the South begs for mercy; indeed, I know, and you know, that the end would be reached quicker by such a course than by any seeming yielding on our part.

— 17 September 1863, letter to John A. Rawlins

1292 All chicken-thieving expeditions or cotton-stealing parties to be prosecuted.

— 25 October 1863, letter to Stephen A. Hurlbut

1293 As to officers, my rule is, if any officer in the service of the United States, while enjoying a salary, makes one cent by way of profit in any manner traceable to his office, he is guilty of a high crime, and should be punished as a criminal.

— 25 October 1863, letter to Hurlbut

1294 War is cruelty. There is no use trying to reform it. The crueler it is, the sooner it will be over.

— December 1863, remark to a Tennessee woman who had complained about the behavior of his troops on their march to Knoxville

1295 She ranks me.

— 1863, attributed comment about Mrs. Mary A. Bickerdyke, a famous nurse

1296 War is hell.

— 1863, attributed comment near Jackson, Mississippi; he repeated the expression in later years

1297 Now, the question arises, should we treat as absolute enemies all in the South who differ from us in opinion or prejudices, kill or banish them, or give them time to think and gradually change their conduct so as to conform to the new order of things which is slowly and gradually creeping into their country?

— 31 January 1864, letter to Roswell M. Sawyer

1298 The people of the South having appealed to war are barred from appealing to our Constitution, which they have practically and publicly defied.

— 31 January 1864, letter to Sawyer

1299 I believe that some of the rich and slave-holding are prejudiced to an extent that nothing but death and ruin will extinguish, but hope, as the poorer and industrial classes of the South realize their relative weakness and their dependence upon the fruits of the earth and good will of their fellow men, they will…discover the error of their ways.
— 31 January 1864, letter to Sawyer

1300 War is simply power unrestrained by constitution or compact.
— 31 January 1864, letter to Sawyer

1301 All the power of earth cannot restore to them their slaves, any more than their dead grandfathers.
— 31 January 1864, letter to Sawyer

1302 To those who submit to the rightful law and authority all gentleness and forbearance; but to the petulant and persistent secessionists, why, death is mercy, and the quicker he or she is disposed of the better.
— 31 January 1864, letter to Sawyer

1303 I have not seen in this war a cavalry command of 1,000 that was not afraid of the sight of a dozen infantry bayonets.
— January 1864, remark to James B. Steedman

1304 Grant is as good a leader as we can find. He has honesty, simplicity of character, singleness of purpose, and no hope or claim to usurp civil power. His character, more than his genius, will reconcile armies and attach the people.
— 5 April 1864, letter to his brother

1305 All the people of the South, old and young, rich and poor, educated and ignorant, unite in this, that they will kill as vipers the whites who attempt to free their slaves, and also the "ungrateful slaves" who attempt to change their character from slave to free.
— 12 April 1864, letter to Lorenzo Thomas

1306 In peace there is a beautiful harmony in all the departments of life—they all fit together like a Chinese puzzle, but in war all is ajar. Nothing fits, and it is the struggle between the stronger and weaker, and the latter, however much it may appeal to the better feelings of our nature, must kick the beam. To make war we must and will harden our hearts.
— 21 April 1864, letter to Charles A. Dana

1307 War, like the thunderbolt, follows its laws and turns not aside even if the beautiful, the virtuous and charitable stand in its path.
— 21 April 1864, letter to Dana

1308 Strengthen your position, fight anything that comes.
— 11 May 1864, written order to James B. McPherson at Sugar Valley, Georgia

1309 All the people retire before us and desolation is behind. To realize what war is one should follow our tracks.
— 26 June 1864, letter to his wife during the Atlanta campaign

1310 It is enough to make the whole world start at the awful amount of death and destruction that now stalks abroad. Daily for the past two months has the work progressed and I see no signs of a remission till one or both and all the armies are destroyed, when I suppose the balance of the people will tear each other up....I begin to regard the death and mangling of a couple thousand men as a small affair, a kind of morning dash—and it may be well that we become so hardened.
— 30 June 1864, letter to his wife

1311 Atlanta is ours, and fairly won.
— 3 September 1864, message to Henry W. Halleck

1312 If the people raise a howl against my barbarity and cruelty I will answer that war is war, and not popularity-seeking. If they want peace they and their relatives must stop war.
— 4 September 1864, message to Halleck

1313 I have had the question put to me often: "Is not a negro as good as a white man to stop a bullet?" Yes, and a sand-bag is better.
— 4 September 1864, letter to Halleck

1314 Grant has the perseverance of a Scotch terrier. Let him alone, and he will overcome Lee by untiring and unceasing efforts.
— 4 September 1864, letter to Halleck

1315 If forced to choose between the penitentiary and White House for four years,...I would say the penitentiary, thank you.
— 4 September 1864, letter to Halleck

1316 I have deemed it to the interest of the United States that the citizens now residing in Atlanta should remove, those who prefer it to go South and the rest North.
— 7 September 1864, message to John B. Hood

1317 I have ordered renewed activity, and to show no mercy to guerrillas or railroad breakers. It makes a world of difference if "my bull gores your ox, or yours mine."
— 9 September 1864, message to Halleck

1318 You who, in the midst of peace and prosperity, have plunged a nation into war—dark and cruel war—who dared and badgered us to battle, insulted our flag, seized our arsenals and forts that were left in the honorable custody of peaceful ordnance-sergeants, seized and made "prisoners of war" the very garrisons sent to protect your people against negroes and Indians, long before any overt act was committed by the (to you) hated Lincoln Government; tried to force Kentucky and Missouri into rebellion, spite of themselves; falsified the vote of Louisiana; turned loose your privateers to plunder unarmed ships; expelled Union families by the thousands, burned their houses, and declared, by an act of your Congress, the confiscation of all debts due Northern men for goods had and received! Talk thus to the marines, but not to me, who have seen these things.
— 10 September 1864, letter to John B. Hood

1319 If we must be enemies, let us be men, and fight it out as we propose to do, and not deal in hypocritical appeals to God and humanity.
— 10 September 1864, letter to Hood

1320 I have your letter of the 11th, in the nature of a petition to revoke my orders removing all the inhabitants from Atlanta. I have read it carefully, and give full credit to your statements of the distress that will be occasioned by it, and yet shall not revoke my orders, simply because my orders are not designed to meet the humanities of the case, but to prepare for the future struggles in which millions of good people outside of Atlanta have a deep interest.
— 12 September 1864, letter to Atlanta city officials

1321 You cannot qualify war in harsher terms than I will. War is cruelty and you cannot refine it, and those who brought war into our country deserve all the curses and maledictions a people can pour out.
— 12 September 1864, letter to Atlanta city officials

1322 You might as well appeal against the thunder-storm as against these terrible hardships of war.
— 12 September 1864, letter to Atlanta city officials

1323 We don't want your negroes or your horses or your houses or your lands or anything you have, but we do want, and will have, a just obedience to the laws of the United States.
— 12 September 1864, letter to Atlanta city officials

1324 Now that war comes home to you, you feel very different. You deprecate its horrors, but did not feel them when you sent car-loads of soldiers and ammunition and molded shells and shot to carry war into Kentucky and Tennessee, and desolate the homes of hundreds and thousands of good people who only asked to live in peace at their old homes and under the Government of their inheritance.

— 12 September 1864, letter to Atlanta city officials

1325 To be sure, I have made war vindictively; war is war, and you can make nothing else of it; but Hood knows as well as anyone I am not brutal or inhuman.

— mid-September 1864, remark to Bishop Henry C. Lay

1326 I have said to them that some of the people of Georgia are engaged in rebellion, begun in error and perpetuated in pride.

— 17 September 1864, dispatch to Lincoln

1327 We ought to ask our country for the largest possible armies that can be raised, as so important a thing as the self-existence of a great nation should not be left to the fickle chances of war.

— 20 September 1864, letter to Grant

1328 The condition of the prisoners at Andersonville has always been present to my mind, and could I have released them I would have felt more real satisfaction than to have won another battle.

— 22 September 1864, letter to James E. Yeatman of the Sanitary Commission

1329 Where a million of people find subsistence, my army won't starve.

— September 1864, letter to Halleck

1330 Hold fast. We are coming.

— 4 October 1864, flag signal to John M. Corse at Allatoona; in full, "General Sherman says hold fast. We are coming," sent by Sherman's signal officer; the quotation generated the hymn "Hold the Fort; I am Coming"

1331 Until we can repopulate Georgia, it is useless for us to occupy it; but the utter destruction of its roads, houses, and people, will cripple their military resources.

— 9 October 1864, telegram to Grant

1332 I can make this march, and make Georgia howl!

— 9 October 1864, telegram to Grant

1333 I propose to demonstrate the vulnerability of the South and make its inhabitants feel that war and individual ruin are synonymous terms.

— 20 October 1864, letter to George H. Thomas

1334 Our armies are merely paper armies. I have 40,000 Cavalry on paper but less than 5,000 in fact.

— 27 October 1864, letter to his wife

1335 The army will forage liberally on the country during the march....Soldiers must not enter the dwellings of the inhabitants, or commit any trespass.
— 9 November 1864, Special Field Order No. 120

1336 In districts and neighborhoods where the army is unmolested, no destruction of such property should be permitted; but should guerrillas or bushwhackers molest our march, or should the inhabitants burn bridges, obstruct roads, or otherwise manifest local hostility, then army commanders should order and enforce a devastation more or less relentless, according to the measure of such hostility.
— 9 November 1864, Special Field Order No. 120

1337 The true way to be popular with troops is not to be free and familiar with them, but to make them believe you know more than they do.
— 11 November 1864, remark to Bishop Henry C. Lay

1338 I never saw a more confident army. The soldiers think I know everything and that they can do anything.
— 16 December 1864, letter to his wife

1339 I beg to present you as a Christmas gift the City of Savannah with 150 heavy guns & plenty of ammunition & also about 25,000 bales of cotton.
— 22 December 1864, telegram to President Lincoln

1340 The whole army is burning with an insatiable desire to wreak vengeance upon South Carolina. I almost tremble at her fate, but feel that she deserves all that seems in store for her.
— 24 December 1864, letter to Halleck

1341 During the war, the military is superior to civil authority, and, where interests clash, the civil must give way.
— 26 December 1864, special field order when he occupied Savannah

1342 Not more than two newspapers will be published in Savannah; their editors and proprietors will be held to the strictest accountability, and will be punished severely, in person and property, for any libelous publication, mischievous matter, premature news, exaggerated statements, or any comments whatever upon the acts of the constituted authorities.
— 26 December 1864, special field order when he occupied Savannah

1343 No city was ever occupied with less disorder or more system than this of Savannah, and it is a subject of universal comment that though an army of 60,000 men lay camped around it, women and children of an hostile people walk its streets with as much security as they do in Philadelphia.
— 31 December 1864, letter to Thomas Ewing

1344 I will accept no commission that would tend to create a rivalry with Grant. I want him to hold what he has earned and got. I have all the rank I want.
— 22 January 1865, letter to his brother

1345 Poor North Carolina will have a hard time, for we sweep the country like a swarm of locusts. Thousands may perish, but they now realize that war means something else than vain glory and boasting.
— 9 April 1865, letter to his wife

1346 A little more labor, a little more toil on our part, and the great race is won, and our Government stands regenerated, after four long years of bloody war.
— 12 April 1865, announcement to his troops of Lee's surrender

1347 I don't fear an assassin, though I would prefer...to get my quietus in a more honest way, in open manly fight.
— 18 April 1865, letter to his wife

1348 I have replies from Washington to my communications of April 18th. I am instructed to limit my operations to your immediate command, and not to attempt civil negotiations. I therefore demand the surrender of your army on the same terms as were given to General Lee at Appomattox, April 9th instant, purely and simply.
— 24 April 1865, note to Joseph E. Johnston

1349 I have never in my life questioned or disobeyed an order, though many and many a time have I risked my life, my health, and reputation in obeying orders, or even hints, to execute plans and purposes not to my liking.
— 28 April 1865, letter to Grant

1350 The capitulation of Johnston's army at Greensboro completes my Campaign.
— 28 April 1865, letter to his wife

1351 The mass of the people south will never trouble us again. They have suffered terrifically, and I now feel disposed to befriend them.
— 28 April 1865, letter to his wife

1352 I am not yet prepared to receive the negro on terms of political equality for the reasons that it will arouse passions and prejudices at the North, which superadded to the causes yet dormant at the South, might rekindle the war whose fires are now dying out, and by skillful management might be kept down.
— 6 May 1865, letter to Salmon P. Chase

1353 Washington is as corrupt as Hell, made so by the looseness and extravagance of war. I will avoid it as a pest house.
— 8 May 1865, letter to his wife

1354 The legitimate object of war is a more perfect peace.
— 20 July 1865, speech in St. Louis, Missouri

PRIVATE SHIELD

Private Shield was a member of the Virginia Light Artillery.

1355 Now I lay me down to sleep,
While gray-backs oe'r my body creep;
If I should die before I wake,
I pray the Lord their jaws to break.
— humorous prayer

HENRY HOPKINS SIBLEY

Born 25 May 1816 in Natchitoches, Louisiana. West Point class of 1838. Before the Civil War, he invented the Sibley tent. He was promoted to major in the United States Army on 13 May 1861, and on the same day he resigned. Joining the Confederate forces, he became a colonel (16 May 1861) and brigadier general (17 June 1861). After the war, he was a general of artillery for the khedive of Egypt, and in his late years he was a lecturer. Died 23 August 1886 in Fredericksburg, Virginia

1356 To my old comrades in arms, still in the ranks of the usurpers of their Government and liberties, I appeal in the name of former friendship: Drop at once the arms which degrade you into the tools of tyrants, renounce their service, and array yourselves under the colors of justice and freedom!
— 20 December 1861, proclamation to the people of New Mexico

JOHN T. SIBLEY

Sibley was a Confederate soldier.

1357 It distresses me at times when I am cool and capable of reflection to think how indifferent we become in the hour of battle when our fellow men fall around us by scores....My God what kind of a people will we be?
— 10 March 1863, letter to E.P. Ellis

CHARLES FERGUSON SMITH

Born 24 April 1807 in Philadelphia, Pennsylvania. West Point class of 1825. Before the Civil War, he rose to lieutenant colonel (1855). During the war, he became a Union brigadier general of volunteers (August 1861), colonel in the Regular Army (9 September 1861), and major general of volunteers (21 March 1862). While boarding a boat, he scraped his leg, which became infected. He died of the infection on 25 April 1862 in Savannah, Tennessee.

1358 Obedience being the soul of military organization, I hold it the beginning and end of duty. It is the rein in hand by which the superior does his driving.
— September 1861, oral advice to Lew Wallace

1359 The chief duties of a general to his command may be classified—the enforcement of discipline—tactical instruction—care of the health of his men—and they are all important because tending to efficiency, the measure of which is the exact measure of his own efficiency.
— September 1861, oral advice to Lew Wallace

1360 Government furnishes everything actually needful to the good condition of the army; and of us—you and me, for instance—it merely asks in return that we know how to get those things, and to help us to the knowledge it has furnished a system of formal requisitions which fools call "red tape." But I pronounce it the perfection of wisdom, since by it alone the government is enabled to keep accounts, prevent waste, and assert the principle of personal responsibility.
— September 1861, oral advice to Lew Wallace

1361 As the preacher knows his Bible, as the lawyer knows his statutes, every general should know the regulations and articles of war.
— September 1861, oral advice to Lew Wallace

1362 It is not possible for a general always to see with his own eyes, or be in two places at the same time; hence the device of a staff—that is, an *alter ego* for every duty.
— September 1861, oral advice to Lew Wallace

1363 In battle a general's duties, in so far as they are reducible to rule, are—first, to fight; second, to fight to the best advantage.
— September 1861, oral advice to Lew Wallace

1364 Genius is determinable by the manner of obedience. A fort is to be taken; genius consists in finding a way to take it with the least appreciable loss. A campaign is to be planned; genius proves itself by devising the best plan; at the same time, strange as it seems, he the most capable in planning may be the most incapable in execution, making two different qualities. The great genius is he who possesses both the qualities.

— September 1861, oral advice to Lew Wallace

1365 Battle is the ultimate to which the whole life's labor of an officer should be directed. He may live to the age of retirement without seeing a battle; still he must always be getting ready for it exactly as if he knew the hour of the day it is to break upon him. And then, whether it come late or early, he must be willing to fight—he *must* fight.

— September 1861, oral advice to Lew Wallace

1366 No terms with traitors, by God!

— 16 February 1862, reply when Ulysses S. Grant asked for Smith's opinion about what surrender terms to offer the Confederate commander at Fort Donelson; Smith's answer became Grant's famous "unconditional surrender" note

JAMES E. SMITH

Smith was a captain with the 4th New York Battery when he made the following statements.

1367 Give them hell! Give them solid shot! Damn them, give them anything!

— 2 July 1863, order to his gunners at Gettysburg as his supply of canister ran low

1368 For God's sake, men, don't let them take my guns away from me!

— 2 July 1863, plea to his men at Gettysburg as Confederates approached

SOUTHERN ILLUSTRATED NEWS

The Southern Illustrated News *was a newspaper in Richmond, Virginia.*

1369 Unless our farmers and planters put forth their utmost endeavors, there will be something like a famine in the land. It is strange that legislation should be needed in a case like this. None would be if there were no impressments, and no Yankee souls in Southern bodies.

— 14 March 1863

EDWIN MCMASTERS STANTON

Born 19 December 1814 in Steubenville, Ohio. Lawyer who served as attorney general of the United States (1860-61) and as secretary of war (1862-68). Died 24 December 1869 in Washington, D.C.

1370 This army has got to fight or run away;...the champagne and oysters on the Potomac must be stopped.
> — 24 January 1862, letter to Charles A. Dana

1371 We have had no war; we have not even been playing war.
> — 2 February 1862, letter to Dana, concerning the lack of aggressiveness by Union military leaders

1372 Battles are to be won, now, and by us, in the same and only manner that they were ever won by any people since the days of Joshua—by boldly pursuing and striking the foe.
> — 19 February 1862, letter to the *New York Tribune*

1373 Here is the fate of this whole republic at stake, and here is the man around whom it all centers, on whom it all depends, turning aside from this monumental issue to read the God damned trash of a silly mountebank!
> — 11 October 1864, comment to Charles A. Dana, concerning President Lincoln's reading a book by the humorist Petroleum V. Nasby

1374 Now he belongs to the ages.
> — 15 April 1865, attributed comment at President Lincoln's death

EDMUND CLARENCE STEDMAN

Born 8 October 1833 in Hartford, Connecticut. Poet, essayist, and literary critic. During the Civil War, he was a war correspondent with the New York World. *After the war, he had a seat on the New York Stock Exchange and wrote in his spare time. Died 18 January 1908 in New York City.*

1375 Before we can possess and advance beyond the scientific intrenchments with which the skill of disloyal officers has made those Virginia forests so fearfully and mysteriously deathful to our patriotic soldiery, we must discover the executive leader whose genius shall oppose new modes of subduing a novel, and thus far successful method of warfare, and whose alert action shall carry his devices into resistless effect.
> — 21 July 1861, article after the Union defeat at 1st Bull Run

ALEXANDER HAMILTON STEPHENS

Born 11 February 1812 in Taliaferro County, Georgia. Before the Civil War, he was a lawyer and politician. During the war, he served as the vice president of the Confederacy. After the war, he returned to law and politics, being elected to the United States Congress and to the Georgia governorship. Died 4 March 1883 in Atlanta, Georgia

1376 Our new government's foundations are laid, its cornerstone rests, upon the great truth that the Negro is not equal to the white man, that slavery—subordination to the superior race—is his natural and normal condition.
— 21 March 1861, speech

1377 Nothing could be more unwise than for a free people, at any time, under any circumstances, to give up their rights under the vain hope and miserable delusion that they might thereby be enabled to defend them.
— 29 August 1863, letter to Howell Cobb, who had proposed a Confederate dictator

1378 But if the people quietly yield the citadel of their liberties they are lost forever. Liberty once lost will never be recovered without blood.
— 12 March 1864, letter to Herschel V. Johnson

1379 Tell me not to put confidence in the president! That he will never abuse the power attempted to be lodged in his hands! The abuses may not be by the president. He will not execute the military orders that will be given. This will necessarily devolve upon subordinates, scattered all over the country, from the Potomac to the Rio Grande. He would have to possess two superhuman attributes to prevent abuses—omniscience and omnipresence....Why put it in the power of any man on earth to order the arrest of another on a simple charge to which nobody will swear? Who is safe under such a law?...I look upon this habeas corpus suspension act as unwise, impolitic, unconstitutional, and dangerous to public liberty.
— 16 March 1864, speech to Georgia legislature

1380 Away with the idea of getting independence first and looking after liberty afterward. Our liberties once lost, may be lost forever.
— 16 March 1864, speech to Georgia legislature

GEORGE HUME STEUART

Born 24 August 1828 in Baltimore, Maryland. West Point class of 1848. In April 1861, he resigned as a captain in the United States Army. During the Civil War, he became a Confederate captain (spring 1861), lieutenant colonel (spring

1861), colonel (21 July 1861), and brigadier general (6 March 1861). After the war, he was a farmer. Died 22 November 1903 in South River, Maryland.

1381 My poor boys! My poor boys!
— 3 July 1863, exclamation after defeat at Gettysburg

WILLIAM R. STILLWELL

Stillwell was a Confederate soldier from Georgia

1382 I have but little or no fears that the Yanks will ever git down to whare you are, but I think that you will be pesterde by our own soldiers...strowling about...and stealing your chickens, etc. I had almost as leave have the Yanks around my hous as our own men, except they will not insult ladies.
— 8 July 1864, letter to his wife

SAMUEL STORROW

Storrow was a Union soldier.

1383 All the fresh meat we had came in the hard bread...and I preferring my game cooked, used to toast my biscuits.
— 26 November 1862, letter to his parents

HARRIET BEECHER STOWE

Born 14 June 1811 in Litchfield, Connecticut. Her original name was Harriet Elizabeth Beecher, and one of her brothers was Henry Ward Beecher. She married Calvin Stowe, an educator. Harriet Beecher Stowe wrote many books, including Uncle Tom's Cabin *(first published serially, 1851-52). Died 1 July 1896 in Hartford, Connecticut.*

1384 Slavery will be sent out by this agony. We are only in the throes and ravings of the exoricsm. The roots of the cancer have gone everywhere, but they must die—will.
—31 July 1862, letter to the Duchess of Argyll

GEORGE TEMPLETON STRONG

Born 26 January 1820 in New York City. Lawyer who, during the Civil War, was the treasurer of the United States Sanitary Commission. Died 21 July 1875 in New York City.

1385 All the indications are that this treasonable inflammation—*secessionitis*—keeps on making steady progress week by week.
—31 January 1861, diary

1386 I think there's a clank of metal in it.
— 5 March 1861, diary entry on President Lincoln's 1st Inaugural Address

1387 The bird of our country is a debilitated chicken, disguised in eagle feathers. We have never been a nation; we are only an aggregate of communities, ready to fall apart at the first serious shock and without a centre of vigorous national life to keep us together.
— 11 March 1861, diary

1388 It's a notable coincidence that the first blood in this great struggle is drawn by Massachusetts men on the anniversary of Lexington. This is a continuation of the war that Lexington opened—a war of democracy against oligarchy.
— 19 April 1861, diary entry on an incident in which a Massachusetts regiment had been attacked by a Baltimore mob

1389 I never knew before what rankness of stench can be emitted by unwashed humanity....It poisons the whole building and, of course, prevails in a concentrated form in the story they occupy, where it is abolutely stercoraceous and of ammoniacal intensity—nauseous and choking. It half strangles me as I go upstairs.
— 28 May 1861, diary entry on billeted soldiers in his office building

1390 Today will be known as BLACK MONDAY. We are utterly and disgracefully routed, beaten, whipped by secessionists.
— 22 July 1861, diary entry after 1st Bull Run

1391 Scrape the "Southern Gentleman's" skin, and you will find a second-rate Comanche underneath it.
— 25 July 1861, diary

1392 We are not yet fighting in earnest, *not even yet.* Our sluggish, good-natured, pachydermatous Northern people requires a deal of kicking to heat its blood.
— 15 August 1861, diary

1393 We have been humbugged by the rebels. Their position at Centreville is strong..., but their works on the crest of the hill were flimsy and armed with logs painted black instead of heavy guns.
> — 16 March 1862, diary

1394 Emancipation in the District of Columbia has passed both Houses by more than two to one....Only the damnedest of "damned abolitionists" dreamed of such a thing a year ago. Perhaps the name of abolitionist will be less disgraceful a year hence. John Brown's "soul's a-marching on," with the people after it.
> — 12 April 1862, diary

1395 Stalwart young vixens and withered old hags were swarming everywhere, all cursing the "bloody draft" and egging on their men to mischief.
> — 13 July 1863, diary entry on the New York City draft riots

1396 She deserves it all. Sowing the wind was an exhilarating pastime. Shelling Anderson out of Sumter was pleasant; resisting the whirlwind is less agreeable; to be *shelled back* is a bore.
> — 29 December 1863, diary entry on the Union bombing of Charleston, South Carolina

1397 Could we but inspire our people with one-hundredth of the earnestness and resolution the rebel leaders shew, all would be well, and that right early.
> — 6 August 1864, diary

1398 Even our comparatively intelligent mechanics (or many of them) are too brutally stupid to see that Lincoln is their representative and is fighting their battle against "Little Mac," the champion of sympathy with and concession to a rebellion that asserts the rightful supremacy of capital over labor.
> — 17 September 1864, diary

JAMES EWELL BROWN STUART

Born 6 February 1833 in Patrick County, Virginia. Known as J.E.B. (or "Jeb") Stuart. West Point class of 1854. He rose to captain in the United States Army before resigning in May 1861. Stuart joined the Virginia forces as a lieutenant colonel (10 May 1861) and then, in the Confederate army, became a captain (24 May 1861), colonel (16 July 1861), brigadier general (24 September 1861), and major general (25 July 1862). Mortally wounded 11 May 1864 at Yellow Tavern, he died the following day in Richmond, Virginia.

1399   We gallop toward the enemy, and trot away, always.
> — summer 1861, advice to his new troops

1400   The noble, the chivalric, the *gallant* Pelham, is no more.
> — 19 March 1863, general order announcing the death of John Pelham

1401   Troops should be taught to take pride in other branches of service than their own. Officers, particularly general officers, should be the last, by word or example, to inculcate in the troops of their commands a spirit of jealousy and unjust detraction toward other arms of service, where all are mutually dependent and mutually interested, with functions differing in character but not in importance.
> — 25 April 1863, report on the campaign in northern Virginia (16 August to 2 September 1862)

1402   Go back! go back! and do your duty, as I have done mine, and our country will be safe. Go back! Go back!
> — 11 May 1864, exhortation to his retreating troops after he had been mortally wounded at Yellow Tavern

1403   I had rather die than be whipped.
> — 11 May 1864, statement to his men

1404   Go back to the front. I will be well taken care of. I want you to do your duty to your country as I always have through my life.
> — 11 May 1864, order to his men

1405   I must be prepared for another world.
> — 12 May 1864, remark to Henry B. McClellan

1406   I am going fast now. I am resigned. God's will be done.
> — 12 May 1864, last words

CHARLES SUMNER

Born 6 January 1811 in Boston, Massachusetts. Lawyer, abolitionist lecturer, and United States senator (1851-74). Died 11 March 1874 in Washington, D.C.

1407   Hand of iron: velvet glove.
> — March 1861, remark to Charles Francis Adams, Jr., concerning President Lincoln's 1st Inaugural Address

1408 Whether the Union stands or falls, I believe the profession of arms will henceforth be more desirable and more respected than it has been hitherto.

> — April 1861

1409 These are dark hours.

> — January 1863, comment on the bad reaction to the Emancipation
> Proclamation

1410 *We are too victorious.* I fear more from our victories than from our defeats.

> — 31 July 1863, letter to John Bright after Union wins at Gettysburg
> and Vicksburg; Sumner feared that Northerners would become
> satisfied with military success and ignore his goal of abolishing
> slavery

1411 Where Slavery is, there Liberty cannot be; and where Liberty is, there Slavery cannot be.

> — 5 November 1864, speech in New York City

GEORGE WILLIAM TAYLOR

Born 1808 in New Jersey. As a young man, he served in both the navy and the army before turning to mining and manufacturing. During the Civil War, he became a Union colonel (4 June 1861) and brigadier general (9 May 1862). Wounded 27 August 1862 during the 2nd Bull Run campaign, he died 31 August.

1412 With their comrades falling around they stood up like a wall of iron, losing over one-third of their number, and gave not an inch of ground until their ammunition was expended and the retrograde movement became general.

> — 4 July 1862, report on Gaines's Mill

TEMPERANCE ASSOCIATION OF MUSKINGAM COUNTY, OHIO

The Temperance Association of Muskingam County, Ohio, wrote to President Lincoln through a committee consisting of A.A. Guthrie, John Taylor, Jr., and Henry Bandy.

1413 We greatly fear that many officers have become addicted to habits of intemperance, and are not only leading their men by example, into ruinous

habits of vice, but by their recklessness, and unfitness to command, have occasioned the needless sacrifice of thousands of valuable lives.
— 4 December 1863, letter to President Lincoln

GEORGE HENRY THOMAS

Born 31 July 1816 in Southampton County, Virginia. West Point class of 1840. During the Civil War, he became a Union lieutenant colonel (25 April 1861), colonel (3 May 1861), brigadier general of volunteers (3 August 1861), major general of volunteers (25 April 1862), brigadier general in the Regular Army (27 October 1863), and major general in the Regular Army (15 December 1864). After the war, he remained in the army. Died 28 March 1870 in San Francisco.

1414 This army does not retreat.
— 31 December 1862, attributed comment at Stones River

1415 Mix 'em up. I'm *tired* of States' Rights.
— 26 November 1863, reply to a chaplain who had asked if the dead should be buried by state

1416 I am well aware that extreme outposts are always exposed, and for that reason they should be sleeplessly vigilant. If we do not run risks we never shall know anything of the enemy.
— 24 April 1864, message to Absalom Baird

HENRY J.H. THOMPSON

Thompson was a Union soldier.

1417 To tell the plain truth we are between a sh-t and a sweat out here.
— summer 1861, letter to his wife, from "Camp Sh-t"

THEODORE TILTON

Born 2 October 1835 in New York City. A journalist who, during the Civil War years, worked for The Independent, *an abolitionist periodical. Died 25 May 1907 in Paris, France.*

1418 *God bless you* for a *good deed!*
— 24 September 1862, letter to President Lincoln after the preliminary Emancipation Proclamation

HENRY TIMROD

Born 8 December 1828 in Charleston, South Carolina. Known as the Poet Laureate of the Confederacy. Died 7 October 1867 in Columbia, South Carolina.

1419   At last, we are / A nation among nations; and the world / Shall soon behold in many a distant port / Another flag unfurled! / Now, come what may, whose favor need we court? / And, under God, whose thunder need we fear?

> — February 1861, poem published 23 February 1861 as "Ode on Occasion of the Meeting of the Southern Congress" in the *Charleston Daily Courier* and 31 January 1862 in the same newspaper under its permanent title, "Ethnogenesis"

1420   Fling down thy gauntlet to the Huns,
And roar the challenge from thy guns;
Then leave the future to thy sons,
Carolina!

> — 8 March 1862, "Carolina," poem published in the *Charleston Daily Courier*

1421   Calm as that second summer which precedes
    The first fall of the snow,
In the broad sunlight of heroic deeds,
    The city bides the foe.

....

God has inscribed her doom;
And, all untroubled in her faith, she waits
    The triumph or the tomb.

> — 3 December 1862, "Charleston," poem published in the *Charleston Mercury*

ROBERT AUGUSTUS TOOMBS

Born 2 July 1810 in Wilkes County, Georgia. Before the Civil War, he was a lawyer and politician. During the war, he was briefly the Confederate secretary of state and then served as a brigadier general (19 July 1861 to 4 March 1863). During the rest of the war, he criticized the Confederate government. After the war, he returned to his law practice. Died 15 December 1885 in Washington, Georgia.

1422   Can you get in here, sir? That's the Department of State, sir!

> — February 1861, angry response, while pointing to his hat, to an office seeker

1423 You will wantonly strike a hornet's nest which extends from mountains to ocean, and legions, now quiet, will swarm out and sting us to death. It is unnecessary; it puts us in the wrong; it is fatal.

> — 10 April 1861, oral warning to Jefferson Davis during debate about the proposed firing on Fort Sumter

1424 The army is dying...and it will not survive the winter. Set this down in your book, and set down opposite to it its epitaph, "*died of West Point.*"

> — September 1861, letter to Alexander H. Stephens, referring to the caution of professional soldiers

1425 We have patched a new government with old cloth, we have tied the living to the dead.

> — September 1861, letter to Alexander H. Stephens

1426 Jeff Davis can make a general, but it takes God Almighty to make a soldier.

> — 30 August 1862, attributed remark to his men at 2nd Bull Run

PRESCOTT TRACY

Tracy was a Union soldier with the 82nd New York.

1427 For a man to find, on waking, that his comrade by his side was dead, was an occurrence too common to be noted. I have seen death in almost all the forms of the hospital and battlefield, but the daily scenes in Camp Sumter exceeded in the extremity of misery all my previous experience.

> — 1864, deposition concerning his term as a prisoner at Andersonville (Camp Sumter), Georgia

ISAAC RIDGEWAY TRIMBLE

Born 15 May 1802 in Culpepper County, Virginia. West Point class of 1822. He resigned from the army in 1832 to work as a railroad engineer. During the Civil War, he became a colonel in the Virginia state forces (May 1861) and then a Confederate army brigadier general (9 August 1861) and major general (23 April 1863, to rank from 17 January). After the war, he returned to engineering. Died 2 January 1888 in Baltimore, Maryland.

1428 If the troops I had the honor to command today couldn't take that position, all hell can't take it.

> — 3 July 1863, comment at Gettysburg

JOHN BASIL TURCHIN

Born 30 January 1822 in Russia. His original name was Ivan Vasilevitch (or Vasilovitch) Turchininoff (or Turchinoff). He rose to colonel in the Russian army before immigrating to the United States in 1856. During the Civil War, he became a Union colonel (17 June 1861) and brigadier general (6 August 1862, to rank from 17 July). Ill health forced him to resign in October 1864. After the war, he was a lawyer, civil engineer, and solicitor of patents. Died in an insane asylum 19 June 1901 in Anna, Illinois.

1429   I shut mine eyes for von hour.

> — May 1862, remark to his troops, inviting them to loot and burn Athens, Alabama, as punishment for the actions of local guerrillas

JOHN TYLER

Born 29 March 1790 in Charles City County, Virginia. Lawyer and politician. During 1841-45 he was president of the United States. Died 18 January 1862 in Richmond, Virginia.

1430   The contest into which we enter is one full of peril, but there is a spirit abroad in Virginia which cannot be crushed until the life of the last man is trampled out.

> — April 1861, letter to his wife

WILLIAM H. UNDERWOOD

Underwood was a lawyer who had worked with Abraham Lincoln in Illinois.

1431   Prosecute this war with the utmost vigor and put down this accursed rebellion against God and man, and posterity north and south will bless you forever.

> — 6 December 1863, letter to President Lincoln

THEODORE FRELINGHUYSEN UPSON

Born 5 May 1845 in Orland, Steuben County, Indiana. His original name was James Madison Doyne; his parents died when he was very young, and his adoptive parents gave him his permanent name. In April 1862, at the age of 16, he joined the 100th Indiana. After the war, he manufactured carriages and wrote a book about his experiences in the conflict, partly from memory and partly from his wartime journal and letters. He lived in Lima (now called Howe), Indiana. Died 29 January 1919.

1432 If a fellow wants to go with a girl now he had better enlist. The girls sing "I Am Bound to Be a Soldier's Wife or Die an Old Maid."
— 6 July 1862, journal

1433 Every one was given a suit, hat, coat, pants and shoes—also shirts and drawers....Most of the boys had never worn drawers and some did not know what they were for and some of the old soldiers who are here told them they were for an extra uniform to be worn on parade and they half believed it.
— 1 August 1862, letter home

1434 It looked pretty hard to see him without any coffin or box, wrapped in his blanket and buried in a shallow grave without ever a prayer or a shot fired over him. But we are too busy to spend much time over the dead.
— 8 January 1863, journal

1435 Good officers know that when wine is in, wit is out. They know too that the men distrust and have no confidence in an intemperate officer, in fact will make fun of him. And an officer whose men make fun of him had better resign as some *have done*, for his usefulness is at an end.
— 2 April 1864, letter to his mother

A.L.P. VAIRIN

Vairin was an orderly sergeant with the 2nd Mississippi.

1436 Made my first detail...for guard duty to which most men object because they said they did not enlist to do guard duty but to fight the Yankies—all fun and frolic.
— 1 May 1861, diary

CLEMENT LAIRD VALLANDIGHAM

Born 29 July 1820 in New Lisbon, Ohio. Lawyer and politician. During the Civil War, he was a well-known copperhead who was banished to the Confederacy in 1863 by President Lincoln. He returned to the United States in 1864 and practiced law after the war. Died 17 June 1871 in Lebanon, Ohio.

1437 The Constitution as it is, the Union as it was.
— May 1862, campaign slogan

1438 I may die for the cause, but the immortal fire shall outlast the humble organ which conveys it.

> — 1862, comment during his campaign for the United States Congress

ZEBULON BAIRD VANCE

Born 13 May 1830 on Reems Creek, near Asheville, Buncombe County, North Carolina. Lawyer and politician. During the Civil War, he became a Confederate captain (3 May 1861) and colonel (27 August 1861). He then served as governor of North Carolina (1862-66, and 1876-78) and United States senator (1879-94). Died 14 April 1894 in Washington, D.C.

1439 Drenched with rain, blistered feet, without sleep, many sick and wounded, and almost naked, they toiled on through the day and all the weary watches of the night without murmuring, cheerfully and with subordination, evincing most thoroughly those high qualities in adversity which military men learn to value still more than courage upon the field.

> — 17 March 1862, report on New Bern

1440 If God Almighty had yet in store another plague worse than all others which he intended to have let loose on the Egyptians in case Pharoah still hardened his heart, I am sure it must have been a regiment or so of half-armed, half-disciplined Confederate cavalry.

> — 1863, letter to the War Department, concerning cavalry thefts from civilians

MRS. SARAH H. VANDEGRIFT

Mrs. Vandegrift was a civilian from Chester, Pennsylvania.

1441 I have called on you for some help I am a widir woman with sixth children I was doing pirty well but since this war bisness commence it has cost me a good bit of truble I am willing to do with less for the sake of are union to stand I want you please to help me a little as I standly badly in need of som help.

> — 8 July 1861, letter to President Lincoln

EARL VAN DORN

Born 17 September 1820 near Port Gibson, Mississippi. West Point class of 1842. He resigned from the United States Army as a major on 3 January 1861. During the Civil War, he became a brigadier general (c. January 1861) and major general (c. February 1861) of Mississippi state troops and then a Confederate colonel (16 March 1861), brigadier general (5 June 1861), and major general (19 September 1861). Murdered on 7 May 1863 (by Dr. George B. Peters for either personal or political reasons) at Spring Hill, Tennessee.

1442 So many mistakes have occurred during this war by the similarity of flags that I have had a battle-flag made, one of which I send you for our army.

> — 7 February 1862, letter to Sterling Price

1443 In the recent operations against the enemy on Sugar Creek I found the want of military knowledge and discipline among the higher officers to be so great as to counteravail their gallantry and the fine courage of their troops.

> — 17 March 1862, letter from Arkansas to Samuel Cooper

1444 I cannot convey to you a correct idea of the crudeness of the material with which I have to deal in organizing an army out here. There is an absolute want of any degree of sound military information, and even an ignorance of the value of such information.

> — 17 March 1862, letter from Arkansas to Samuel Cooper

1445 I hate all men, and were it not for the women, I should not fight at all.

> — 1863, attributed remark to a young woman who had advised him to stay away from women during the war

ELI VEAZIE

Veazie was a Union soldier from Massachusetts.

1446 I had a gay old time I tell you. Lager Beer and a horse and Buggy [and] in the evening Horizontal Refreshments or in Plainer words Riding a Dutch gal—had a good time generally I tell you.

> — 20 April 1863, letter to Jeremiah Norris, concerning Veazie's visit to Washington, D.C.

VICKSBURG DAILY CITIZEN

The Vicksburg Daily Citizen *was a newspaper in Vicksburg, Mississippi.*

1447 The great Ulysses—the Yankee Generalissimo, surnamed Grant—has expressed his intention of dining in Vicksburg on Saturday next, and celebrating the 4th of July by a grand dinner....Ulysses must get into the city before he dines in it. The way to cook a rabbit is "first catch the rabbit."

> — 2 July 1863 (composed by Confederates; printed by Union forces 4 July 1863)

1448 The banner of the Union floats over Vicksburg. Gen. Grant has "caught the rabbit."

> — 4 July 1863, "Note" composed by Union forces and added after the previous quotation

CHARLES SHIELS WAINWRIGHT

Born 31 December 1826 in New York, New York. Before the Civil War, he was a farmer. During the war, he became a Union major (17 October 1861), lieutenant colonel (30 April 1862), colonel (1 June 1862), and brevet brigadier general (1 August 1864). After the war, he returned to farming. Died 13 September 1907 in Washington, D.C.

1449 It is astonishing how little snap men have generally. I suppose we have as good a lot of officers as any regiment among the volunteers;...yet I have not come across more than half a dozen in the lot who can get fairly wakened up. Their orders come out slow and drawling, and then they wait patiently to see them half-obeyed in a laggard manner, instead of making the men jump to it sharp, as if each word of the order was a prod in their buttocks.

> — 12 December 1861, diary

1450 Whatever may have been the cause, whether it was having so much to do, or whether it was excitement, or both together. I know not, but I cannot recall having felt the least personal fear while under fire....I certainly never was more conscious nor did my mind ever see things more coolly or reason clearer. As to seeing men shot, dead or dying, I had no feeling but one of perfect indifference. When Lieutenant Eakin fell against me, and cried out that he was "a dead man," I had *no* more feeling for him, than if he had tripped over a stump and fallen; nor do I think it would have been different had he been my brother.

> — 5 May 1862, diary

1451 Fighting a battle, I find, is the smallest part of a campaign. The repairing of damages, writing reports, and getting ready to go at it again is infinitely more fatiguing.

> — 7 May 1862, diary

1452 In every respect the two armies are so well balanced that the assaulting party is sure to fall if the other has time to post itself and do anything at entrenching.

— 4 July 1863, diary

WILLIAM HENRY TALBOT WALKER

Born 26 November 1816 in Augusta, Georgia. West Point class of 1837. He resigned from the United States Army as a captain on 20 December 1860. During the Civil War, he became a major general of Georgia troops (April 1861), Confederate army brigadier general (May 1861), Georgia major general again (October 1861), Confederate brigadier general again (March 1863), and Confederate major general (to rank from 23 May 1863). Killed in action 22 July 1864 at Atlanta.

1453 Hood has "gone up like a rocket." It is to be hoped that he will not come down like a stick.

— July 1864, letter to his wife, concerning John Bell Hood

SAM WARD

Born 27 January 1814 in New York, New York. Northern banker and congressional lobbyist. Died 19 May 1884 in Pegli, Italy.

1454 While you are planning, these people are acting. They have been anticipating every contingency for months, perhaps years, and have concerted measures for every emergency.

— 16 April 1861, letter to George E. Baker of the State Department, concerning Southern leaders

GOUVERNEUR KEMBLE WARREN

Born 8 January 1830 in Cold Spring, New York. West Point class of 1850. When the Civil War began, he was a 1st lieutenant and later won promotions to Union lieutenant colonel (14 May 1861), captain (9 September 1861), colonel (11 September 1861), brigadier general of volunteers (26 September 1862), captain of engineers (3 March 1863), major general of volunteers (3 May 1863), and major of engineers (25 June 1864). After the war, he remained in the army. Died 8 August 1882 in Newport, Rhode Island.

1455 For thirty days now it has been one funeral procession past me, and it is too much!

— June 1864, comment to a friend after Cold Harbor

THOMAS WARRICK

Warrick was a Confederate soldier from Alabama.

1456 I can inform you that I have Seen the Monkey Show at last and I dont Waunt to see it no more I am satsfide with Ware Martha I Cant tell you how many ded men I did see...But I can tell you that there Was a meney a ded man where I was men Was shot Evey fashinton that you mite Call for Som had there hedes shot of and som ther armes and leges Won was sot in too in the midel I can tell you that I am tirde of Ware.
— 11 January 1863, letter to his wife, after Murfreesboro

WASHINGTON TELEGRAPH

The Washington Telegraph *was a newspaper in Washington, Arkansas.*

1457 We have despised the enemy and laughed at their threats, until, almost too late, we find ourselves in their power.
— 26 February 1862

STEPHEN HINSDALE WEED

Born 17 November 1831 in Potsdam, New York. West Point class of 1854. During the Civil War, he became a Union captain (14 May 1861) and jumped to brigadier general (6 June 1863). Killed in action 2 July 1863 at Gettysburg.

1458 I'm as dead a man as Julius Caesar.
— 2 July 1863, statement after being mortally wounded

STEPHEN MINOT WELD

Born 4 January 1842 in Jamaica Plain, Massachusetts. He graduated from Harvard in 1860 and during the Civil War became a Union second lieutenant (27 January 1862), first lieutenant. (1 November 1862), captain (1863), lieutenant colonel (2 January 1864, to rank from 25 December 1863), colonel (31 May 1864), and brevet brigadier general (13 March 1865). After the war, he was a manufacturer and lived in Dedham, Massachusetts. Died 16 March 1920.

1459 The feeling here in the army is that we have been absolutely butchered, that our lives have been periled to no purpose, and wasted.
— 21 June 1864, letter from Petersburg to his father

EDWIN WELLER

Born 9 April 1839 in Chemung County, New York. During the Civil War, he joined the 107th New York and rose to lieutenant. After the war, he was a merchant in Havana (later called Montour Falls), New York. Died 1908.

1460   When we first Started from our position as a reserve to the Woods near where the Rebels were, I thought of Home, friends, and most everything else, but as Soon as we Entered the Woods where the Shells and Balls were flying thick and fast I lost all fear..., and a Reckless don't care disposition Seemed to take possession of me. Then was two of our Company Shot down near me and Even their Shrieks and yells did not affect me in the least. This is the way I felt and I have heard other Soldiers Say the Same.
        — 6 January 1863, letter to Antoinette Watkins, whom he married
        in November 1865

1461   I am all safe, have passed through one of the most fierce and hardest fought Battles of the war but thank fortune the fatal Bullett has again missed me.
        — 5 July 1865, letter to his father, after Gettysburg

GIDEON WELLES

Born 1 July 1802 in Glastonbury, Connecticut. Journalist and politician who served as the United States secretary of the navy from 1861 to 1869. Died 11 February 1878 in Hartford, Connecticut.

1462   McClellan is an intelligent engineer and officer, but not a commander to head a great army in the field. To attack or advance with energy and power is not in him; to fight is not his forte....The study of military operations interests and amuses him. It flatters him to have on his staff French princes and men of wealth and position; he likes show, parade, and power. Wishes to outgeneral the Rebels, but not to kill and destroy them.
        — 3 September 1862, diary

1463   Halleck is heavy-headed; wants sagacity, readiness, courage, and heart. I am not an admirer of the man.
        — 5 January 1863, diary

1464   Halleck was good for nothing then, nor is he now.
        — 9 January 1863, diary

1465   Should April open, as we hope, with success at Charleston and Vicksburg, there will be a change in the deportment and conduct of England. Her arrogance and subtle aggression will be checked by our successes, and by that alone. She has no magnanimity, no sense of honor or of right. She is cowardly, treacherous, and mean, and hates and fears our strength. In that alone is our security.

— 31 March 1863, diary

1466 He has suggested nothing, decided nothing, done nothing but scold and smoke and scratch his elbows.

— 16 July 1863, diary entry on Henry W. Halleck

1467 There was...an aristocratic purpose in this Rebellion. An aristocracy of blood and wealth was to have been established. Consequently a contrary effect would work benignantly. Were a few of the leaders to be stripped of these possessions, and their property confiscated, their familes impoverished, the result would be salutary in the future.

— 1 June 1864, diary

1468 There is fatuity in nominating a general and warrior in time of war on a peace platform.

— 3 September 1864, diary entry on the Democratic nomination of George B. McClellan for president

1469 What mischief has the press performed and is still doing in the Rebel States by stimulating the people to crime by appeals to their manhood, to their courage, to all that they hold dear, to prosecute the war against the most benignant government that a people ever had!...The suppression for a period of the Rebel press in Richmond, Charleston, and one or two other points would do more than armies in putting an end to this unnatural war.

— 1 January 1865, diary

1470 Charleston and Columbia have come into our possession without any hard fighting. The brag and bluster, the threats and defiance which have been for thirty years the mental ailment of South Carolina prove impotent and ridiculous. They have displayed a talking courage, a manufactured bravery, but no more, and I think not so much inherent heroism as others. Their fulminations that their cities would be Saragossas were mere gasconade.

— 21 February 1865, diary

1471 This Rebellion which has convulsed the nation for four years, threatened the Union, and caused such sacrifice of blood and treasure may be traced in a great degree to the diseased imagination of certain South Carolina gentlemen, who some thirty and forty years since studied Scott's novels, and fancied themselves cavaliers, imbued with chivalry, a superior class, not born to labor but to command, brave beyond mankind generally, more intellectual, more generous, more hospitable, more liberal than others.

— 7 April 1865, diary

CHATHAM ROBERDEAU WHEAT

Born 9 April 1826 in Alexandria, Virginia. Before the Civil War, he was a lawyer and politician. During the war, he held the rank of major and commanded the 1st Louisiana Special Battalion, known as the "Tigers." Killed in action 27 June 1862 at Gaines's Mill, Virginia.

1472 I don't feel like dying yet.
> — 21 July 1861, comment after being seriously wounded at 1st Bull Run

1473 Bury me on the field, boys.
> — 27 June 1862, request after being mortally wounded at Gaines's Mill

WILLIAM HENRY CHASE WHITING

Born 22 March 1824 in Biloxi, Mississippi. West Point class of 1845. He rose to captain (1858) in the United States Army before resigning (20 February 1861). He became a Confederate major (early 1861), brigadier general (28 August 1861, to rank from 21 July), and major general (1863). On 15 January 1865, he was wounded at Fort Fisher. Taken prisoner, he was removed to Fort Columbus, Governors Island, New York, where he died on 10 March.

1474 What are they sending me unarmed and new recruits for? Don't want them. They will only be in my way. Can't feed them nor use them. I want re-enforcements, not recruits.
> — 16 November 1861, message to Samuel Cooper

1475 I have come to share your fate.
> — 13 January 1865, comment to William Lamb at Fort Fisher

WALT WHITMAN

Born 31 May 1819 near Huntington, Long Island, New York. A poet who, during the Civil War, served as a volunteer helper in Washington, D.C., military hospitals. Famous for his Leaves of Grass, *a book of poetry first published in 1855 but revised many times in later years. Died 26 March 1892 in Camden, New Jersey.*

1476 Beat! beat! drums!—blow! bugles! blow!
> — 1861, "Beat! Beat! Drums!" a Union recruiting poem first published 28 September 1861

1477   I had a good view of the President last evening—he looks more careworn even than usual—his face with deep cut lines, seams, & his *complexion gray*, through very dark skin, a curious looking man, very sad.
— 30 June 1863, letter to his mother

1478   Mother, one's heart grows sick of war, after all, when you see what it really is—every once in a while I feel so horrified & disgusted—it seems to me like a great slaughter-house & the men mutually butchering each other—then I feel how impossible it appears, again, to retire from this contest, until we have carried our points—(it is cruel to be so tossed from pillar to post in one's judgment).
— 7 July 1863, letter to his mother

1479   He is one of the thousands of our unknown American young men in the ranks about whom there is no record or fame, no fuss made about their dying so unknown, but I find in them the real precious & royal ones of this land, giving themselves up, aye even their young & precious lives, in their country's cause.
— 10 August 1863, letter to the parents of Erastus Haskell

JOHN GREENLEAF WHITTIER

Born 17 December 1807 in Haverhill, Massachusetts. Poet and abolitionist. His works include Snow-Bound *(1866). Died 7 September 1892 in Hampton Falls, New Hampshire.*

1480   "Shoot, if you must, this old gray head, / But spare your country's flag," she said.
— October 1863, "Barbara Frietchie," published in *Atlantic Monthly*

EDWARD K. WIGHTMAN

Wightman was a journalist who joined the 3rd New York, became a sergeant, and, at the age of 29, was killed in action on 15 January 1865 at Fort Fisher.

1481   I'd rather Johnny'd be where them eggs is breaking than me.
— 26 December 1864, letter to "Bro.," written as shells were bursting over Fort Fisher

CADMUS MARCELLUS WILCOX

Born 29 May 1824 in Wayne County, North Carolina. West Point class of 1846. On 8 June 1861, he resigned as a captain in the United States Army. During the Civil War, he became a Confederate colonel (May 1861), brigadier general

(21 October 1861), and major general (3 August 1863). After the war, he held government appointments. Died 2 December 1890 in Washington, D.C.

1482 In an hour you'll be in hell or glory.
> — 3 July 1863, comment to George E. Pickett before his charge at Gettysburg

MRS. JOSEPHINE WILCOX

Mrs. Wilcox was a civilian from Adrian, Michigan.

1483 The eagle of American liberty from her mountain eyrie has at intervals during the past few years given us faint warnings of danger. Now she swoops down on spreading pinions with unmistakable notes of alarm; her cries have reached the ears of freemen, and brave men rush to arms. She has perched on this banner which we now give to your keeping. Let your trust be in the God of battles to defend it.
> — 21 June 1861, speech to the 4th Michigan as it received its colors from the ladies of Adrian, who had made the flag

MRS. WILLIAMS

Mrs. Williams was a Union army wife at Fort Riley, Kansas.

1484 Brave heroes rest beneath this sculptured stone;
In unfair contest slain by murderous hands:
They knew no yielding to a cruel foe—
And thus, this tribute to their memory stands—
Our country's honor, and a Nation's pride;—
'Twas thus they nobly lived, and bravely died.
> — July 1864, inscription on a marble monument to 8 Union cavalrymen of the 2nd Colorado bushwhacked near Fort Riley, Kansas

CHARLES W. WILLS

Wills enlisted as a private in an Illinois regiment and became an officer during the war.

1485 The army is becoming awfully depraved. How the civilized home folks will ever be able to live with them after the war, is, I think, something of a question. If we don't degenerate into a nation of thieves, 'twill not be for lack of example set by a fair sized portion of our army. Do you remember that I

used to write that a man would no sooner lose his morality in the army than at home? I now respectfully beg to recall the remark.
— 12 December 1862, letter

DAVID WILLS

Wills was a Gettysburg resident who spearheaded the drive to establish a national cemetery in Gettysburg and planned the program for the 19 November 1863 dedication ceremonies.

1486 I am authorized by the Governors of the different States to invite you to be present and participate in these ceremonies, which will doubtless be very imposing and solemnly impressive.

It is the desire that, after the Oration, You, as Chief Executive of the Nation, formally set apart these grounds to their Sacred use by a few appropriate remarks.
— 2 November 1863, letter to President Lincoln, inviting him to the dedication of the national cemetery at Gettysburg

JAMES HARRISON WILSON

Born 2 September 1837 near Shawneetown, Illinois. West Point class of 1860. He began his Civil War service as a Union second lieutenant (10 June 1861) and rose to brigadier general (30 October 1863) and major general (21 June 1865, to date from 6 May). In 1870 he left the army to become an engineer and railroad executive. He returned to military service during the Spanish-American War. Died 23 February 1925 in Wilmington, Delaware.

1487 Let's crush the head and heart of the rebellion, and the tail can then be ground to dust or allowed to die when the sun goes down.
— 15 January 1864, letter to Charles A. Dana; the "head" was Atlanta

ROBERT CHARLES WINTHROP

Born 12 May 1809 in Boston, Massachusetts. Lawyer, orator, writer, historian, and politician. Died 16 November 1894 in Boston.

1488 A star for every State, and a State for every star.
— 1862, speech in Boston

HENRY ALEXANDER WISE

Born 3 December 1806 in Drummondtown, Virginia. Before the Civil War, he was a lawyer and politician. During the war, he became a Confederate brigadier general (5 June 1861) and major general (6 April 1865). After the war, he returned to his law practice. Died 12 September 1876 in Richmond, Virginia.

1489 The militia are nothing for warlike uses here. They are worthless who are true, and there is no telling who is true.
> — 1 August 1861, letter from Bunger's Mill, Virginia, to Robert E. Lee

1490 Our teams are shoeless, and there are but very few blacksmiths. This delays me as much as any other cause.
> — 11 August 1861, letter to Lee

1491 Disasters have come, and disasters are coming, which you alone, I fear, can repair and prevent.
> — 11 September 1861, letter to Lee

1492 Country be damned! There is no country. There has been no country, General, for a year or more. You're the country to these men. They have fought for you, without pay or clothes or care of any sort. There are still thousands of us who will die for you.
> — 7 April 1865, statement to Lee

JANE STUART WOOLSEY

Woolsey was a New York City girl.

1493 It seems as if we never were alive till now; never had a country till now. How could we ever have laughed at Fourth-of-Julys?
> — 10 May 1861, letter to a friend in Paris

1494 A friend asked an Ohio man the other day how the West was taking it. "The West?" he said, "the West is all one great Eagle-scream!"
> — 10 May 1861, letter to a friend in Paris

JOHN LORIMER WORDEN

Born 12 March 1818 in Ossining, New York. He joined the navy as a teenager and became a lieutenant in 1846. During the Civil War, he commanded the first Union ironclad, the U.S.S. Monitor, and rose to commander (12 July 1862) and captain (3 February 1863). After the war, he became a rear admiral and served as the superintendent of the United States Naval Academy. Died 18 October 1897 in Washington, D.C.

1495 I cannot see, but do not mind me. Save the *Minnesota* if you can.
— 9 March 1862, order to his crew on the *Monitor* during its battle with the C.S.S. *Virginia*; he was temporarily blinded

HENRY CLAY WORK

Born 1 October 1832 in Middletown, Connecticut. Songwriter. Died 8 June 1884 in Hartford, Connecticut.

1496 "Hurrah! hurrah! we bring the Jubilee!
Hurrah! hurrah! the flag that makes you free!"
So we sang the chorus from Atlanta to the sea,
While we were marching through Georgia.
— 1865, "Marching through Georgia," song

WILLIAM LOWNDES YANCEY

(For biography and 21 May 1861 quotation, see Ambrose Dudley Mann.)

1497 The man and the hour have met.
— 18 February 1861, speech introducing Jefferson Davis

YAZOO DAILY YANKEE

The Yazoo Daily Yankee *was a newspaper in Yazoo City, Mississippi.*

1498 Gentle stranger drop a tear
The C.S.A. lies buried here;
In youth it lived and flourished well
But like Lucifer, it fell.
Its body's here—its soul in...well,
Even if I knew I would not tell.
Rest from every care and strife,
Your death were better than your life,
And this one line shall grace your grave:
Your death gave freedom to the slave.
— 20 July 1863, lines accompanying a cut of a cemetery scene

Y-O-TO-WAH

Y-O-To-Wah was a spokesman for the Weas, Peorias, Miamis, and Piankashaws—Indian peoples from Indiana.

1499 I came to get arms and a force to guard our frontier. I told General Hunter we would gladly fight with white soldiers, and go wherever wanted....

The tomahawk is buried under our orchards, and we want to go as men. We don't want to pull the tomahawk—we would rather prune our trees....I will make a child's bargain with the Missouri rebels—if they'll let me alone, I'll let them alone....

I give my most cordial feeling to the people of Kansas and to the First and Second Kansas regiments who have fought so bravely for us.

This is my story. You can put in the pinks, and roses, and flowers.

> — 11 January 1862, statement to William P. Dole, commissioner of Indian affairs

FELIX KIRK ZOLLICOFFER

Born 19 May 1812 in Bigbyville, Maury County, Tennessee. Journalist and politician who, during the Civil War, became a brigadier general in the Tennessee state forces (April 1861) and then a brigadier general in the Confederate army (9 July 1861). Killed in action 19 January 1862 at Fishing Creek, near Mill Springs, Kentucky.

1500 The news I am receiving indicates a mischievous purpose on the part of the Federals and their leaders in Johnson County. You will seize the leaders who commit overt acts of a hostile character, as much as possible endeavoring to pursue a conciliatory course towards their misguided followers.

> — 1 September 1861, General Order No. 12, directed at W.E. Baldwin in Knoxville, Tennessee

1501 The population here is so generally hostile I cannot push spies through. The male population has nearly disappeared between here and Barboursville.

> — 26 September 1861, letter from Camp Buckner, east Tennessee, to William W. Mackall

1502 I regret to have to report that I learn that some of our soldiers committed discreditable trespasses on the property of private citizens on the route, which I will investigate and endeavor to have properly punished.

> — 30 September 1861, report on an expedition from Cumberland Ford, Kentucky

SAMUEL KOSCIUSZKO ZOOK

Born March 1822 (some sources give 1821 or 1823) in Chester County, Pennsylvania. Before the Civil War, he was a superintendent with a telegraph company. During the war, he became a lieutenant colonel with the New York state militia (7 July 1861) and then a Union colonel (19 October 1861) and brigadier general (29 November 1862). Mortally wounded 2 July 1863 at Gettysburg, he died the next day and was posthumously breveted a major general.

1503 If you can't get out of the way, lie down and we will march over you.
— 2 July 1863, command to Brigadier General James Barnes's retreating troops near the Wheat Field, Gettysburg

KEYWORD INDEX

249

aristocrats

(733) What will the aristocrats do

arm

(817) He has lost his left arm, but I have lost my right arm

armistice

(788) no armistice on sea or land, until all...are subjugated or exterminated

arms

(406) would make fine companies if there were arms for them

(503) I am sorely pressed for want of arms

(691) Arms is a profession that...requires an officer do what he fears may be wrong

(851) if the army cannot protect them, the arms will be of little use

(1266) The arms sent us are...European muskets of uncouth pattern

(1408) the profession of arms will henceforth be more desirable

army

(11) army is a great place to learn philosophy

(15) no force on earth which could resist this Army

(117) Man that is born of woman and enlists in Jackson's Army

(118) brass-mounted army

(131) our two armies ain't nothing but howling mobs

(637) The Rebel army...is now the legitimate property of the Army of the Potomac

(689) an army of the living God

(826) the eyes and ears of my army

(834) the transfer of the army into Maryland

(857) Has the army dissolved

(947) nothing I could say or do could make the Army move

(948) Our army held the war in the hollow of their hand

(1329) my army won't starve

(1334) Our armies are merely paper armies

(1444) the crudeness of the material...in organizing an army

(1452) the two armies are so well balanced

(1485) The army is becoming awfully depraved

arrest

(571) I was advised to arrest you on your return

artillery

(743) fear artillery unreasonably

assassin

(1276) to the assassin who fires from the river bank

assassinated

(271) he will be poisoned or assassinated

(880) I would rather be assassinated on this spot than to surrender

assassination

(1233) Assassination is not an American practice

Atlanta

(156) Atlanta is this great strategic point

(1311) Atlanta is ours, and fairly won

(1316) The citizens now residing in Atlanta should remove

atone

(155) I cannot live to atone

attack

(533) I propose to attack at daylight

(638) a suspension in the attack today will embolden the enemy to attack

(891) if they will not attack us, we will not attack them

(1182) why did we not attack them and drive them into the river

attacking

(1189) attacking the man in the moon

awkward

(32) this is a very awkward business

baboon

(1044) The Presdt is nothing more than a well meaning baboon

backs

(90) With their backs to the field

bad

(1192) If he be the best, they must all be exceedingly bad

KEYWORD INDEX

baggage
(447) The road to glory cannot be followed with much baggage

bands
(345) measures are scattering and scaring the bands

banner
(1210) Furl that banner

base
(1050) Never did such a change of base

battle
(337) This is my last battle
(371) if a battle is fought without many errors and failures
(522) There is the battle
(527) The battle is...to him that holds on to the end
(741) The battle is there
(1188) I was in the first battle..., and I was in the last
(1372) Battles are to be won...by boldly pursuing and striking the foe

bayonet
(322) I...will hold my position at the point of the bayonet
(525) Fix bayonets and go for them
(667) we'll give them the bayonet
(701) sweep the field with the bayonet
(1303) afraid of the sight of a dozen infantry bayonets

beast
(1245) the Valley...will have but little in it for man or beast

bed
(1179) a bed of pine boughs better than one of feathers

befriend
(1351) I now feel disposed to befriend them

behaved
(983) If the people over the river had behaved themselves

bell
(298) Seward's lettle bell reigns supreme
(1232) I can touch a bell on my right hand and order the imprisonment

Bible
(986) Both read the same Bible, and pray to the same God

big
(538) You will find him big enough

bird
(1387) The bird of our country is a debilitated chicken, disguised in eagle feathers

bitterness
(871) Do not cherish bitterness

black
(939) black soldiers...would end the rebellion at once
(1390) Today will be known as BLACK MONDAY

blame
(924) I blame you for blaming me

blankets
(312) the most of the boys are mighty anxious to get a lick at them for some blankets

blindfolded
(703) I am willing to follow him blindfolded

blizzard
(1020) Give them blizzards
(1206) give them a blizzard, and then charge with cold steel

blood
(94) A lady's thimble will hold all the blood
(177) My business is stanching blood
(251) worse than the shedding of blood
(330) we are prepared for the "needless effusion of blood"
(340) blood ran from the table into a tub
(515) sprinkle blood in the face of the people
(649) the precious blood of our sons
(858) I reciprocate your desire to avoid useless effusion of blood
(987) until every drop of blood drawn with the lash
(1092) The ground was in a perfect slop and mud with blood
(1132) The smell of blood is sickening

251

(1162) The very moment that blood is shed, old Virginia will make common cause

(1289) young bloods of the South

blow

(643) Blows, not marches, are to kill the rebellion

(874) We must strike them a blow

Blücher

(185) thou Blücher of the day

blue

(1004) His face to the sky of blue

blunder

(757) What a blunder France and England made

boasting

(798) I wish them to take a firm, dignified course, free from bravado and boasting

boat

(507) I would rather see the devil than that boat

bodies

(470) Their bodies were swollen, black, and hideously unnatural

bodyguard

(919) it is only McClellan's bodyguard

boldness

(1222) boldness in execution is nearly always necessary

boot

(1015) I never like to go into battle with one boot off

booty

(183) their war-cry is "Beauty and booty"

bore

(625) War is an organized bore

borrow

(904) does not want to use the army, I would like to borrow it

bottom

(903) The bottom is out of the tub

bowels

(146) you look like your bowels wuz so reglar

(1213) you and I are apt to be afflicted with disordered bowels

boys

(1381) My poor boys

Bragg, Braxton

(76) Bragg a Boo and Morgan, too

bragging

(347) both come out of hiding-places,...calling names and bragging

branches

(1401) Troops should be taught to take pride in other branches of service

brave

(706) all would be equally brave

breastworks

(111) fond of charging breastworks

(123) Hood's boys are great at storming breastworks

(482) I am not going to make breastworks of you

breath

(1165) when my last breath escapes me on the battle field, it will whisper your name

brick

(1027) an expression as if he had determined to drive his head through a brick wall

bridge-burner

(199) hang every bridge-burner you can catch

brigade

(675) the First Brigade in our second War of Independence

(681) I never found anything impossible with this brigade

brigadier

(1133) I shall come out of this fight a live major general or a dead brigadier

British

(1021) I hate the British government

Brown, John

(52) John Brown's body lies a-mould'ring

(1394) John Brown's "soul's a-marching on," with the people after it

bullet

(624) A bullet has a most villanous greasy slide

(781) The Rebel bullet that can kill me

(954) appeal from the ballot to the bullet

(1125) Every bullet has its billet

(1313) Is not a negro as good as a white man to stop a bullet

(1461) the fatal Bullett has again missed me

Bull Run

(498) It is a Bull Run to the Navy

bugles

(1476) blow! bugles! blow

buried

(1498) Gentle stranger drop a tear/The C.S.A. lies buried here

burn

(68) If I don't burn you, I'll be damned

burned

(325) The whole heart of the town is burned

bury

(836) bury these poor men and let us say no more about it

(1473) Bury me on the field

butchery

(342) It was not a battle; it was a butchery

Butler, Benjamin F.

(368) I...declare the said Benjamin F. Butler to be a felon, deserving of capital punishment

(379) Butler, who knows everything, controls everything, and should be held responsible for everything

(1030) Butler...is the strangest sight

Butterfield, Dan

(75) Dan, Dan, Dan Butterfield

buttocks

(1449) as if each word of the order was a prod in their buttocks

buzzards

(277) Buzzards could not eat it

capital

(1398) the supremacy of capital over labor

capture

(1248) don't capture me

carcass

(560) I look on the carcass of a man now...as I would do were it a horse or dog

carnage

(1144) one of great carnage

Carolina

(1420) leave the future to thy sons, Carolina

carpenter

(568) a carpenter who is required to build a bridge with...rotten timber

cast iron

(56) He thinks everybody's made of cast iron

casualties

(1244) I do desire resolute and actual fighting, with necessary casualties

cause

(326) a waning cause tottering on its last legs

(328) this wild adventurous work of crushing the Southern Cause

(1080) the most sacred cause that ever called men to arms

cavaliers

(1471) fancied themselves cavaliers

cavalry

(91) Whoever saw a dead cavalryman

(116) Jine the Cavalry

(523) ragtag, bobtail cavalry

(614) The cavalry constitute the eyes and ears of the army

(697) Oh, that my cavalry were in place

central idea

(444) if I came as near to the central idea of the occasion, in ten hours, as you did in ten minutes

chance

(1073) War is a game of chance

(1153) The chances are death, capture, glory, and promotion

Chancellorsville

(714) Keep closed on Chancellorsville

champagne

(1102) Keep the champagne, but return the negro

(1370) the champagne and oysters on the Potomac must be stopped

charge
(210) our men made a charge which will be the theme of the poet
(474) I will charge under my own orders
(479) Charge them both ways
(524) they don't know any better than to charge up there
(1136) their gallant unsupported charge

cheaper
(702) cheaper to feed them than to fight them
(1167) The Boys generally get it a little cheaper

Chickamauga
(1241) Remember Chickamauga

chicken
(27) A chicken could not live in that field

Christ
(352) the bulliest day since Christ

Christmas
(1339) I beg to present you as a Christmas gift the City of Savannah

cities
(436) apathy and opposition in the cities

citizens
(844) they are citizens defending their country
(868) if you make as good citizens as you have soldiers

clank
(1386) there's a clank of metal in it

coax
(1087) Don't coax the rebel chiefs, but pound them

coffin
(58) dis here iron coffin
(480) I will be in my coffin
(1434) without any coffin or box

color
(264) I never will ask the color of the man who exposes his life to protect mine

colors

(314) Receive...these colors woven by our feeble but reliant hands
(585) do you see those colors

Comanche
(1391) you will find a second-rate Comanche underneath it

coming
(513) We are coming, Father Abraham

command
(569) Give me command in the West
(682) With such interference in my command

commander
(225) changes of command and commanders
(586) a corps commander's life does not count
(819) there is the difficulty—proper commanders

commissary
(169) the "Commissary" is at fault

common people
(192) This is the common people's war

communications
(189) never to abandon our country

competency
(750) evidence of competency

compromise
(785) we will make a compromise and save slavery
(1135) the cold-blooded Puritan and the cock-hatted Huguenot and Cavalier would have made a compromise

concentrate
(187) We must give up some minor points, and concentrate our forces

conciliating
(864) do much toward conciliating our people

conciliatory
(1500) pursue a conciliatory course towards their misguided followers

concluded
(228) I concluded they ment me

creature
(363) The creature has been exalted above its creators

creeper
(780) The Virginia Creeper

criminal
(217) too great a soul to die like a criminal

cross
(1207) Cross yourselves and march forward

crow
(546) crows flying over it...will have to carry their provender
(553) we can crow loud
(1250) A crow could not fly over it without carrying his rations with him

crueler
(1294) The crueler it is the sooner it will be over

cruelty
(652) transcends, in studied and ingenious cruelty, all acts...in the dark history of war

crusade
(660) unholy crusade

Custer, George A.
(1026) Custer...looks like a circus rider gone mad

cut
(530) cut our way out

damned
(109) take the battery and be damned

danger
(317) a little spice of danger, every day, is an excellent thing
(1265) when danger threatens...I am and will be at my post

Davis, Jefferson F.
(52) hang Jeff Davis on a sour apple tree
(1217) I am amazed that any man of judgment should hope for the success of any cause in which Jefferson Davis is a leader

day
(246) the day is ours

dead

(73) Are you all dead
(304) I have felt as if all were dead within me
(408) wish them all dead
(593) dead as the clods they load
(620) I thought it would do one some good to see dead federals
(1173) if you ain't dead, get inside
(1174) Ain't dead yet
(1176) Hallo, Sam. I'm dead
(1237) we lay down among the dead
(1435) we have tied the living to the dead
(1458) I'm as dead a man as Julius Caesar

death
(69) This means death
(162) the last sleep before that of death
(860) I would rather die a thousand deaths
(1150) I have seen death in so many shapes
(1169) no escape except by death
(1270) The very object of war is to produce results by death and slaughter

deathful
(1375) forests so fearfully and mysteriously deathful

deed
(1418) God bless you for a good deed

deceive
(708) If I can deceive my own friends

defeat
(404) call a defeat a reconnaissance
(462) Any man who is prepared for defeat
(1410) I fear more from our victories than from our defeats

defeated
(839) If defeated, there will be nothing left to live for

defending
(815) no better way of defending a long line

defenseless
(1053) I have not come here to wage war upon the defenseless

defensive
(1128) we had best stick to the defensive

defer
(946) It is better that I...should defer to him

"Dixie"
(995) I have always thought "Dixie" one of the best tunes

document
(33) A poor document but a mighty act

dodge
(521) Just count each blot a dodge

dodging
(63) I believe in dodging

dog
(57) don't run like dogs
(1260) If you attempt to leave without orders,...I will shoot you like a dog

doom
(1009) the impending doom of a nation

draft
(1395) all cursing the "bloody draft"

drawers
(1433) Most of the boys had never worn drawers

dream
(652) the dream is over

drill
(1116) drill, then drill, then drill again

drummer boy
(605) the drummer boy who prayed before he died

drunk
(580) is the majority always drunk

duck
(957) confused and stunned like a duck hit on the head

dulce
(782) Dulce et decorum

duty
(61) we'll obey duty's call
(204) I died at my post doing my duty
(250) He who does his duty to the Union, does his duty to the state
(365) the measure of duty was full
(401) Success is not in my hands; to do my duty is
(432) When Duty whispers low, Thou must,/The youth replies, I can

(458) There's a hotter fire than that waiting for those who don't do their duty
(493) our duty to divest ourselves of all such feelings
(628) the duty of fighting has ceased for me
(642) No one will consider the day as ended until the duties it brings have been discharged
(723) Duty is ours; consequences are God's
(725) My duty is to obey orders
(1362) a staff—that is, an alter ego for every duty
(1402) do your duty, as I have done mine
(1404) do your duty to your country

dying
(19) Here we are dying by inches
(26) dying royally
(728) the dying fell with their faces to the foe
(791) the difference between dyeing to day and to morrow is not much but we all prefer to morrow
(1472) I don't feel like dying yet

eagle
(1483) The eagle of American liberty
(1494) the West is all one great Eagle-scream

Early, Jubal A.
(1187) Early was late

early risers
(707) I do not want to make an appointment on my staff except of such as are early risers

editors
(1342) editors and proprietors will be held to the strictest accountability

efficiency
(1359) the exact measure of his own efficiency

egg
(915) Broken eggs can never be mended
(935) broken eggs can not be mended
(990) we shall sooner have the fowl by hatching the egg than by smashing it
(1481) I'd rather Johnny'd be where them eggs is breaking than me

election
(976) he will have secured his election on such ground

elephant
(999) When you have got an elephant by the hind leg
(1226) They couldn't hit an elephant

Ellsworth, Elmer
(38) Remember Ellsworth

emancipation
(907) gradual, and not sudden emancipation, is better for all

end
(926) Whichever way it ends,...I shan't last long after it's over
(964) I shall not live to see the end

ending
(554) I feel now like ending the matter

enemy
(182) not only willing, but are anxious, to meet the enemies of our country
(283) Don't let anybody stop me except the enemy
(333) the enemy fell like grass before the mower
(339) Seeing an enemy wounded and helpless
(572) find the enemy and fight him
(588) throw the masses of your troops on the fractions of the enemy
(635) The enemy is in my power
(739) our enemies a moment ago
(778) all enemies must yield before us
(803) I begin to fear the enemy will not attack us
(821) neglect no honorable means of dividing and weakening our enemies
(823) If the enemy is there, we must attack him
(824) The enemy is here, and if we do not whip him, he will whip us
(827) The enemy is there, and I am going to strike him
(872) expect the enemy to do what he should do

(920) when you assume that you can not do what the enemy is constantly doing
(978) he did not want to hurt the enemy
(1043) the enemy have from 3 to 4 times my force
(1064) We part as friends, but on the field of battle we meet as enemies
(1258) A fatal mistake in war is to underrate...an enemy
(1272) the possession of the Mississippi River by us is an advantage to our enemy
(1297) should we treat as absolute enemies all in the South who differ from us
(1416) If we do not run risks we never shall know anything of the enemy

England
(8) Touch England through her pocket

enslaved
(196) may it wave over a nation neither enslaved nor enslaving

entrenched
(773) both parties entrenched up to the eyes

entrenching
(973) he is intrenching

entrenchments
(545) A battle with them outside of intrenchments cannot be had

equal
(265) an equal space in ranks while he lives, and an equal grave when he falls

error
(653) the one great error of your life

eternity
(465) Drive them into the Potomac or into eternity
(928) responsible through time and eternity
(933) he will yet send us all into eternity
(1205) the first bullet may send you to eternity

events
(967) events have controlled me

evil
(664) the sum of all evils
(808) this evil, which has increased instead of diminished

(810) act upon probabilities and endeavor to avoid greater evils

Europe
(2) privileged classes all over Europe
(1106) the savageries of old Europe

exorcism
(1384) We are only in the throes and ravings of the exorcism

expectations
(833) How can I fulfil the expectations of others

explosion
(41) We know that with every explosion

eyes
(1429) I shut mine eyes for von hour

face
(1175) can't get his face straightened out

failure
(961) the little I did say was not entirely a failure

fall
(78) Fall in, ye poor devils

families
(671) not permitted to go and see their wives and families

fan
(1269) fan the flames of local hatred

farewell
(867) I bid you an affectionate farewell

fatal
(1423) It is unnecessary; it puts us in the wrong; it is fatal

fate
(492) I will share the fate of my men
(1340) I almost tremble at her fate
(1475) I have come to share your fate

father
(84) Our Father who art in Washington
(100) I have seen Father Abraham and felt him
(952) The Father of Waters

fatigue

(921) what the horses of your army have done...that fatigue anything

fault
(540) the fault is not with you
(828) all this has been my fault
(830) All this has been my fault

favor
(1263) I have closely minded my business, which is a bad sign for favor

fear
(18) Pain is the only thing I should fear
(167) more to fear from the opinions of our friends than the bayonets of our enemies
(194) Fear was stronger than faith
(376) I fear it will be disastrous for our people
(443) Darkness was upon us, and Jackson was on us, and fear was on us
(700) Never take counsel of your fears
(1273) They cannot be made to love us, but may be made to fear us
(1465) She...hates and fears our strength

field
(587) I pray God I may never leave this field

fight
(21) fight some small man and lick him
(46) won't fight to free the nigger
(97) Them as wants to fight
(129) We will fight them, sir, till hell freezes
(202) he is not going to fight
(207) No victory has ever been won without bringing about a fight
(278) The edge of the fight rolled backward and forward
(280) fight men in arms, but not babes in arms
(490) We have made our last fight
(496) Shoot any man who won't fight
(543) propose to fight it out on this line
(583) I propose to fight
(584) fight without a star
(639) he must fight me on my own ground
(737) I would fight them if they were a million
(767) the oftener we are beaten the sooner we will learn to fight

(854) do my duty and fight to the last

(910) I can't spare this man; he fights

(1028) will fight while he has a division or a day's rations left

(1103) if you won't fight get out of the way

(1127) the more we fight, the less we like it

(1246) Don't cheer me. Fight

(1249) My practice has always been to fight in the front rank

(1308) fight anything that comes

(1319) If we must be enemies, let us be men, and fight it out

(1347) to get my quietus in a more honest way, in open manly fight

(1363) first, to fight; second, to fight to the best advantage

(1365) he must be willing to fight
—he must fight

(1462) to fight is not his forte

fighting

(49) enough of fighting to last my lifetime

(596) I don't quite understand what we are fighting for

(754) Fighting is a sport

(770) You'll find lovely fighting all along the line

(884) when...you cease fighting, the identical old questions...are again upon you

(1089) We are fightin' for de Union

(1392) We are not yet fighting in earnest

(1451) Fighting a battle, I find, is the smallest part of a campaign

file closers

(336) If any man runs I want the file closers to shoot him

fire

(1163) I could not fire the first gun of the war

(1438) the immortal fire shall outlast the humble organ which conveys it

firearms

(259) The Negro...has acquired a great horror of fire-arms

fired

(279) fired his pistol at my head with one hand, while he handed me his sword with the other

first

(478) got there first with the most men

fish

(582) other fish to fry

fitted

(439) a man so fitted to the event

fizzle

(1134) great things threatened only to realize fizzles

(1177) There's a fizzle

flag

(191) not the flag only, but the nation itself

(327) drop that Rebel flag

(382) If anyone attempts to haul down the American flag

(1034) the bonnie blue flag

(1095) the flag of our Union forever

(1100) Lay me down and save the flag

(1419) the world/Shall soon behold in many a distant port/Another flag unfurled

(1442) mistakes have occurred during this war by the similarity of flags

(1480) "Shoot, if you must, this old gray head,/But spare your country's flag," she said

fleeing

(407) now that the opportunity is offered, you are fleeing from it

follow

(127) We'll follow you, Marse George

folly

(1180) reaping the fruits of their folly

fool

(529) fools...bring upon themselves all the horrors of war

(629) Get down, you damn fool

forage

(1335) The army will forage liberally on the country

force

(753) My small force is melting away

(800) an effective blow by a concentration of our forces

(905) we have the greater numbers, and the enemy has the greater facility of concentrating forces

formalities
(656) formalities are absurd in the face of such realities

Forrest, Nathan B.
(310) Gen. Forrest ordered them shot down like dogs

fort
(441) a hundred rounds cannot silence a fort
(472) Nothing but God Almighty can save that fort

Fort Donelson
(532) Fort Donelson will hearafter be marked in capitals

Fort Sumter
(181) demand the evacuation of Fort Sumter
(289) he will open the fire of his batteries on Fort Sumter in one hour

fortunes
(380) not wishing to risk their lives to make fortunes for others
(381) too willing to permit his friends to make fortunes

fought
(567) You fought and stood well

4th of July
(1493) How could we ever have laughed at Fourth-of-Julys

Fredericksburg
(60) Fredericksburg
(232) the fatal field of Fredericksburg
(308) The city of Fredericksburg was a trap

free
(917) all persons held as slaves...shall be then, thenceforward, and forever free
(1055) let them...relieve me & I shall once more be a free man
(1088) a miserable creature who has no chance of being free

freedom
(387) Freedom for all, or chains for all
(849) giving immediate freedom to all who enlist
(850) We should not expect slaves to fight for prospective freedom
(980) so costly a sacrifice upon the altar of Freedom
(1200) A country good for slavery and not good for freedom

Frémont, John C.
(50) Frémont and the Union

friend
(956) that friend shall be down inside of me

fugitives
(712) a mass of disordered fugitives

fun
(603) you will see some fun
(1436) all fun and frolic

funeral
(1455) For thirty days now it has been one funeral procession

furlough
(150) I'm feeling for a furlough

fury
(1219) to restrain the fury of the noncombatants

future
(234) You have your future in your own hands

gallant
(1400) the gallant Pelham, is no more

game
(1277) You initiate the game, and...your people will regret it

general
(341) Until we have good generals, it is useless to fight battles
(686) something more is required to make a general
(744) I still rightfully hold the rank of first general
(755) Our generals will resolve never to survive a defeat

(756) Our generals never modify their reports of victories

(1193) he has earned and well merits the title of General

(1361) every general should know the regulations and articles of war

gentleman

(766) as a gentleman I felt called on to act

(1032) I will die as a gentleman

Georgia

(727) Come on, Georgia

(1331) Until we can repopulate Georgia

Gettysburg

(1079) another Gettysburg in front of us

(1185) Gettysburg will curse the Rebels

ghost

(1083) their ghosts and babies fight very well

(1195) rise to welcome his stern ghost

girl

(1432) If a fellow wants to go with a girl now he had better enlist

git

(142) a hell of a git you got

glory

(213) You have added glory to the sky

(614) Glory, glory, hallelujah

(1482) In an hour you'll be in hell or glory

going

(1406) I am going fast now

goodness

(26) real goodness is never wasted

goods

(180) we abuse the Yankees to our heart's content, but buty their goods still

government

(161) to help maintain this government

(247) utter one word against the Government

(274) defeating the objects of the Government by their personal or political quarrels

(418) The country...has a government at last

(508) Better lose a million men in battle

than allow the government to be overthrown

(510) God reigns, and the government at Washington still lives

(657) If we are right in passing this measure, we were wrong in denying to the old government

(882) no government...had a provision in its organic law for its own termination

(887) no administration...can very seriously injure the government

(894) Must a government, of necessity, be too strong... or too weak

(959) government of the people, by the people, for the people, shall not perish from the earth

(979) government, not too strong..., can be strong enough

(1035) rebelled against a mild and paternal government

(1287) Our government should become a machine

Grant, Ulysses S.

(14) The feeling about Grant is peculiar

(132) Where is Grant a-going to elbow us again

(238) God—Grant—Victory

(570) Grant has resumed his bad habits

(577) Grant, who was behind at Fort Henry, drunk at Donelson, surprised at Shiloh

(840) Grant has managed his affairs remarkably well

(1186) If we were under any other General except Grant I should expect a retreat

(1304) Grant is as good a leader as we can find

(1344) no commission that would tend to create a rivalry with Grant

grave

(34) go to Anderson and see the graves there

(395) the government and your liberty in the same hopeless grave

(889) from every battle-field, and patriot grave

(1140) to sleep for all time in an unknown grave

grease

(1254) There won't be a grease spot of 'em left

greatest
(878) greatest good to the greatest number

Greeley, Horace
(1074) Greeley's enmity he might stand, but his friendship will kill him

green
(892) you are all green alike

gruel
(178) I make gruel—not speeches

guardian
(640) the guardian of its own history and its own fame

gun
(152) shoots the biggest gun
(153) We want men with guns in their hands
(281) every man should stand by his guns
(353) We've cleaned them out of their guns and got ours back
(993) if Grant is wise he will leave them their guns
(1113) Every gun fired in this struggle
(1156) so many ill effects from leaving guns
(1184) a National Salute with shotted guns was fired
(1368) don't let them take my guns away

gunpowder
(416) Sometimes gunpowder smells good

habeas corpus
(893) suspend the writ of Habeas Corpus
(918) The Writ of Habeas Corpus is suspended

hairs
(1085) You are responsible for my gray hairs

Halleck, Henry W.
(1464) Halleck was good for nothing

hallowed
(594) your deeds have made this crest, your resting place, hallowed ground

hand
(390) to fight with your white hand, and allow your black to remain tied

(391) striking with the iron hand of the black man
(393) unchain...her powerful black hand
(1204) your fate is mainly in your own hands
(1407) Hand of iron: velvet glove

hang
(549) hang them without trial
(1123) hang every one he caught

hanging
(499) their peculiar habits of hanging, shooting, &c.

harass
(805) harass if we cannot destroy them

hard bread
(1383) All the fresh meat we had came in the hard bread

hard crackers
(87) hard crackers, come again no more

hardened
(1310) it may be well that we become so hardened

hardship
(790) that men could stand such hardship

hardtack
(67) What we want is hardtack
(88) hardtack, hardtack, come again no more

heads
(630) grieve for the course intrusted to such heads

heart
(375) with unconquered and unconquerable hearts
(399) My hand and heart are in it
(598) they chose that which necessarily lay nearest the heart
(1025) With the heart that beat a charge, he fell
(1197) the anguish of my heart is stretched to the utmost
(1274) We cannot change the hearts of those people of the South

(451) massacred in every conceivable form of horror

horses
(12) I do my best for my horses
(972) not best to swap horses when crossing streams
(1261) horses running about riderless with blood streaming from their nostrils

hospitals
(466) the informal hells called hospitals

hot
(171) I have a hot place picked out for some of you

hotter
(128) It's hotter here than it was in front

hottest
(611) go in where it is hottest
(742) Go where the fire is hottest

hour
(1409) These are dark hours
(1497) The man and the hour have met

howl
(1332) I can make this march, and make Georgia howl

hug
(21) I wanted to hug the army

humanities
(1320) my orders are not designed to meet the humanities of the case

humbug
(1284) Vox populi, vox humbug

humbugged
(1393) We have been humbugged by the rebels

husband
(354) your very gallant husband

imbecility
(195) an incurable consumption of Central Imbecility

independence
(372) We are fighting for independence and that, or extermination, we will have
(645) You may...win Southern independence...but I doubt it

Indian
(324) to conciliate the Indian nations

indifference
(1450) As to seeing men shot,...I had no feeling but one of perfect indifference

infantry
(722) Pass the infantry to the front

infatuation
(764) The most fatal infatuation

inflexible
(997) principles may, and must, be inflexible

information
(842) He never brought me a piece of false information

inherited
(974) he holds on to it as if he had inherited it

insane
(307) Gen. William T. Sherman...is insane

insolence
(269) Their insolence is beyond endurance

Institute
(715) The Institute will be heard from today

intemperance
(1413) many officers have become addicted to habits of intemperance

intervention
(1231) independence on this continent against European intervention

intrigued
(267) He intrigued to get me out and behold the result

invader
(945) Drive the invader from our soil

invasion
(287) an invasion to have been more foolish and disastrous
(1130) I am tired of invasion

invincible
(831) I thought my men were invincible

iron
(1065) I regard the possession of an iron-ar-

laurel
(411) The laurel is a running vine

laws
(1323) we do want, and will have, a just obedience to the laws of the United States

leaders
(648) the howls of their jackal leaders
(771) it is to the disadvantage of a constituted command to take men from their habitual leaders

leather
(242) the state of the leather market in the Confederacy

Lee, Robert E.
(144) love you just as well as ever, General Lee
(148) General Lee to the rear
(763) I doubt if he will ever forgive Gen. Lee
(1047) I prefer Lee to Johnston
(1077) We're on Lee's flank
(1137) If General Lee had Grant's resources
(1143) Lee seems to have become as weak as Burnside

legs
(18) barring a few lives and legs
(152) longest legs to run

letter
(85) Soldier's letter, nary red

liberty
(394) Liberty won by white men would lose half its luster
(1378) if the people quietly yield the citadel of their liberties
(1411) where Liberty is, there Slavery cannot be

lick
(534) lick 'em tomorrow

lie
(113) and here we lie

life
(966) often a limb must be amputated to save a life

(1063) you may take not only my sword but my life
(1430) until the life of the last man is trampled out

Lincoln, Abraham
(285) King Lincoln
(410) we've scared Abe Lincoln
(578) Lincoln would have spared them

liquors
(253) intoxicating liquors...will be seized and destroyed

listening
(616) listening to the sound of hostile shot and shell

Longstreet, James
(825) what can detain Longstreet

looking
(70) I've been looking for for the last four years

lost
(684) If this Valley is lost
(1380) Our liberties once lost, may be lost forever

love
(272) don't fall in love nor the enemy's hands

lunatic
(489) a fit subject for a lunatic asylum

lying
(1126) lying reports of our general and reporters

McClellan, George B.
(233) They will not do anything without McClellan, but will they do anything with him
(348) I have more confidence in General McClellan than in any man living
(426) McClellan ebbed like a sea
(746) No one but McClellan could have hesitated to attack
(898) I will hold McClellan's horse

McPherson, James B.
(1007) McPherson and revenge

mad

(1373) the God damn trash of a silly mountebank

movable

(740) this force can be made useful...by
rendering it movable

move

(1037) not to move until I know that
everything is ready

mud

(119) Burnside stuck in the mud

(227) I could have drank out of a mud
puddle

mule

(37) Here's your mule

(80) Forward the Mule Brigade

(359) Forward harness and wagons; can't do
anything with mules without them

(1283) If they will send me the mules, they
can keep the brigadiers

murder

(997) Every life that is now lost in this war
is murder

(1099) it is murder, but it's the order

murdered

(1104) I have been basely murdered

music

(676) The sweetest music I have ever heard

muskets

(198) It is not men we lack, but muskets

(595) I am too old to shoulder a musket
myself

mystify

(726) mystify, mislead, and surprise the
enemy

name

(792) Were it possible for human lips to
raise your name heavenward

nation

(623) One nation, evermore

naval

(1068) Naval education and training

needle

(818) Straight as the needle to the pole he
advanced to the execution of my purpose

Negro

(300) people who still believe negroes to be
property

(343) negro prisoners were the most efficient foes

(374) the raising of negro troops

(389) The Negro is the key of the situation

(398) The negro is the stomach of the
rebellion

(847) choose between employing negroes
ourselves and having them employed
against us

nerve

(1157) men of nerve to command

news

(1281) Tis folly to say the people must have
news

newspaper

(249) We want no newspaper government

(670) My brigade is not a brigade of newspaper correspondents

nigger

(135) Take the white man! Kill the nigger

Nightingale, Florence

(1108) All our women are Florence Nightingales

noble

(329) the noble that fall and the ignoble that
remain

nominating

(1408) nominating a general and warrior in
time of war on a peace platform

North

(1278) The North must rule or submit to
degradation

Northern

(231) the Northern States will manage
somehow to muddle through

(286) the hope of success vanish from the
Northern mind

Northerners

(779) I know the Northerners to be so
contemptible

nothing

(688) Say nothing about it

(1042) He understands nothing, appreciates nothing

(1466) He has suggested nothing, decided nothing, done nothing

nurse

(25) the nurse with the bottle

(175) I can stand and feed and nurse them

occupied

(1343) No city was ever occupied with less disorder

offensive

(1117) We must take the offensive and destroy their army

officer

(266) Competent officers make good soldiers

(367) Tender consideration for worthless and incompetent officers

(461) one of the requisite studies for an officer is man

(665) it is unmilitary and unlike an officer to write news respecting one's post

(677) If officers desire to have control over their commands

(950) the ranking officer must be obeyed

(1072) the officers...are ignorant, inefficient and worthless

(1154) This war is not being conducted for the benefit of officers

(1158) an officer will be kept by the compass

(1293) if any officer...makes one cent by way of profit

(1443) the want of military knowledge and discipline among the higher officers

operations

(658) Operations so extensive and important

order

(777) such an order can only be prompted by cowardice or treason

(814) The greatest difficulty I find is in causing orders and regulations to be obeyed

(1349) I have never in my life questioned or disobeyed an order

Orphan Brigade

(229) My poor Orphan Brigade

outmaneuver

(1017) In order to whip him we must outmanoeuver him

outrages

(257) outrages committed at and near Kennerville

overboard

(783) wanted to be throd overboard

ox

(1317) It makes a world of difference if "my bull gores your ox, or yours mine"

pain

(18) Pain is the only thing I should fear

(556) The pain in my head seemed to leave me the moment I got Lee's letter

paper

(1057) a paper with which if I cannot whip Bobbie Lee

paradise

(576) ravaged but still beautiful Paradise

pardoned

(902) The Doll Jack is pardoned

pardons

(837) pardons...will not only make all the blood that has been shed for the maintenance of discipline useless

parlor

(1194) made parlor pets by some of the social noodles

paroled

(865) be paroled and go to your homes

passions

(1275) If we allow the passions of our men to get full command

(1352) arouse passions and prejudices at the North

patriotic

(488) singleness of purpose that might almost be called patriotic

patriotism
(211) It is hard to maintain one's patriotism on ashcake and water
(351) my patriotism and my desire to be and remain with my darling
(1170) it's tough on patriotism

patriots
(578) two parties now,—Traitors & Patriots

peace
(42) the Peapple is in for making Peas
(420) a hasty peace restoring the old rottenness
(421) the peace of the man who has forsworn the use of the bayonet
(852) They cannot barter manhood for peace
(1082) these two armies would...make peace in an hour
(1218) Wayward Sisters, depart in peace
(1234) peace agitators in time of war ultimately bring about an abandonment of the conflict
(1252) when they have to bear their burden...they will cry for peace
(1354) The legitimate object of war is a more perfect peace

pear
(1148) Mobile...would fall to us like a mellow pear

people
(1357) what kind of people will we be

periled
(1459) our lives have been periled to no purpose

personality
(597) fling his lank personality into the chair of state

pest
(1353) I will avoid it as a pest house

pharoah
(40) Pharoah's army going to the Red Sea

picket
(197) The picket's off duty forever

Pickett, George E.

(1016) I would stop Pickett now, but that General Lee has ordered it

pillar
(1478) it is cruel to be so tossed from pillar to post

pilot
(378) you are the only Pilot to lead the Ship

place
(511) Who can fill his place

plague
(1440) If God Almighty had yet in store another plague worse than all others

planning
(1364) the most capable in planning may be the most incapable in execution
(1454) While you are planning, these people are acting

plans
(969) The particulars of your plans I neither know, or seek to know

plunderer
(1239) to degenerate into a plunderer and robber

poisoned
(1115) selling poisoned pies to the soldiers

policy
(912) The severest justice may not always be the best policy
(1110) no policy so fatal as having no policy

political
(1038) no one is to be molested merely because of political opinions

politicians
(299) The Confederacy done to death by the politicians
(561) influenced by...fossil politicians

Polk, Leonidas
(133) killed our old Gen. Polk

poor
(36) A rich man's war and a poor man's fight

population
(1501) The male population has nearly disappeared

(51) All quiet on the Potomac

(197) All quiet along the Potomac

quinine

(77) Come and get your quinine

rabbit

(1447) The way to cook a rabbit is "first catch the rabbit"

(1448) Gen. Grant has "caught the rabbit"

race

(895) to afford all, an unfettered start, and a fair chance, in the race of life

racer

(1105) the Yankee racers

rake

(59) Just hunt me up with an oyster rake

rally

(1202) rally round the flag, boys

ranks

(622) Fill up the ranks that have opened for you

(1124) No man who runs away ranks me

(1295) She ranks me

Ransom, Robert

(203) few meaner men unhung than this Robert Ransom

ready

(890) the necessity of being ready increases

rear

(54) ain't got any rear

(350) Where in hell is the rear

(358) a successful battle in his rear would settle all trouble

(450) their pants are out at the rear

(1146) disaster and shame lurk in the rear

Rebel

(235) Grape for the rebel masses, and hemp for their leaders

(1397) the earnestness and resolution the rebel leaders shew

rebellion

(261) that rebellion is treason, and that treason, persisted in, is death

(467) embarrassed by this unholy rebellion

(1090) The backbone of the Rebellion is this day broken

(1431) put down this accursed rebellion

Rebs

(243) the Rebs couldn't make anything of them fellers

reckless

(1460) a Reckless don't care disposition Seemed to take possession of me

red tape

(1360) a system of formal requisitions which fools call red tape

reenforcements

(1474) I want re-enforcements, not recruits

regiment

(901) He who does something at the head of one Regiment

rein

(1358) It is the rein in hand by which the superior does his driving

rejoicing

(559) the best sign of rejoicing after the victory will be to abstain from all demonstrations

relation

(397) The relation subsisting between the white and colored people

remarks

(1486) set apart these grounds to their Sacred use by a few appropriate remarks

remember

(736) Remember the precious stake involved

reputation

(427) something rotten about a sensitive reputation

resistance

(506) if not surprised, they did not offer a sufficient resistance

(661) to defend it with terrific resistance

resolution

(853) do not permit them to impair our resolution

responsibility

(861) If it is right, then I will take all the responsibility

retreat
(149) He's hell on retreat
(268) lose less men in a defence...than you will in a retreat
(1013) Retreat! Hell
(1247) Retreat, hell
(1414) This army does not retreat

retreating
(106) they were retreating after us
(302) not retreating before irresistable veterans

Revere, Paul
(1012) Listen, my children, and you shall hear/Of the midnight ride of Paul Revere

revolution
(360) it is by the abuse of language that their act has been denominated revolution
(735) One revolution at a time is enough
(793) Secession is nothing but revolution

rich
(36) A rich man's war and a poor man's fight

Richmond
(44) On to Richmond
(104) look away to Richmond town
(760) the very name of Richmond is a terror
(774) Richmond would have been ours
(963) I have...given passes to two hundred and fifty thousand men to go to Richmond
(1111) Forward to Richmond

ridicule
(958) I have endured a great deal of ridicule

right
(885) their constitutional right of amending it, or their revolutionary right to dismember
(1112) the supremacy of the rights of man
(1377) Nothing could be more unwise than for a free people...to give up their rights

rioters
(590) the insane fury of the rioters

risks

(1076) I am tired of this playing war without risks

river
(453) Fighting is nothing to the evil of the river

rocket
(1453) Hood has "gone up like a rocket"

roses
(1044) no bed of roses on which to recline

Rosy
(83) Old Rosy is our man

rout
(241) the rout was complete

royal
(1479) the real precious & royal ones of this land

ruined
(224) Universal suffrage, furloughs, and whisky have ruined us

rules
(873) Private and public life are subject to the same rules

run
(98) de man what made old massa run
(125) If I was an old hare, I'd run too
(694) Surely they need not have run

running
(140) I'm running' cause I can't fly

sacrifice
(275) a bloody sacrifice on the altar of my adopted country
(1049) you have done your best to sacrifice this Army

sacrificed
(186) I would readily have sacrificed my life

sad
(1477) a curious looking man, very sad

saddle
(1147) My headquarters will be in the saddle

safer
(512) nothing that you can do will make you safer in one place than another

salute
> (551) I have ordered a salute to be fired with shotted guns

sash
> (415) a yellow sash or six feet of ground

savages
> (364) In moral and social condition they had been elevated from brutal savages

saved
> (1) saved the present trials from their children

scare
> (481) keep up the scare
> (486) Keep the scare on 'em

scared
> (412) The Yankees got whipped; we got scared

science
> (20) science will be the masters of man

Scott, Winfield
> (7) Scott's campaign

scoundrel
> (1054) the most unmitigated scoundrel I ever knew

scour
> (960) That speech won't scour

sea
> (651) the sea of eternity beyond

secede
> (1121) guess dis chile will secede once moah

secession
> (794) I...cannot see the good of secession

secessionists
> (172) rendered secessionists so scarce
> (1302) to the petulant and persistent secessionists, why, death is a mercy

secessionitis
> (1385) this treasonable inflammation

see
> (1495) I cannot see, but do not mind me

self-defense
> (1209) the first great law of nature, the right of self-defense

service
> (377) they any no serviz to us at home

sheathe
> (731) never sheathe it in the bosom of my mother

sheep
> (173) If sheep attack you

shell
> (335) Shell and be damned
> (1011) Every shell...bursts not only on the battle-field, but in far-away homes
> (1159) lodging the shell before it explodes
> (1396) to be shelled back is a bore

Shenandoah Valley
> (550) we want the Shenandoah Valley to remain a barren waste

shepherd
> (968) The shepherd drives the wolf from the sheep's throat

Sheridan, Philip
> (542) Did Sheridan say that

Sherman, William T.
> (761) Sherman's army is doomed
> (1031) Sherman...is a very remarkable-looking man

shoddy
> (221) to puff up all the shoddy in the world
> (1109) This is the age of shoddy

shoddycracy
> (1118) Shoddycracy is pretty large in New York

shoes
> (284) all a Yankee is now worth is his shoes

shoot
> (693) shoot them where they stand
> (699) Shoot the brave officers, and the cowards will run away
> (1198) I wish that some of our own men would shoot me
> (1224) if I should show the white feather, shoot me dead in my tracks

shooters
> (619) Shooters are more needed than tooters

shooting

(769) They're shooting at me, not at you

shot

(30) I shall await the first shot

(601) Some men seem born to be shot

shrouds

(107) to wear our own burial shrouds

sick

(72) All ye sick men

siege

(841) This army cannot stand a siege

Sigel, Franz

(82) I fights mit Sigel

signals

(456) none of this Nelson business...about not seeing signals

silence

(459) The minute he opens, I silence him

silent

(294) silent and strong, biding their time

sin

(137) War is the result of a nation's sins

(1023) the sheathed blade may rust with darker sin

sink

(1236) If we only went in for sink or swim, we should finish the thing up

sinned

(1164) wee sinned as a nation

skill

(552) a skill and ability...unsurpassed, if not unequalled

skinning

(970) Those not skinning can hold a leg

skulk

(617) skulk at home as the cowardly exempts do

swords

(663) draw your swords and throw away the scabbard

slain

(634) the slain lay in rows

slander

(975) Truth is generally the best vindication against slander

slave

(311) If slaves will make good soldiers

(431) The slave is the owner

(500) to liberate the very race who they are most anxious should be slaves

(504) their slaves...are hereby declared freeman

(505) the article respecting the liberation of slaves

(848) we must decide whether...slaves be used against us, or use them ourselves

(982) I never knew a man who wished himself to be a slave

(1010) a slave's collar of iron

(1301) All the power on earth cannot restore to them their slaves

slavery

(10) This war is killing slavery

(384) which of the two, Freedom or Slavery, shall give law to this republic

(428) Slavery is a divine institution

(650) the knell of slavery

(965) If slavery is not wrong, nothing is wrong

(989) Whenever [I] hear any one, arguing for slavery

(1070) The public mind here is entirely opposed to... slavery

(1199) Had it not been for slavery, we would have had no war

(1201) take slavery by the throat

(1376) slavery...is his natural and normal condition

sleep

(1172) went to sleep to dream of the hideous sights

slows

(932) McClellan's got the slows

smash

(306) The grand smash has come

smashing

(1253) I'm ready to strike out tomorrow and go to smashing things

snow

(1183) I would like to have some of those "On to Richmond" fellows out here with us in the snow

society
(344) Society is terribly mutilated

soldier
(92) Who wouldn't be a soldier
(103) more harm than our own soldiers have done
(105) a soldier's wife I'll be
(222) no idea of what it is to be a soldier
(263) one thing...stands between you and your government—and that is slavery
(319) Soldiers may be gentlemen but they can't live like gentlemen
(491) a man who has been a good soldier can be a good citizen
(517) paying them as American Soldiers, not as menial hirelings
(544) a gallant soldier and a Christian gentleman
(599) whether he is a soldier or not
(602) A dead rebel soldier was today fished out of the well
(674) soldiers not only to defend, but able and willing both to defend and protect
(762) fast becoming...machine soldiers
(765) a better soldier than those who treat me so cavalierly
(845) soldiers know their duties better than general officers
(1211) exterminate these citizen soldiers
(1235) We have a very pleasant feeling towards Rebel soldiers now
(1262) Our men are not good soldiers
(1426) it takes God Almighty to make a soldier
(1502) some of our soldiers committed discreditable trespasses

soldiering
(276) Soldiering is a good deal like going to school
(442) I am heartily sick of soldiering
(1181) Soldiering is not fun

sorrows
(1114) the cup of sorrows which the Rebels

souls
(1131) may God have mercy on their guilty souls

soupy
(86) Soupy, soupy, soupy, without any bean

South
(320) God pity this south land when we are done with it

South Carolina
(48) South Carolina villains

Southern
(255) I am a friend of Southern rights now, but I came here to put down Southern wrongs

spies
(1280) I will never again command an army in America if we must carry along paid spies

spout
(136) Old Imboden's gone up the spout

stable
(79) Go to the stable, as quick as you're able

Stanton, Edwin M.
(908) Stanton's navy is as useless as the paps of a man

stars
(1075) If I survive, my two stars are secure

Stars and Stripes
(174) to raise the Stars and Stripes above our Capitol
(206) There is among us but one thought, one object, one end, one symbol—the Stars and Stripes

starved
(30) we shall be starved out in a few days

state
(866) help to build up the shattered fortunes of our old state
(1488) A star for every State, and a State for every star

states' rights
(1415) Mix 'em up. I'm tired of States' rights

steel
(154) Give them the cold steel

((1036) foemen worthy of your steel

stench
(1389) I never knew before what rankness of stench can be emitted by unwashed humanity

stocking
(896) what the girl said when she stuck her foot into the stocking

straggler
(613) The straggler is generally a thief
(806) Stragglers are usually those who desert their comrades in peril
(1191) We cease to wonder at the number of stragglers

straggling
(627) straggling and marauding have become a great evil

strategy
(604) We...regard strategy as it is called—a humbug

strength
(223) Our strength consists in the enemy's weakness

stripes
(254) they shall fear the stripes if they do not now reverence the stars of our banner

strong
(633) I am as strong as I can expect to be

struggle
(3) wanton and wicked struggle

subdue
(1145) How can you subdue such a nation as this

substitute
(370) To ask me to substitute you...is to demand for me an impossibility

succeed
(679) cannot afford to keep a man who does not succeed

success
(188) Your success has been signal
(509) measureless ruin or complete success

(813) successes that inflict no loss upon the enemy beyond the actual loss in battle
(1081) Be not over-elated by reported successes
(1243) I shall expect nothing short of success
(1271) Success is demanded, and yet the means to attain success are withheld

suffer
(122) kill me—don't let me suffer
(801) Our poor sick I know suffer much
(856) we who are left are the ones to suffer

suffered
(270) they deny being whipped because they have not yet suffered

suffering
(469) If a man wants to see human suffering

Sunday
(690) concerned at my attacking on Sunday

superfluous
(4) It would be superfluous in me

superior
(1052) as faithfully as subordinate ever served superior

surprised
(615) The officers and men who permit themselves to be surprised

surrender
(124) If you can't feed us, you had better surrender us
(157) Mississippians don't know, and refuse to learn, how to surrender
(477) I must demand an unconditional surrender of your force
(484) I demand the unconditional surrender of this garrison
(531) No terms except unconditional and immediate surrender
(555) the surrender of that portion of the C.S. Army known as the Army of Northern Virginia
(557) I propose to receive the surrender of the Army of Northern Virginia
(607) Surrender! Never

(863) ascertain upon what terms you would receive the surrender of my army

(869) It is with pain that I announce...the surrender

(1018) If General Lee doesn't know when to surrender

(1255) If the thing is pressed I think Lee will surrender

(1348) I therefore demand the surrender of your army ..., purely and simply

surrendered

(494) the government to which you have surrendered

surrendering

(473) these people are talking about surrendering

swear

(1240) Unless I swear like hell

swearing

(355) his swearing made my hair stand straight up

sweat

(695) sweat them tonight, that I may save their blood tomorrow

(1417) we are between a sh-t and a sweat

sword

(793) Save in her defense, I will draw my sword no more

(795) Save in defence of my native State, I never desire again to draw my sword

(796) save in defence of my native State,...I hope I may never be called on to draw my sword

(1212) I can clean this country with fire and sword

symbol

(644) the musical symbol of a new nationality

tardy

(214) What are you waiting for, tardy George

task

(362) I...will not shrink from the task imposed upon me

(829) the task was too great for you

teams

(1490) Our teams are shoeless

Tennessee River

(738) we will water our horses in the Tennessee River

tenting

(787) Tenting on the old camp ground

terms

(236) ungenerous and unchivalrous terms

(1019) unless he offers us honorable terms

terrier

(1314) Grant has the perseverance of a Scotch terrier

territory

(927) territory is the only part which is of certain durability

terror

(1160) our lives would be spent in terror and sorrow

Texan

(501) no Texan walks a yard if he can help it

theory

(373) Died of a theory

Thermopylae

(665) the spirit which actuated the defenders of Thermopylae

thick

(1005) kill them—where they are thick

thorough

(698) let us make thorough work of it

three years

(71) All in the three years

thunderstorm

(1322) You might as well appeal against the thunder-storm

tin can

(96) tin can on a shingle

titles

(748) how fond all Americans are of titles

tomahawk

(1499) We don't want to pull the tomahawk—we would rather prune our trees

lic from one upon slavery...for a question upon union

United States
(244) assert the authority of the United States

untouched
(631) yet I am untouched

useless
(220) Useless, useless

victory
(295) this victory will be our ruin
(485) I will always lead you to victory
(518) till the sun goes down or victory is won
(641) the earliest moments of dawning victory
(938) go forward, and give us victories
(1048) Victory has no charms for me when purchased at such cost
(1122) Let your work this day be for victory or death

views
(914) I shall adopt new views so fast as they shall appear to be true views

Virginia
(692) Old Virginia has waken up
(1138) Don't forget today that you are from Old Virginia

virtue
(284) with peace...will come national virtue
(1091) female virtue...seems now almost a perfect wreck

volley
(710) deliver one deadly, deliberate volley

volunteers
(581) carrying on a war by Volunteers is utterly suicidal

vote
(66) Vote as you shoot

wagon dogs
(147) Come all you wagon dogs

wail
(95) The wail of lost souls

walk
(934) I never walk back

war
(23) I've often longed to see a war
(193) absolute, terrible, and immeasurable war
(205) I have had enough of the glory of war
(262) a war of the aristocrats against the middling men
(282) no decree of death in war
(292) The cry to day is war
(309) the time for playing war is past
(315) War is not a question of valor, but a question of money
(349) Glorious War
(369) This war is ours; we must fight it ourselves
(386) war for the destruction of liberty must be met with war for the destruction of slavery
(388) a war for slavery dominion
(405) service during war but not war service
(419) The war goes on educating us
(422) It is...a war of Instincts
(424) The war is...a chivalrous sport to him
(425) War, the searcher of character
(429) The war...brought with it the immense benefit of drawing a line
(430) The war is our sole and doleful instructor
(433) War disorganizes, but it is to reorganize
(434) War ennobles the age
(437) I shall always respect War hereafter
(438) The War at last appoints the generals
(547) the saddest affair I have witnessed in the war
(659) war on a scale inaugurated by this rebellion
(662) People who are anxious to bring on war don't know what they are bargaining for
(711) the secret of successful war
(752) Our people are tired of war
(759) willing to wage the war against quadruple their number
(811) It is well that war is so terrible

(1214) Weeping, sad and lonely

West Point
(1424) died of West Point

whip
(487) We'll whip 'em in five minutes

whipped
(316) We are somewhat whipped
(916) we are whipped again
(1403) I had rather die than be whipped

White House
(1315) If forced to choose between the penitentiary and White House

wicked
(696) a wicked fellow

wickedness
(564) I have seen little of the wickedness and depravity of man until I Joined the Army

widow
(101) Better a widow than married to a craven

wife
(672) love your wife more than your country

win
(1058) if we can keep this up, we win

wind
(1286) they have sowed the wind and must reap the whirlwind

wine
(1435) Good officers know that when wine is in, wit is out

wiped
(303) wiped off the face of the earth

wolves
(562) we have fought wolves with the devices of sheep

woman
(24) women could carry on the war better than the men
(47) son or husband of some woman
(258) liable to be treated as a woman of the town plying her avocation

(297) these times make all women feel their humiliation in the affairs of the world
(446) women would make a grand brigade—if it was not for snakes and spiders
(786) The celebrated Woman Order...was exactly what was required
(925) the little woman who wrote the book that made this great war
(1285) the deep and bitter enmity of the women of the South
(1445) were it not for the women, I should not fight at all

wooden
(452) It don't hurt a bit to be shot in a wooden leg
(1067) Naval engagements between wooden frigates

world
(1405) I must be prepared for another world

wound
(414) I would like first rate to get such a wound
(687) a kind Providence may enable us to inflict a terrible wound

wounded
(112) you aren't wounded; you are only bruised
(716) I have always been kind to their wounded
(1238) the perfect calmness of the wounded men

wrongs
(334) Rather bear the wrongs you have than fly to others

Yankee
(110) all this Yankee scoundrel got
(323) They...would be a terror to the Yankees
(463) I expect to murder every Yankee I ever meet
(475) if you want a heap of fun and to kill some Yankees
(655) The Yankees are behaving very well
(1119) I would like to shoot a Yankee
(1369) Yankee souls in Southern bodies

Yanks

KEYWORD INDEX

SUBJECT INDEX

(866) help to build up the shattered fortunes of our old state

(1019) unless he offers us honorable terms

arguments

(928) time for mere catch arguments

aristocrats

(733) What will the aristocrats do

Armistead, Lewis A.

(155) I cannot live to atone

armistice

(788) no armistice on sea or land, until all...are subjugated or exterminated

arms

(406) would make fine companies if there were arms for them

(503) I am sorely pressed for want of arms

(691) Arms is a profession that...requires an officer do what he fears may be wrong

(851) if the army cannot protect them, the arms will be of little use

(1408) the profession of arms will henceforth be more desirable

army

(11) army is a great place to learn philosophy

(15) no force on earth which could resist this army

(40) Pharoah's army going to the Red Sea

(117) Man that is born of woman and enlists in Jackson's Army

(118) brass-mounted army

(375) with an army free to move from point to point

(545) Lee's army is really whipped

(548) They have robbed the Cradle and the grave equally

(554) We will all act together as one army

(564) I have seen but little of the wickedness and depravity of man until I Joined the Army

(582) I am getting tired of the army

(689) an army of the living God

(761) Sherman's army is doomed

(785) neither army shall get much advantage of the other

(844) These men are not an army

(849) The surest foundation upon which the fidelity of an army can rest

(948) Our Army held the war in the hollow of their hand

(970) Those not skinning can hold a leg

(1082) these two armies would...make a peace in an hour

(1161) This army moves as a disciplined body—not an armed mob

(1327) We ought to ask our country for the largest possible armies

(1329) my army won't starve

(1334) Our armies are merely paper armies

(1335) The army will forage liberally on the country

(1338) I never saw a more confident army

(1424) The army is dying

(1444) the crudeness of the material...in organizing an army

(1452) the two armies are so well balanced

(1485) The army is becoming awfully depraved

Army of Northern Virginia

(867) the Army of Northern Virginia has been compelled to yield to overwhelming numbers and resources

(943) If the head of Lee's army is at Martinsburg and the tail of it on the Plank road

Army of the Potomac

(89) We are the boys of Potomac's ranks

(637) The Rebel army...is now the legitimate property of the Army of the Potomac

(640) the Army of the Potomac will give or decline battle whenever its interest or honor may demand

(919) it is only McClellan's bodyguard

(1046) the proud consciousness that we belonged to the Army of the Potomac

(1049) If I save this Army...I owe no thanks to you

artillery

(742) fear artillery unreasonably

assassination

(944) if anybody wants to kill me he will do it

(1064) We part as friends, but on the field of battle we meet as enemies

blankets

(312) the most of the boys are mighty anxious to get a lick at them for some blankets

blockades

(498) It is a Bull Run to the Navy

blood

(94) A lady's thimble will hold all the blood

(251) worse than the shedding of blood

(515) sprinkle blood in the face of the people

(1132) The smell of blood is sickening

blows

(643) Blows, not marches, are to kill the rebellion

(874) We must strike them a blow

boasting

(347) both come out of hiding-places,...calling names and bragging

(542) Let him go ahead and do it

(798) I wish them to take a firm, dignified course, free from bravado and boasting

(940) The hen is the wisest

(1134) great things threatened only to realize fizzles

(1262) They brag, but do not perform

(1470) The brag and bluster...of South Carolina prove impotent and ridiculous

boat

(507) I would rather see the devil than that boat

body

(560) I look on the carcass of a man now...as I would do were it a horse or dog

bonds

(889) Though passion may have strained, it must not break our bonds of affection

Booneville, Mo.

(358) a successful battle in his rear would settle all trouble

Booth, John Wilkes

(217) too great a soul to die like a criminal

bowels

(1213) you and I are apt to be afflicted with disordered bowels

Bragg, Braxton

(76) Bragg a Boo and Morgan, too

(149) He's hell on retreat

breastworks

(111) fond of charging breastworks

(123) Hood's boys are great at storming breastworks

(482) I am not going to make breastworks of you

bridge-burner

(199) hang every bridge-burner you can catch

brigade

(675) the First Brigade in our second War of Independence

(681) I never found anything impossible with this brigade

Bristoe Station

(836) bury these poor men and let us say no more about it

Brown, John

(52) John Bown's body lies a-mould'ring

bull

(1317) It makes a world of difference if "my bull gores your ox, or yours mine"

bullet

(624) A bullet has a most villanous greasy slide

(781) The Rebel bullet that can kill me

(1125) Every bullet has its billet

burning

(1062) I regret that is is necessary to burn your vessel

burying

(395) bury the government and your liberty

(1415) Mix 'em up

(1434) too busy to spend much time over the dead

Butler, Benjamin F.

(271) he will be poisoned or assassintaed

competency
(750) evidence of competency

Confederacy
(360) the sovereign states here represented
(373) Died of a theory
(1256) a Speedy termination to this Southern Confederation

Confederates
(502) the destruction of such a gallant race

Confederate weakening
(5) the disease cannot last

conscription
(692) Old Virginia has waken up

conspiracy
(1010) It is not a revolution, but a Catalinian conspiracy

Constitution
(881) no purpose to construe the Constitution or laws, by any hypercritical rules
(1167) the Constitution, as it is, against insane abolitionism on one side and rebellious secessionism on the other
(1437) The Constitution as it is, the Union as it was

control
(459) I have him under my control
(967) events have controlled me

convalescent camp
(469) If a man wants to see human suffering

cookies
(45) These cookies are expressly for the sick soldiers

cooperation
(290) heed not the universal babbling of some nor the deliberate malice of many

corpse
(1172) eat with a corpse for a table

corruption
(356) The mania for sudden fortunes...has to an alarming extent corrupted and demoralized the army
(380) military authorities are so corrupt that they will take all means to make money

councils

(575) councils of war never fight

country
(141) I'll be damned if I ever love another country
(160) If it is necessary that I should fall on the battle field for my county
(164) love of Country comes over me like a strong wind
(168) Don't you love your country
(219) Tell mother I die for my country
(275) a bloody sacrifice on the altar of my adopted country
(509) A nation is not worthy to be served
(565) Stand by her, boy, as you would stand by your mother
(566) no man deserved less at her hands
(589) Our country calls us
(622) your country is calling
(623) One nation, evermore
(678) All I am and all I have is at the service of my country
(736) offer battle to the invaders of your country
(782) Dulce et decorum
(797) the country will have to pass through a terrible ordeal
(885) This country, with its institutions, belongs to the people who inhabit it
(927) A nation may be said to consist
(959) Four score and seven years ago
(1040) called upon to save my country
(1056) Again I have been called upon to save the country
(1059) I've done all I can for my country
(1080) the eyes of the whole country are looking
(1145) How can you subdue such a nation as this
(1216) our country has been wonderfully prosperous
(1264) The bluer the times the more closely should one cling to his country
(1387) We have never been a nation; we are only an aggregate of communities
(1419) At last, we are/A nation among nations

292

(1212) I can clean this country with fire and sword

(1336) order and enforce a devastation more or less relentless

determination

(240) determination to suffer death rather than give up an inch of ground

dictatorship

(937) What I now ask of you is military success, and I will risk the dictatorship

disasters

(1491) Disasters have come, and disasters are coming

discipline

(855) discipline contributes no less to thier safety than to their efficiency

disparity

(200) the disparity of numbers

"Dixie's Land"

(104) look away to Richmond town

(644) the musical symbol of a new nationality

(995) I have always thought "Dixie" one of the best tunes

dodging

(63) I believe in dodging

(521) Just count each blot a dodge

dogmas

(929) The dogmas of the quiet past

draft

(955) Has the manhood of our race run out

draft riots

(590) the insane fury of the rioters

(1395) all cursing the "bloody draft"

dream

(652) the dream is over

(998) I soon began to dream

(1000) I had this strange dream again last night

drill

(1116) drill, then drill, then drill again

drums

(1476) Beat! beat! drums

drunkenness

(580) is the majority always drunk

duty

(61) we'll obey duty's call

(204) I died at my post doing my duty

(250) He who does his duty to the Union, does his duty to the state

(362) I...will not shrink from the task imposed upon me

(401) Success is not in my hands; to do my duty is

(458) There's a hotter fire than that waiting for those who don't do their duty

(468) duty to put down rebellion and nothing more

(493) our duty to divest ourselves of all such feelings

(628) the duty of fighting has ceased for me

(642) No one will consider the day as ended until the duties it brings have been discharged

(723) Duty is ours; consequences are God's

(725) My duty is to obey orders

(854) do my duty and fight to the last

(1181) duty keeps us in the ranks

dying

(591) I died for her and my country

(1196) better die by Rebel bullets than Union Quackery

(1227) I consider it a privilege to die for my country

(1405) I must be prepared for another world

(1406) I am going fast now

Early, Jubal A.

(1187) Early was Late

economy

(1236) there should be no economy which is sure to be waste in the end

editors

(1269) They are the chief cause of this unhappy war

eggs

(915) Broken eggs can never be mended

elections

(923) too big to cry, and far too badly hurt to laugh

(1231) independence on this continent against European intervention

evil

(627) straggling and marauding have become a great evil

(810) act upon probabilities and endeavor to avoid greater evils

Ewell, Richard S.

(1193) he has earned and well merits the title of general

exaggeration

(1081) Be not...over-depressed by exaggerated rumors

execution

(471) shot dead in cold blood at the iron decree of military law

exempts

(617) skulk at home as the cowardly exempts do

extermination

(1211) extermination alone can achieve the end expected

Fair Oaks

(728) encouraged their comrades to press on

fate

(1204) your fate is mainly in your own hands

fault

(540) the fault is not with you

fear

(18) Pain is the only thing I should fear

(194) Fear was stronger than faith

(700) Never take counsel of your fears

(1036) I fear now but one thing

(1450) I cannot recall having felt the least personal fear while under fire

(1460) as Soon as we Entered the Woods where the Shells and Balls were flying thick and fast I lost all fear

Federals

(1500) a mischievous purpose on the part of the Federals

fighting

(49) enough of fighting to last my lifetime

(97) Them as wants to fight

(129) We will fight them, sir, till hell freezes

(202) he is not going to fight

(278) The edge of the fight rolled backward and forward

(280) fight men in arms, but not babes in arms

(372) We are fighting for independence and that, or extermination, we will have

(480) before I will fight again under your command

(495) mix with 'em

(496) Shoot any man who won't fight

(562) we have fought wolves with the devices of sheep

(595) I am too old to shoulder a musket myself

(596) I don't quite understand what we are fighting for

(737) I would fight them if they were a million

(754) Fighting is a sport

(767) the oftener we are beaten the sooner we will learn to fight

(862) They would be compelled to rob and steal

(1037) success by maneuvering rather than by fighting

(1066) fighting with iron against wood

(1083) their ghosts and babies fight very well

(1088) nothing which he is willing to fight for

(1103) if you won't fight get out of the way

(1127) the more we fight, the less we like it

(1244) I do desire resolute and actual fighting

(1276) willing to meet you anywhere and everywhere in manly fight

(1370) This army has got to fight or run away

fire

(611) Face the fire

firing

(710) deliver one deadly, deliberate volley

(1158) broadsides might be fired in the wrong direction

(1159) The object is to lodge the shell in the parapets
(1177) There's a fizzle
(1475) I have come to share your fate
(1481) I'd rather Johnny'd be where them eggs is breaking than me

Fort Pemberton
(1020) Give them blizzards

Fort Pillow
(310) Gen. Forrest ordered them shot down like dogs
(484) I demand the unconditional surrender of this garrison

Fort Sumter
(29) it is a demand with which I regret
(30) I shall await the first shot
(31) If we never meet in this world again
(181) demand the evacuation of Fort Sumter
(206) The assault on Fort Sumter started us all to our feet
(289) he will open the fire of his batteries on Fort Sumter in one hour
(1163) I could not fire the first gun of the war
(1219) to restrain the fury of the noncombatants
(1423) You will wantonly strike a hornet's nest

4th of July
(1184) Was ever the Nation's Birthday celebrated in such a way before

France
(757) What a blunder France and England made

Franklin, Tennessee
(1092) I could hardly step without stepping on dead and wounded men

Frayser's Farm
(608) if you will not follow me, I'll die alone

Fredericksburg
(232) the fatal field of Fredericksburg
(308) The city of Fredericksburg was a trap
(341) The slaughter is terrible
(342) It was not a battle; it was a butchery

(705) sometimes failed to take a position, but to defend one, never

freedom
(384) which of the two, Freedom or Slavery, shall give law to this Republic
(387) Freedom for all, or chains for all
(1055) let them...relieve me & I shall once more be a free man
(1202) Shouting the battle-cry of Freedom

furlough
(150) I'm feeling for a furlough
(671) not permitted to go and see their wives and families

Gaines's Mill
(442) one of the hardest fought battles ever known
(631) these dead and suffering men
(1412) they stood up like a wall of iron
(1473) Bury me on the field

gardens
(1180) detail a good many men to protect the gardens

garrison
(680) The treadmill of the garrison

generals
(744) I still rightfully hold the rank of first general
(755) Our generals will resolve never to survive a defeat
(756) Our generals never modify their reports of victories
(768) a chief of proven military prestige
(1041) "The Young General" has no bed of roses
(1096) we should have to go over two Hills, then get over a Stonewall
(1289) young bloods of the South
(1359) The chief duties of a general
(1361) every general should know the regulations and articles of war
(1363) a general's duties...are—first, to fight; second, to fight to the best advantage
(1426) Jeff Davis can make a general

Georgia
(727) Come on Georgia

(1129) the people would soon bring the government to it

(1287) A government resting immediately on the caprice of a people is too unstable to last

(1346) our Government stands regenerated

(1360) Government furnishes everything actually needful to the good condition of the army

(1425) We have patched a new government with old cloth

Grant, Ulysses S.
(14) The feeling about Grant is peculiar
(62) He looks as if he meant it
(132) Where is Grant a-going to elbow us again
(238) God—Grant—Victory
(302) not retreating before irresistable veterans
(570) Grant has resumed his former bad habits
(571) I was advised to arrest you on your return
(577) Grant, who was behind at Fort Henry, drunk at Donelson, surprised at Shiloh
(840) Grant has managed his affairs remarkably well
(910) I can't spare this man
(969) You are vigilant and self-reliant
(974) When Grant once gets possession of a place
(1017) that man will fight us every day and every hour
(1027) an expression as if he had determined to drive his head through a brick wall
(1304) His character, more than his genius
(1314) Grant has the perseverance of a Scotch terrier
(1447) Ulysses must get into the city before he dines in it
(1448) Gen. Grant has "caught the rabbit"

grief
(417) Grief and pride ruled the hour

guerrillas
(1123) hang every one he caught

guerrilla war

(260) bring that uncivilized system of warfare to a sudden termination by an equally uncivilized remedy

gun
(152) shoots the biggest gun
(153) We want men with guns in their hands
(281) every man should stand by his guns
(1156) so many ill effects from leaving guns

gunpowder
(416) Sometimes gunpowder smells good

Halleck, Henry W.
(946) Halleck knows better than I what to do
(1463) Halleck is heavy-headed
(1464) Halleck is good for nothing
(1466) He has suggested nothing, decided nothing, done nothing

hanging
(549) hang them without trial

hardtack
(67) what we want is hardtack
(87) hard crackers, come again no more
(88) hardtack, hardtack, come again no more

Harpers Ferry
(740) opposing his advance into the country
(834) To prolong a state of affairs in every way desirable

Harrisburg
(487) We'll whip 'em in five minutes

hat
(1422) That's the Department of State, sir

headquarters
(1147) My headquarters will be in the saddle

hell
(120) We've given 'em h-ll
(139) You go to hell. I've been there
(332) I am short a cheek-bone and an ear, but am able to whip all h—l yet
(408) I wish them all in Hell

Hill, A.P.
(856) He is at rest now

(898) I will hold McClellan's horse

(904) If General McClellan does not want to use the army

(906) couldn't the General have known whether a boat would go through a hole or a lock

(909) you must act

(920) Are you not over-cautious

(932) McClellan's got the slows

(973) he is intrenching

(978) I began to fear he was playing false

(1039) I could become Dictator

(1052) I will do so as faithfully as ever subordinate served superior

(1074) the reaction in favor of McClellan since he has had some men killed is very great

(1189) McClellan...thinks no more of attacking the Confederate Army

(1192) If he be the best, they must all be exceedingly bad

(1462) Wishes to outgeneral the Rebels, but not to kill and destroy them

(1468) nominating a general and warrior in time of war on a peace platform

maggot

(28) maggots always carried it

(159) Short and Sweet just like rosted maget

Malvern Hill

(777) such an order can only be prompted by cowardice or treason

marching

(78) Fall in, ye poor devils

(226) won by marching, not fighting

(516) when Johnny comes marching home

(572) March where you please

(709) I had rather lose one man in marching

(790) that men could stand such hardship

(891) Our men are not moles, and can't dig under the earth

(1203) Tramp! Tramp! Tramp! the boys are marching

(1496) While we were marching through Georgia

(1503) we will march over you

marines

(1151) A ship without Marines

Marye's Heights

(27) A chicken could not live in that field

Maryland

(1168) Maryland! My Maryland

Maryland Heights

(666) the spirit which actuated the defenders of Thermopylae

Meade, George G.

(74) damned goggle-eyed old snapping turtle

(822) General Meade will commit no blunder in my front

(1075) if I fall, you will have my reputation to live on

means

(878) means which will give the greatest good to the greatest number

mess call

(86) Soupy, soupy, soupy, without any bean

military education

(686) something more is required to make a general

militia

(1489) The militia are nothing for warlike uses here

Mine Run

(1079) another Gettysburg in front of us

Missionary Ridge

(357) the men were not to be held back

(526) all hell can't stop them

(537) It's all right if it turns out all right

(1241) Remember Chickamauga

(1242) If you can't run, then holler

Mississippi River

(952) again goes unvexed to the sea

(1272) the possession of the Mississippi River by us is an advantage to our enemy

Missouri

(660) Not one man will the State of Missouri furnish

mistake

(846) When a man makes a mistake

mob

(1313) Is not a negro as good as a white man to stop a bullet

(1352) not yet prepared to receive the negro on terms of political equality

(1376) the Negro is not equal to the white man

New Bern

(246) the day is ours

New Madrid

(514) a pyrotechnic display

newspaper

(249) We want no newspaper government

(1342) editors and proprietors will be held to the strictest accountability

newspaper correspondents

(670) My brigade is not a brigade of newspaper correspondents

(835) prefer sowing discord to inculcating harmony

(1280) I will never again command an army in America if we must carry along paid spies

noble

(329) the noble that fall and the ignoble that remain

nonsense

(37) Here's your mule

North

(231) the Northern States will manage somehow to muddle through

(286) the hope of success vanish from the Northern mind

(500) The people who can't pay $300

(779) I know the North to be so contemptible

(1022) Their offense is that they are free

(1392) Our sluggish, good-natured, pachydermatous Northern people

North Carolina

(1345) we sweep the country like a swarm of locusts

nursing

(25) the nurse with the bottle

(175) I can stand and feed and nurse them

(177) My business is stanching blood

(178) I make gruel—not speeches

obedience

(1358) the beginning and end of duty

odors

(1389) I never knew before what rankness of stench can be emitted by unwashed humanity

officer

(266) Competent officers make good soldiers

(367) Tender consideration for worthless and incompetent officers

(461) one of the requisite studies for an officer is man

(568) a dull ax, a broken saw, and rotten timber

(615) The officers and men who permit themselves to be surprised

(665) it is unmilitary and unlike an officer to write news respecting one's post

(677) If officers desire to have control over their commands

(699) Shoot the brave officers, and the cowards will run away

(950) the ranking officer must be obeyed

(1072) the officers...are ignorant, inefficient and worthless

(1293) if any officer...makes one cent by way of profit in any manner traceable to his office

(1413) many officers have become addicted to habits of intemperance

(1435) Good officers know that when wine is in, wit is out

(1449) Their orders come out slow and drawling

olive branch

(732) the olive branch in one hand and the Constitution in the other

ordeal

(273) through the ordeal as gold thro' the refiner's fire

orders

(1349) I have never in my life questioned or disobeyed an order

Orphan Brigade

Potomac
(51) All quiet on the Potomac
(197) All quiet along the Potomac

powder
(413) We have faith in God and dry Powder

power
(1232) I can touch a bell on my right hand and order the imprisonment

presidency
(1190) A gentleman in the Presidency would give mortal offense

principles
(997) principles may, and must, be inflexible

press
(1281) What defeats and will continue to defeat our best plans here and elsewhere? The press
(1469) What mischief has the press performed

prison
(396) The iron gate of our prison stands half open

prisoner
(16) depots of prisoners
(702) It is cheaper to feed them than to fight them
(993) They will never shoulder a musket in anger again
(1170) we don't care which licks, what we want is to get out of this pen
(1173) if you ain't dead, get inside
(1174) Ain't dead yet
(1175) can't get his face straightened out again

promotion
(685) Merit should be the only basis of promotion

promptness
(618) Promptness is the greatest of military virtues

property
(1038) private property whether of secessionists or others must be strictly respected

protection
(455) the best protection against the enemy's fire

punishment
(254) they shall fear the stripes if they do not now reverence the stars of our banner
(261) that rebellion is treason, and that treason, persisted in, is death
(804) For the bad behavior of a few it would not appear just to punish the whole

Quakers
(977) opposed to both war and oppression, they can only practically oppose oppression by war

quiet
(51) All quiet on the Potomac
(197) All quiet along the Potomac

racial relations
(397) all-consuming question for this age and nation to solve

rank
(1344) I have all the rank I want

Ransom, Robert
(203) few meaner men unhung than this Robert Ransom

readiness
(890) the necessity of being ready increases

Reams's Station
(587) I pray God I may never leave this field

rebellion
(1090) The backbone of the Rebellion is this day broken
(1326) rebellion, begun in error and perpetuated in pride
(1467) There was...an aristocratic purpose in this rebellion

Rebels
(235) Grape for the rebel masses, and hemp for their leaders
(598) they chose that which necessarily lay nearest the heart
(1393) We have been humbugged by the rebels

(267) He intrigued to get me out and behold the result

snow

(1183) I would like to have some of those "On to Richmond" fellows out here with us in the snow

society

(344) Society is terribly mutilated

soldier

(92) Who wouldn't be a soldier

(103) more harm than our own soldiers have done

(105) a soldier's wife I'll be

(201) The men in many cases really will not go home

(222) no idea of what it is to be a soldier

(243) the Rebs couldn't make anything of them fellers

(276) Soldiering is a good deal like going to school

(319) Soldiers may be gentlemen but they can't live like gentlemen

(491) a man who has been a good soldier can be a good citizen

(494) You have been good soldiers; you can be good citizens

(517) paying them as American Soldiers, not as menial hirelings

(674) soldiers not only to defend, but able and willing both to defend and protect

(762) fast becoming...machine soldiers

(765) a better soldier than those who treat me so cavalierly

(845) soldiers know their duties better than the general officers

(868) if you make as good citizens as you have soldiers

(939) blacks soldiers...would end the rebellion at once

(1029) Their great characteristic is their stoical manliness

(1089) we're de bully soldiers of de "First of Arkansas"

(1191) one-fourth of whom were entirely barefooted

(1194) drones in uniform

(1260) You are a soldier, and must submit to orders

(1267) young men of the best families did not like to be killed

(1382) I had almost as leave have the Yanks around my hous as our own men

(1436) they did not enlist to do guard duty

(1439) they toiled on...without murmuring

(1479) thousands of our unknown American young men in the ranks

(1502) some of our soldiers committed discreditable trespasses

South

(320) God pity this south land when we are done with it

(578) In killing the President the South has lost their best friend

(649) The soil of our beloved South

(759) no terror for the Southern people

(1107) Southern heavens are overcast

(1298) The people of the South having appealed to war

(1305) they will kill as vipers the whites who attempt to free their slaves

(1333) I propose to demonstrate the vulnerability of the South

(1351) The mass of the people south will never trouble us again

(1391) Scrape a "Southern Gentleman's" skin

South Carolina

(48) South Carolina villains

(1340) an insatiable desire to wreak vengeance upon South Carolina

(1420) Fling down thy gauntlet to the Huns

(1471) This Rebellion...may be traced in a great degree to the diseased imagination of certain South Carolina gentlemen

Southern army

(464) the Southern army was better manned and officered

Southern rights

(255) I am a friend to Southern rights now, but I came here to put down Southern wrongs

Spangler's Spring, Gettysburg

CIVIL WAR QUOTATIONS

(1348) I am instructed...not to attempt civil negotiations

swearing

(355) his swearing made my hair stand straight up

(1240) Unless I swear like hell

sword

(663) draw your swords and throw away the scabbard

(731) never sheathe it in the bosom of my mother

Taylor, Richard

(696) a wicked fellow

tenacity

(527) to him that holds on to the end

Texans

(499) their peculiar habits of hanging, shooting, &c.

(501) no Texan walks a yard if he can help it

thirst

(227) I could have drank out of a mud puddle

13th Amendment

(983) If the people over the river had behaved themselves

Thompson, Jacob

(999) an elephant by the hind leg

thoughts

(626) one cannot at the same time keep home, parents and such thoughts as they suggest in his mind

titles

(748) how fond all Americans are of titles

torpedoes

(460) Damn the torpedoes

trains

(541) so few men left that they will not want any trains

traitors

(528) two parties now,—Traitors & Patriots

transfugees

(563) transfugees from the rebel army

treason

(730) he that is guilty of treason

(734) treason must be made odious

(877) treason of the darkest hue

Treasury aides

(1149) A greater pack of knaves never went unhung

Trent affair

(900) One war at a time

(1021) I hate the British government

(1093) such slatternly abuse of us

Trevilian Station

(350) Where in hell is the rear

(583) I propose to fight

troops

(704) Who could not conquer, with such troops as these

(1337) make them believe you know more than they do

(1401) Troops should be taught to take pride in other branches of service

truth

(975) Truth is generally the best vindication against slander

tub

(903) The bottom is out of the tub

tyranny

(366) The tyranny of an unbirdled majority

tyrants

(218) Sic semper tyrannis

(1356) the tools of tyrants

uniform

(600) Everywhere some insignia of soldiership were to be seen

(859) I must make my best appearance

(1433) Most of the boys had never worn drawers

Union

(6) aloof from the conflict

(43) anything to preserve the Union

(879) the good old ship of the Union

(966) often a limb must be amputated to save a life

(438) The War at last appoints the generals

(457) the chances of war

(559) The war is over, the rebels are our countrymen again

(574) This is cruel warfare

(625) War is an organized bore

(647) as horrible as his Satanic Majesty could desire

(659) war on a scale inaugurated by this rebellion

(662) all the horrors that must accompany such an event

(664) the sum of all evils

(711) the secret of successful war

(747) a species of warfare at which we can never win

(752) Our people are tired of war

(772) War—strangles youth

(811) It is well that war is so terrible

(812) But what a cruel thing is war

(884) Suppose you go to war, you cannot fight always

(888) In your hands,...and not in mine, is the momentous issue of civil war

(911) I expect to maintain this contest

(922) If I had had my way, this war would never have been commenced

(964) This war is eating my life out

(985) Both parties deprecated war

(987) Fondly do we hope...that this mighty scourge of war

(994) Let the thing be pressed

(1008) Weary days with wars and rumors of wars

(1009) The civil war grumbles and growls and gathers

(1011) What an infernal thing war is

(1051) It should not be, at all, a War upon a population

(1053) I have not come here to wage war upon the defenseless

(1073) War is a game of chance

(1076) we cannot carry on war without fighting

(1084) The war is over

(1086) what misery this dreadful war has produced

(1098) let a man say war to me and I will choke him

(1117) We've been fooling about this thing long enough

(1118) the hideous offspring of the monster war

(1120) the destruction of human life is revolting in the extreme

(1135) The war was never really contemplated in earnest

(1141) War and its horrors, and yet I sing and whistle

(1154) This war is not being conducted for the benefit of officers

(1234) The advocates of war...generally gain their fearful end

(1257) I have seen enough of war not to be caught by its first glittering bait

(1258) A fatal mistake in war is to underrate...an enemy

(1259) as soon as real war begins, new men...will emerge from obscurity

(1270) The very object of war is to produce results by death and slaughter

(1274) we can make war so terrible

(1275) indeed will this war become a reproach to the names of liberty and civilization

(1278) war must go on—it can't be stopped

(1282) this universal burning and wanton destruction of private property is not justified in war

(1288) War was not the remedy for grievances

(1290) War...should be "pure and simple"

(1291) I would make this war as severe as possible

(1294) War is curelty

(1296) War is hell

(1300) War is simply power unrestrained by consitution

(1306) To make war we must and will harden our hearts

(1307) War, like the thunderbolt, follows its laws

(1312) war is war, and not popularity-seeking

SUBJECT INDEX

(297) How are the daughters of Eve punished

(446) women would make a grand brigade—if it was not for snakes and spiders

(1091) female virtue...seems now almost a perfect wreck

(1108) All our women are Florence Nightingales

(1115) selling poisoned pies to the soldiers

(1285) the deep and bitter enmity of the women of the South

(1445) were it not for the women, I should not fight at all

Woman Order

(258) liable to be treated as a woman of the town plying her avocation

(269) Never has anything been more deserved

(786) It brought ladies to their senses

wooden leg

(452) It don't hurt a bit to be shot in a wooden leg

wound

(112) you aren't wounded; you are only bruised

(228) I concluded they ment me

(414) I could limp and complain of the "old wound"

(716) I have always been kind to their wounded

(1238) the perfect calmness of the wounded men

writ of habeas corpus

(893) you...are authorized to suspend that writ

(918) The Writ of Habeas Corpus is suspended

(1379) I look upon this habeas corpus suspension act as...dangerous to public liberty

wrongs

(334) Rather bear the wrongs you have than fly to others

Yankee

(110) all this Yankee scoundrel got

(146) you look like yer bowels wuz so reglar

(180) we curse the Yankees to our heart's content, but buy their goods still

(183) their war-cry is "Beauty and booty"

(209) a yankee twang that grates against my nerves

(463) I expect to murder every Yankee I ever meet

(475) if you want a heap of fun and to kill some Yankees

(655) The Yankees are behaving very well

(1094) Suppose I should unconsciously entrap some magnificient Yankee

(1105) the Yankee racers

(1369) Yankee souls in Southern bodies

Yellow Tavern

(1402) do your duty, as I have done mine

(1403) I had rather die than be whipped

(1404) Go back to the front

zouaves

(93) Zou! Zou! Zou!